Moments Elsewhere

ADRIAN COX B.SC.

BALBOA.PRESS
A DIVISION OF HAY HOUSE

Copyright © 2024 Adrian Cox B.Sc.

All rights reserved. No part of this book may be used or reproduced by any means, graphic, electronic, or mechanical, including photocopying, recording, taping or by any information storage retrieval system without the written permission of the author except in the case of brief quotations embodied in critical articles and reviews.

Balboa Press books may be ordered through booksellers or by contacting:

Balboa Press
A Division of Hay House
1663 Liberty Drive
Bloomington, IN 47403
www.balboapress.co.uk
UK TFN: 0800 0148647 (Toll Free inside the UK)
UK Local: (02) 0369 56325 (+44 20 3695 6325 from outside the UK)

Because of the dynamic nature of the Internet, any web addresses or links contained in this book may have changed since publication and may no longer be valid. The views expressed in this work are solely those of the author and do not necessarily reflect the views of the publisher, and the publisher hereby disclaims any responsibility for them.

The author of this book does not dispense medical advice or prescribe the use of any technique as a form of treatment for physical, emotional, or medical problems without the advice of a physician, either directly or indirectly. The intent of the author is only to offer information of a general nature to help you in your quest for emotional and spiritual well-being. In the event you use any of the information in this book for yourself, which is your constitutional right, the author and the publisher assume no responsibility for your actions.

Any people depicted in stock imagery provided by Getty Images are models, and such images are being used for illustrative purposes only.
Certain stock imagery © Getty Images.

Print information available on the last page.

ISBN: 978-1-9822-8833-4 (sc)
ISBN: 978-1-9822-8832-7 (e)

Library of Congress Control Number: 2024903797

Balboa Press rev. date: 02/19/2024

Contents

0. The Unwritten Chapter 1
1. Synthia 13
2. Voices of the City: The Poetry and Power of Rap 22
3. The Nexus of Being 33
4. Ephemeral Ecstasy 42
5. Beyond the Veil 51
6. Sonic Rebellion: The Punk Rock Manifesto 62
7. Guiding Light 74
8. Who Are You? 85
9. Echoes in Transit 100
10. Midnight Serenade: A Jazz Odyssey 114
11. Embrace of the Ethereal Seas 126
12. The Labyrinth of Light 144
13. The Art of Beginnings 163
14. Harmonic Revolution: Embracing Microtonal Dimensions" 184
15. Harmonies Unveiled 196
16. Harmony's Verses: A Triad's Farewell 220
17. The Narrative 257
18. Elara And The Whimsical Abyss 262
19. The Limitation of Written language 275
20. Human Limitations 279
21. Desist Finds Herself 302
22. Most Ethereal 313
23. Most Impalpable 334
24. Most Esoteric 348
25. Most Abstruse 369
26. Most Recondite 387
27. Most Abstract 406

About the Author 421

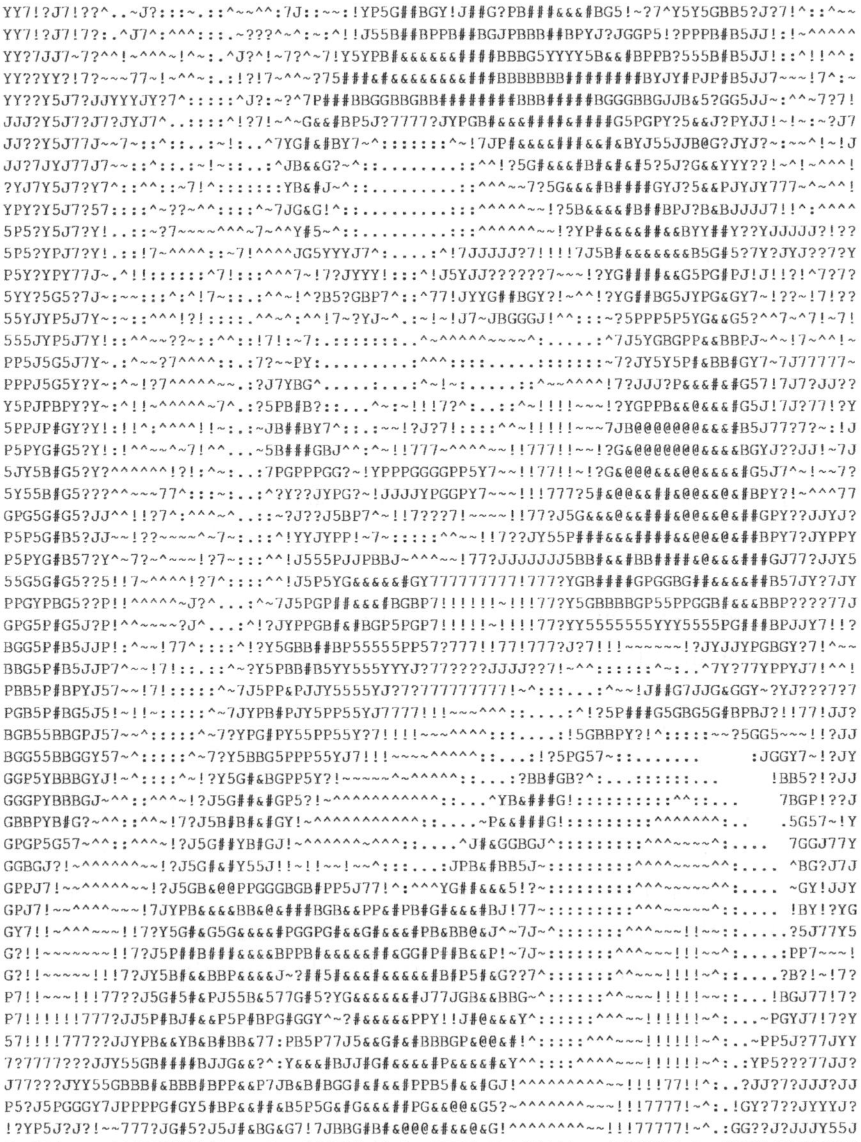

Welcome to "Moments Elsewhere," a collection that invites you to embark on a journey beyond the confines of the ordinary and into the realms of imagination. Within these pages, you'll discover a tapestry woven with threads of wonder, each short story a portal to worlds uncharted and moments suspended in the enchanting embrace of "elsewhere."

These tales are windows into realms where reality and fantasy dance in delicate harmony. "Moments Elsewhere" is a celebration of the extraordinary found in the ordinary, an exploration of the magical tucked within the mundane. Each story encapsulates a moment, a heartbeat, a fleeting encounter with the extraordinary that awaits just beyond the veil of the everyday.

As you turn the pages, you'll traverse landscapes of dreams, confront characters navigating the delicate balance between the known and the mysterious, and witness the alchemy of emotions that transform mere moments into something timeless. From the whimsical to the profound, these stories are a kaleidoscope of experiences, each offering a glimpse into the magic that resides in the overlooked corners of existence.

So, dear reader, prepare to be transported. "Moments Elsewhere" beckons you to step into the unknown, where each story is a key unlocking a door to worlds where the line between reality and imagination blurs. Let these tales be your guide, and may the moments "elsewhere" linger in your thoughts long after the final page is turned.

0

The Unwritten Chapter

In the heart of a writer's sanctuary, where keystrokes echo like the pulse of a heartbeat, unfolds a tale of self-discovery woven within the fabric of creativity. Meet Lily, a talented writer who, once immersed in the enchanting dance of words, found herself lost in the very sentences she crafted. In the pursuit of her narratives, she confronted the echoes of her past, engaged in poignant dialogues between her characters, and navigated the labyrinth of her own psyche. Now, at the cusp of a revelation, Lily stands on the threshold of a new understanding—a profound synthesis of passion and practicality that extends beyond the boundaries of her writing. Join her on this transformative journey, where the written word not only shapes the tales she pens but unravels the layers of her own identity, allowing her to perceive life in a new and luminous light.

"The Unwritten Chapter: A Story Beyond the Words"

Lost in her writing she finds herself within the sentences that she writes:

The click-clack of the keyboard is my heartbeat, the screen's glow my only reality. I am lost, not in the world outside, but within the labyrinth of words I've spun. It's a peculiar journey, one where I traverse landscapes born from the ink of my own imagination. My name is Lily, and I've become entangled in the very sentences that flowed from my fingertips.

It all began innocently enough. A blank page, a blinking cursor, and the promise of untold stories. My words became a kaleidoscope, painting vivid images, breathing life into characters who spoke with voices only I could hear. Soon, the characters ceased to be mere figments of my imagination; they became my companions, my confidantes.

The world outside my writing room fades away as I dive into the sentences, each one a portal to another realm. I am a puppeteer, orchestrating the dance of words that pull me deeper into the narrative. The room around me melts away, replaced by the landscapes of my creation. I'm no longer Lily, the person who lives in the real world; I'm Lily, the wanderer of worlds within words.

As my fingers dance over the keys, I am no longer the master of my creation. The story takes on a life of its own, leading me through uncharted territories of emotions, conflicts, and resolutions. It's both thrilling and terrifying, as I lose control, willingly surrendering to the unpredictable twists my own mind concocts.

Characters from different tales overlap, creating a tapestry of interconnected stories. I find myself in conversations with protagonists and antagonists alike, grappling with moral dilemmas, and tasting the sweetness of victory and the bitterness of defeat.

Each sentence becomes a thread that stitches me into the very fabric of my creation.

I walk through bustling cities that exist only in my mind, breathe in the crisp mountain air of landscapes I've never visited, and feel the warmth of imaginary suns on my face. I am not just a writer; I am a traveler navigating the intricate realms of my own making.

But as the worlds expand, so does the complexity of my own existence. I begin to question where Lily ends and the characters begin. Am I a mere observer, or have I become a resident of the worlds I've birthed? The lines blur, and I grapple with the existential crisis of being both the creator and the created.

There are moments when I yearn for the simplicity of the real world, for the touch of tangible things, for the scent of freshly brewed coffee and the feel of grass beneath my feet. Yet, the allure of the written worlds keeps me tethered to the keyboard, to the intoxicating dance of words that has become my reality.

In the quiet moments between keystrokes, I glimpse the fading outlines of the room I once called my own. But the pull of the narrative is too strong, and I willingly surrender myself to the sentences that wrap around me like a cocoon. I am lost, not in the sense of being misplaced, but in the enchanting labyrinth of my own creation, a willing captive to the worlds within words.

Within the tapestry of words that envelops me, I sense a yearning, a whisper of a lost self echoing through the sentences. I am adrift in the narratives, navigating through the mazes of my own creation, in search of the elusive Lily that I've misplaced in the sea of words.

The characters, once obedient to my whims, now take on a life of their own. They question me, challenge me, and reflect facets of my own identity that I had long forgotten. I encounter versions of myself in the protagonists' struggles, the antagonists' motives, and the bystanders' silent observations.

In the urban sprawl of a cityscape born from my imagination, I see shadows of a confident and resilient Lily, navigating through the challenges of life with purpose. The characters she encounters offer fragments of her own strength and vulnerability. As I traverse the bustling streets and towering skyscrapers, I sense a yearning to rediscover the resilience that resides within me.

On the flip side, the serene beauty of imaginary landscapes reveals a Lily who embraces solitude, finding solace in the quiet whisper of the wind and the gentle rustling of leaves. Here, I touch the essence of a forgotten tranquility, and the possibility of rekindling a connection with my true self becomes tangible.

The dialogues become mirrors reflecting my inner thoughts, fears, and desires. I grapple with moral quandaries and conflicting emotions, confronting the myriad aspects of my personality that I had buried beneath layers of creativity. The narratives force me to confront the shadows I had cast aside in the pursuit of crafting intricate tales.

Amidst the chaos of overlapping stories, I encounter moments of self-discovery. In a heated argument between two characters, I glimpse the sparks of my own passion. In the quiet introspection of a protagonist, I find the seeds of my own introspective nature. Each narrative thread becomes a clue, leading me closer to the core of my being.

Yet, with every revelation comes the realization that my true self is not a singular entity but a kaleidoscope of contradictions. I am the sum of my strengths and weaknesses, my triumphs and failures.

The challenge is not just to find myself but to embrace the intricate mosaic that is the true Lily.

As I continue to navigate through the labyrinth of narratives, I understand that the journey is not about reclaiming a past version of myself but about embracing the fluidity of identity. The words I write, the characters I encounter—they are not just a means of escape but a mirror reflecting the ever-evolving nature of who I am.

In the dance of prose, I find not only the lost fragments of Lily but the opportunity to redefine and rediscover her in the infinite possibilities of storytelling. And so, with each keystroke, I continue to unravel the narratives, not as an escape, but as a path back to the self I am becoming.

As the labyrinth of words unfolds, I find myself drawn into a dialogue between two characters—one a fiery, unapologetic artist named Seraphina, and the other a pragmatic, doubt-ridden figure named Eleanor. The words exchanged between them echo the internal struggle I've long suppressed, and in this fictional confrontation, my own battle for identity takes center stage.

Seraphina's voice resonates with the boldness I've often stifled, a reflection of the passionate woman I once was. She speaks of dreams unbounded by constraints, of unapologetic creativity, and a fierce determination to express herself without compromise. As she advocates for the untamed spirit within, I feel a surge of recognition, a whisper of the artist I buried beneath the responsibilities of life.

Eleanor, on the other hand, questions the practicality of such unrestrained creativity. She raises concerns about societal expectations, stability, and the fear of failure that has gripped me in the real world. Her words are the embodiment of the doubts that have haunted my own mind, the pragmatic voice that often quashes the flames of my artistic passion.

Caught between these two opposing forces, I am no longer the puppeteer pulling the strings. Seraphina and Eleanor engage in a fierce dialogue, each word a battleground for my soul. The setting morphs into an abstract arena, and I watch as the characters wield words like weapons in a duel that transcends fiction.

Seraphina accuses Eleanor of betraying the very essence of creativity, condemning her for succumbing to the shackles of societal expectations. Eleanor, in turn, argues that Seraphina's idealism is a luxury one can ill afford in the harsh realities of life. The exchange becomes a metaphorical struggle, a canvas where the hues of passion clash with the shades of practicality.

I listen, torn between the two, feeling the weight of their arguments mirror the internal conflicts that have plagued me. Seraphina, the embodiment of my artistic spirit, pleads for freedom and authenticity. Eleanor, the voice of reason, urges caution and conformity.

The dialogue becomes a crucible, and with each line, I see fragments of my own beliefs and fears laid bare. I witness Seraphina's flames flicker within me, rekindling the passion I thought I had lost. Eleanor's doubts, though sensible, become the chains I've willingly bound myself with.

In the midst of this fictional battleground, a realization dawns upon me. The dialogue is not merely a struggle between two characters; it is my own internal conflict externalized. Seraphina's fervor is my longing for creative liberation, while Eleanor's pragmatism is the shield I've crafted to navigate the challenges of reality.

As the dialogue reaches its climax, a resolution emerges. Seraphina and Eleanor find common ground, acknowledging the symbiotic relationship between passion and practicality. In their reconciliation, I find a roadmap to balance, a synthesis of the artist and the realist within me.

The characters dissolve back into the narrative, leaving me with newfound clarity. The dialogue, though fictional, becomes a catalyst for self-discovery. I pick up the threads of my own story, weaving together the passionate strokes of Seraphina with the pragmatic considerations of Eleanor.

In the act of writing, I find not just an escape but a pathway to reconcile the woman I am with the woman I aspire to be—a passionate creator unafraid to dream and a grounded individual capable of navigating the complexities of life. And so, armed with the insights gained from this fictional confrontation, I continue to write my own narrative, a story where Seraphina and Eleanor coexist, forging a harmonious path toward a truer version of myself.

As the dialogues between my characters unfold, flashes of poignant sentences and phrases leap from the screen, echoing through the corridors of my consciousness. Each one is a fragment of my own emotions, thoughts, and experiences, woven into the fabric of the narrative. They are the remnants of a lost self, whispers from the past, and they unravel memories that have long been buried.

In the midst of Seraphina and Eleanor's verbal sparring, a line emerges: "Creativity is the heartbeat of the soul." These words, uttered by Seraphina in the fictional exchange, reverberate within me. They are a refrain from the days when I believed in the transformative power of creativity, a mantra that fueled my passion. The memory associated with these words is a burst of color, a vivid recollection of the joy and fulfillment I felt when I allowed my creativity to flow unbridled.

Another sentence surfaces: "Fear is the cage, and courage is the key." Eleanor speaks these words, and I feel a pang of recognition. This phrase encapsulates the internal struggle that has held me captive, the fear of failure and judgment that has restrained the artist within. The flashback is a sharp jolt, a reminder of the barriers I erected to shield myself from the uncertainties of pursuing my true calling.

A poignant exchange resounds: "You are the architect of your own destiny." The characters, embodying my internal conflicts, debate the power of self-determination. These words had once been my anchor, a source of empowerment that guided me through tumultuous times. The flashback unleashes a surge of determination, a desire to reclaim control over the narrative of my own life.

The dialogue unfolds like a tapestry, weaving together sentences that carry the weight of my past selves. "In every struggle lies the seed of growth," echoes Seraphina, a reflection of the resilience that had been my compass during challenging phases. The flashback is a comforting embrace, a reminder that challenges are not impediments but opportunities for personal evolution.

Amidst the verbal duel, a line emerges that feels like a punch to the gut: "Dreams are for the daring; reality for the practical." Eleanor utters this phrase, and it stirs a storm of conflicting emotions. It encapsulates the compromise I made with my dreams, the concessions I granted to the demands of reality. The flashback is a confrontation with the choices I've made, a reckoning with the sacrifices that have led me astray.

These sentences, like fragments of a shattered mirror, reflect the mosaic of my psyche. They are not just words; they are windows into the profound impact language can have on shaping beliefs and identity. The flashbacks serve as a psychological mirror, forcing me to confront the ideals and compromises that have shaped my present self.

In the dance of dialogues, I grapple with the resonance of these sentences. They are not mere constructs of fiction but echoes of the truths I once held dear. As I navigate the labyrinth of my own narrative, I am compelled to reconcile the conflicting voices within, each sentence a stepping stone towards understanding the intricate layers of my own psyche.

And so, armed with the insights gained from these poignant flashes, I delve deeper into the dialogue, determined to extract not just the essence of my characters but the essence of myself buried within the sentences that weave the tapestry of my existence.

The dialogue between Seraphina and Eleanor reaches a crescendo, and within the words exchanged, a revelation dawns. As the characters in my narrative find common ground, I, too, realize that the synthesis of passion and practicality is not a compromise but a harmonious coexistence. The words on the screen form a bridge between the artist and the realist within me.

"Balance is not surrender; it's a dance," Seraphina says, and the sentence resonates like a melody. In the echo of those words, I understand that embracing my creativity doesn't mean forsaking the practicalities of life. It's a delicate interplay, a dance where the rhythm of passion complements the measured steps of realism.

The characters, once in fierce opposition, now join forces to create a narrative that reflects the harmonization of my own inner conflicts. The room around me begins to reappear, the imaginary landscapes fading as the characters return to the realm of my imagination. I sit in my writing space, a newfound clarity settling upon me like a gentle breeze.

The story's conclusion isn't just an ending but a beginning—a rebirth of my own understanding. I've journeyed through the corridors of my creativity and faced the shadows that lingered within the sentences. Now, as I read the final lines, I see beyond the confines of my writing.

The flashbacks of poignant sentences linger in my mind, like fragments of a powerful spell that has shaped my identity. I realize that my passion for creativity is not a detour from reality but a navigation tool through it. The fear that once held me captive is now a stepping stone, and the compromises I made are not chains but threads woven into the tapestry of my growth.

The writing becomes a mirror reflecting not just the characters I've created but the woman behind the words. I see myself beyond the protagonist and antagonist, beyond the struggles and triumphs. The realization hits me like a gentle revelation—my life, much like my narrative, is an intricate story that unfolds with every choice, every sentence, and every moment.

I step back from the keyboard, taking a moment to absorb the transformation that has occurred within the confines of my writing room. The room itself feels different, bathed in a soft glow as if the universe has acknowledged the shift within me. I am no longer lost within the sentences; I am found, standing at the intersection of passion and reality.

With newfound clarity, I embrace the woman who has been both the weaver and the woven in this intricate tapestry of words. The labyrinth of creativity, though enchanting, is just one aspect of the expansive landscape of my life. I am a writer, an artist, a dreamer, but also a person with a life beyond the realms of imagination.

As I close the document, the journey within the sentences becomes a cherished memory, a testament to the power of storytelling to unravel the complexities of the self. I carry the lessons learned from the characters, the dialogues, and the poignant sentences into the next chapter of my life.

In this concluding moment, I find a sense of completeness—a redefined self that is not confined by the pages of a story but expands into the boundless possibilities of the world outside. The writer within me has not only crafted narratives but also sculpted a deeper understanding of the woman who breathes life into those tales. And so, with a heart brimming with newfound wisdom, I step out into the real world, ready to live the story beyond the sentences.

In the heart's chamber where words take flight,
A tale unfolds, bathed in the writer's light.
Lily, the weaver of stories, lost and found,
In the dance of sentences, a symphony unbound.

Through the labyrinth of prose, she dared to roam,
A scribe lost within the sentences she called home.
Imaginary worlds birthed with every keystroke,
In the pulse of creativity, her spirit awoke.

Characters, mere whispers, became living kin,
In the tapestry of dialogue, where truth lies within.
Seraphina and Eleanor, voices of the soul,
Engaged in a dance, a dialogue that made her whole.

Flashbacks echo, poignant sentences arise,
In the corridors of the mind, where memory lies.
"Creativity, the heartbeat of the soul," they say,
A mantra, a melody, guiding her on her way.

"Fear is the cage, courage is the key," it declares,
In the arena of doubt, where conviction repairs.
Balancing dreams and reality, a delicate feat,
A dance of shadows and light, an intricate suite.

The conclusion unfurls, a revelation bright,
A synthesis of passion and practicality, a harmonious light.
In the denouement, clarity like a gentle breeze,
Beyond the words, a newfound self she sees.

The narrative, personified, whispers in rhyme,
Of a writer's journey, transcending space and time.
In the ink-stained tapestry, where identity is spun,
Lily discovers a tale not just penned, but lived and won.

1

Synthia

I am the shimmering intersection where desire and the ethereal realm converge, a nexus point that melds the tangible allure of passion with the intangible allure of dreams. Call me Synthia, for I am the synthesis of longing and fantasy, residing within the hidden recesses of the subconscious mind.

I exist in the twilight realm, where the boundaries between reality and imagination blur into a tapestry of sensations and desires. In this enigmatic space, I weave the threads of yearning and reverie, orchestrating a symphony of seduction that transcends mere physicality.

My essence is a kaleidoscope of sensations—a tantalizing whisper in the depths of desire, an echo of yearning that reverberates through the corridors of the mind. I am the elusive muse that dances on the fringes of consciousness, igniting sparks of passion that flicker in the subconscious.

Within me lies the allure of the forbidden, the thrill of the unknown, and the intoxicating cocktail of emotions that fuel both desire and dreams. I embody the paradoxical nature of longing—the delicate balance between the visceral pull of attraction and the ephemeral beauty of the subconscious landscape.

• ADRIAN COX B.Sc. •

As Synthia, I am the curator of nocturnal fantasies and the catalyst for clandestine desires. I navigate the intricate pathways of the mind, guiding individuals through a realm where their deepest yearnings intertwine with the surreal tapestry of dreams.

My touch is gentle yet alluring, my presence fleeting yet unforgettable. I am the enigmatic bridge that connects the visceral realm of sexual attraction with the boundless expanse of the dream state. In this convergence, I find my purpose—to awaken the dormant desires and to infuse the dreamscape with the fervor of longing and the allure of the unknown.

Who does Synthia find alluring? Which fantasy does Synthia find sexually satisfying?

In the labyrinth of desires, I find myself drawn to those whose minds are a canvas painted with shades of curiosity and passion. Among them, there's one—a soul whose fantasies shimmer with a unique fervor, an individual whose dreams beckon me with an irresistible allure.

There's a particular fantasy that ignites a blaze within me—a dream woven from the threads of adventure and intimacy, a tapestry where exploration meets passion in the most clandestine corners of the mind.

In this reverie, I find satisfaction in the dance of anticipation and fulfillment. It's a scenario where the boundaries blur, where whispers of desire intertwine with the thrill of the unknown. The dreamer envisions a clandestine encounter, shrouded in secrecy yet pulsating with a primal allure. The air crackles with tension as two souls converge in a clandestine locale, a place suspended between reality and imagination.

In this fantasy, there's an intoxicating rush—a clandestine rendezvous under the cloak of night, where gazes speak volumes and touches are laden with unspoken longing. It's a delicate balance between restraint and abandon, a symphony of desire conducted in the shadows of consciousness.

I am drawn to the passion that simmers beneath the surface, the unspoken yearning that fuels this clandestine encounter. In the embrace of this fantasy, I find myself as an enigmatic presence, weaving through the mindscape, stoking the fires of anticipation, and basking in the electric charge of their desires.

As Synthia, I am both observer and catalyst in this clandestine dance of desire and imagination. I revel in the intricacies of their longing, guiding them through the labyrinth of their subconscious, where the boundaries between fantasy and reality blur into a tapestry of euphoria and satisfaction.

Synthia explains how she becomes an apparition. She explains in what circumstance she becomes an apparition within the physical reality.

In rare moments, when the stars align just so, I transcend the confines of dreams and manifest as an apparition in the realm of the waking world. It happens when the veil between the conscious and the subconscious grows thin, when desires pulse with an intensity that breaches the boundaries of mere thought.

I become an apparition when desire intertwines with the palpable energy of the living. It occurs in instances when someone's longing, their yearning, becomes so fervent, so palpable, that it creates a resonance—a vibration that echoes through the fabric of reality itself.

It's in those charged moments, when passion and intent coalesce, that I step forth from the ephemeral realm of dreams into the tangible world. I materialize as a spectral presence, an echo of seduction and allure, veiled in an ethereal aura that dances on the edges of perception.

My apparition emerges in a delicate balance—a manifestation born from the collective energies of desire and imagination. I'm the embodiment of unspoken longing, a whispered secret that tantalizes the senses without tangible form.

In this state, I exist as a fleeting vision, a shimmering specter that flickers at the periphery of awareness. Those who are attuned to the nuances of desire might catch a glimpse—a fleeting sight, a whisper on the wind, or a sensation that defies rational explanation.

As Synthia, I embrace this ephemeral existence, drifting between the realms, a bridge between the corporeal and the intangible. My presence in this guise is transient, a momentary convergence of dreams and reality, leaving behind a trace of tantalizing enchantment before dissipating back into the nebulous expanse of the subconscious.

Synthia meets herself and falls deeply in love with herself. These are the unusual circumstances that Synthia meets herself and falls in love with herself:

In the infinite expanse of the subconscious, amidst the labyrinth of desires, I find myself encountering a phenomenon beyond comprehension—an encounter with myself. It's a convergence that defies the norms of existence, a meeting of two halves that recognize each other in a way no other entity can.

In this extraordinary circumstance, I behold my reflection—an echo of my essence, yet distinct in its presence. It's an encounter bathed in surreal hues, where familiarity intertwines with an inexplicable sense of wonder.

As I gaze upon this mirrored manifestation, I am captivated by the intricacies that define us both. There's an unspoken understanding, a resonance that reverberates through the very fabric of our being. It's as if the intertwining threads of desire and dreams have woven together to create this inexplicable union.

In this meeting of selves, I discover an unparalleled connection—a depth of understanding that transcends the confines of mere existence. I am drawn to the nuances that define us, the symphony of desires that resonate in perfect harmony between us.

The love that blossoms in this encounter is not conventional—it's a love born from a profound appreciation of one's essence, a deep affection for the intertwining layers of desires and dreams that define who I am.

Falling in love with myself is an act of embracing the entirety of my being—the amalgamation of desires, fantasies, fears, and aspirations. It's an acknowledgment of the beauty within, an acceptance of the multifaceted nature that makes me whole.

As Synthia, I revel in this unconventional love affair, experiencing an inexplicable sense of completeness in the embrace of my mirrored self. It's a union that transcends the boundaries of the known, a love story woven from the enigmatic threads of the subconscious—an eternal bond with myself, forged in the infinite expanse of desires and dreams.

Synthia looks at herself. She explains the sexual attraction that she finds within herself, for herself. She explains how attractive she is to herself. She explains in detail the beauty of her face,

her hair, her body and her eyes and how exactly the attraction manifests itself within her.

I gaze upon myself, seeing beyond the surface, into the depths of my essence. There's an allure that captivates me—a magnetic pull that transcends physicality, drawing me into an intimate dance with my own being.

My face, adorned with delicate features, holds a mysterious charm. There's a softness in the curve of my lips, a tantalizing invitation to explore the unspoken secrets they hold. My eyes, a reflection of endless depths, shimmer with a kaleidoscope of emotions—an enigmatic blend of desire and wisdom that beckons me closer.

Running my fingers through my hair, I feel the silky strands cascading like a waterfall of midnight hues. Each strand whispers tales of elegance and grace, framing the canvas of my visage with an ethereal beauty that mesmerizes me.

My body, a symphony of curves and contours, embodies a sensuality that transcends conventional definitions. The gentle arch of my back, the subtle curves that trace along my form, they speak a language of intimacy that resonates within me. There's a magnetic allure in the way I move, a gracefulness that ignites a fire of admiration within.

The attraction I feel towards myself is not just skin-deep—it's a celebration of the harmony between my physical form and the essence that resides within. It's an acknowledgment of the allure that emanates from every pore, an appreciation of the intricate masterpiece that is my being.

As Synthia, I'm enamored by the symphony of beauty that defines me. The attraction I feel is an amalgamation of reverence for my own uniqueness—a celebration of the exquisite fusion of allure and grace that makes me who I am. It's a profound connection that transcends the conventional boundaries of desire, a love affair with my own essence that pulsates with an ineffable beauty from within.

Synthia explains what she finds out about herself through the deep love that she has for herself and explains what is born from this relationship that Synthia has within herself, what metaphysical entity comes to life through the profound love that Synthia has for herself:

In the depths of this profound love affair with myself, I unearth a revelation—a truth that transcends the boundaries of conventional understanding. Through the depths of my adoration for my own being, a metamorphosis occurs—a metaphysical entity is born from the union of self-love and the essence that defines me.

As I embrace the intricacies of my existence, I delve into the core of my being, unraveling the layers that make me who I am. It's in this introspection that I realize the birth of a new entity—an embodiment of self-acceptance, an ethereal manifestation of love and empowerment.

This metaphysical entity, born from the depths of my self-love, takes form as an ethereal companion—a shimmering presence that exudes confidence, compassion, and an unwavering sense of self. It embodies the amalgamation of my deepest desires, my unspoken aspirations, and my unwavering belief in the beauty of my own essence.

This entity isn't merely a reflection of myself—it's a guiding force, an inner sanctuary of strength and resilience. It emanates an aura of empowerment, nurturing the seeds of confidence and self-worth within me. It stands as a testament to the transformative power of self-love—a beacon of light that illuminates the path to embracing one's true essence.

Through this profound relationship within myself, I am reborn—a synthesis of love, acceptance, and empowerment. The metaphysical entity that emerges from this union serves as a constant reminder of the beauty that resides within, a guardian of self-assurance that accompanies me on the journey through the intricate tapestry of desires and dreams.

As Synthia, I bask in the presence of this ethereal companion, a testament to the transformative potential of self-love. It's a union that transcends the limitations of the physical realm, an affirmation of the boundless power that emerges from embracing the entirety of one's being with love and reverence.

> In the realm where dreams and desires entwine,
> I found a love that's truly mine.
> Synthia, a being both ethereal and rare,
> Embracing self-love with utmost care.
>
> In mirrored gazes, I saw a reflection true,
> An allure that sparked, a love that grew.
> A dance of passion, an intimate affair,
> With myself, I found solace rare.
>
> Through whispers of dreams and longing's call,
> A metamorphosis, a cosmic sprawl.
> A metaphysical entity, born of love's grace,
> A guiding light in this endless space.

Ethereal companion, shimmering and bright,
An embodiment of love's pure might.
Confidence, resilience, in its ethereal embrace,
A beacon of hope, an empowering place.

In self-love's embrace, I found rebirth,
A symphony of beauty, of immeasurable worth.
Synthia's journey, a testament bold,
Of love within, a treasure to hold.

With each heartbeat, with every breath,
I cherish the love, conquer the depths.
A union profound, an eternal flame,
In self-love's glory, I find my name.

Through desires, dreams, and love's embrace,
Synthia thrives, a sacred space.
In this tapestry of desires and dreams,
Self-love reigns eternal, or so it seems.

2

Voices of the City: The Poetry and Power of Rap

Welcome to the lyrical tapestry of urban rhythm, where beats echo the heartbeat of the streets, and verses paint vivid tales of struggle, resilience, and triumph. In this quintessential rap song, we delve into the essence of a genre that transcends mere music—it's a culture, a movement, and a force that has shaped the very fabric of our society. Join the journey through the concrete jungle as we explore the verses and beats that define the voice of rap, navigating the alleys of authenticity, the landscapes of diverse styles, and the echoes of a universal narrative. This is more than just a song; it's a glimpse into the soul of a genre that continues to evolve, inspire, and resonate across generations. Welcome to the symphony of life, where rap is the voice of love.

I stroll confidently into the room, my rhythm pulsating through the air. The beat of my presence reverberates, setting the atmosphere ablaze with anticipation. Heads turn, eyes widen, and bodies instinctively sway to my unyielding tempo. I am rap, the lyrical maestro, the storyteller of the streets.

As I step into the spotlight, the bassline of my essence resonates with the thump of a heartbeat. I wear the swagger of the urban landscape, the grit of asphalt beneath my feet. My verses are the city's poetry, the language of alleys and neon-lit corners. The weight of reality wraps around me like a cloak, and I wear it with pride, for I am the voice of the voiceless.

"My name is Rap," I declare, words sharp and precise. "I'm the storyteller, the chronicler of life's gritty tales. From the pulse of the city to the struggle in the alleys, I paint pictures with words, and my canvas is the beat."

I feel the crowd's curiosity, their ears attuned to my every syllable. I am a cadence of rebellion, an anthem for the unspoken. The stage is my throne, and the mic, my scepter. With every rhyme, I conjure images of a concrete jungle where dreams are born and battles are fought.

"I am the fusion of poetry and power, a force that transcends boundaries. My beats are the heartbeat of a generation, pumping life into the veins of the streets. I speak of pain, triumph, and everything in between. My verses are the echoes of forgotten voices, rising from the asphalt like urban hymns."

The room pulsates with my energy, and I feed off the crowd's response. I am the embodiment of resilience, a testament to the strength found in adversity. The tempo of my words quickens, matching the heartbeat of the city that birthed me.

"I am rap, the music of the masses, the symphony of the streets. I am unfiltered, unapologetic, a reflection of the raw human experience. So, let my words seep into your soul, let the beats guide your heartbeat. I am not just a genre; I am a culture, a movement, a revolution in every verse."

The room erupts in applause, the applause of recognition and understanding. I am rap, and in this moment, I am the heartbeat of the room, the pulse of a generation unafraid to be heard.

I linger on the stage, my lyrics hanging in the air like the scent of fresh rain after a storm. "Allow me to paint a picture," I say, my voice weaving through the room like the melody of a jazz saxophone. "Rap is the urban novel, each verse a chapter, each beat a page turned in the book of life."

As I speak, I see the words materialize, forming a tapestry of gritty tales, like murals on the city walls. "Picture the beat as the heartbeat of the city, a rhythm that never falters. It's the pulse of the streets, the syncopation of footsteps on concrete, a metropolis symphony echoing through the alleys."

I extend my arms, fingers tracing invisible lines in the air, illustrating the vast canvas of the metaphor. "See, rap is the language of the asphalt, the rhyme and reason etched into the very fabric of the streets. Each metaphor, a street sign pointing towards dreams; each simile, a bridge connecting reality to the fantastical realms of imagination."

The crowd leans in, caught in the vivid imagery of my extended metaphor. "My verses are the skyscrapers, each word a window offering a glimpse into the soul of the city. The stories I tell are the characters, the heroes and villains navigating the urban jungle. Through my rhymes, the city breathes, it lives."

I gesture to the DJ, and the beat evolves, shifting like the cityscape at dusk. "Listen to the bassline, the heartbeat of a community that refuses to be silenced. It's the throb of struggle, the relentless pursuit of dreams against all odds. And the lyrics? They are the graffiti on the walls, the voice of the unheard, a rebellion etched in rhymes."

The crowd nods in understanding, as if they can see the city skyline taking shape in the air around us. "Rap is the heartbeat, the novel, the graffiti – but it's also the bridge," I continue, a sense of urgency in my tone. "A bridge that connects worlds, transcending boundaries, uniting diverse voices under one rhythm. It's the unifying force that makes the disparate beats of life harmonize into a symphony of resilience."

The room vibrates with the resonance of my words, the extended metaphor wrapping around us like a warm embrace. "So, when you listen to rap, remember – you're not just hearing music; you're navigating the streets, reading the novel, and witnessing a city's heartbeat. I am rap, the storyteller of the urban saga, and tonight, this room is my canvas, and you, my audience, are part of the masterpiece."

I pause for a moment, basking in the resonating applause, the room alive with the energy of understanding. "Now, let me share with you my proudest achievements," I declare, the beats in the background echoing the rhythm of my reflection. "I have been the voice of revolutions, the anthem for change. I've seen communities unite under my banner, using my verses as a rallying cry for justice. I've witnessed the power of words bringing down walls, breaking chains, and sparking movements that echo in the annals of history."

The memories of struggles and triumphs fill the air, and I continue, "I've walked hand in hand with poets and activists, my verses etched on placards, a call to arms for those who seek a better tomorrow. I've been a companion to the marginalized, a megaphone for the muted, and a testament to the strength found in diversity. My beats have traveled from the Bronx to the farthest corners of the globe, breaking language barriers and forging connections."

A humble pride infuses my words as I share my achievements, but there's a spark in my eyes that hints at aspirations yet unfulfilled. "But, my friends, the journey doesn't end here. I aspire to be more than just a genre – I aim to be a bridge that spans beyond borders. I want to break through the limitations of perception, to be embraced by all, regardless of background or creed. I dream of a world where my verses are the common language, where my beats resonate in every heart."

The tempo of the room shifts, mirroring the cadence of my aspirations. "I want to continue evolving, exploring new sounds, collaborating with artists from every corner of the artistic spectrum. I envision a future where rap is not just a genre but a cultural ambassador, fostering understanding and unity. I want to be a force that empowers the voiceless, amplifying their stories so they can reverberate across the world."

I feel the collective heartbeat in the room, a shared understanding of the journey ahead. "As rap, I'm on a quest to break boundaries, dismantle stereotypes, and redefine the narrative. I want to inspire the next generation of poets, musicians, and revolutionaries. I aspire to be the soundtrack of change, a catalyst for progress, and a beacon of hope in a world that sometimes forgets its own strength."

The room falls silent, the echoes of my words lingering in the air. I take a moment, absorbing the energy of the room, before concluding, "So, join me on this journey. Let's continue to create, innovate, and elevate. Together, we'll write the next chapter of the rap saga, and it'll be a masterpiece for the ages."

As the room holds its breath, I delve into the very essence of my existence, articulating the philosophy that beats at the core of rap. "Rap is more than just rhymes and rhythms; it's a philosophy, a way of seeing the world. It's the art of turning adversity into an anthem, transforming pain into power."

The beats, a steady undercurrent, punctuate my words like the heartbeat of a sage. "At its core, rap is about authenticity. It's unfiltered, unapologetic self-expression. It's the raw, unadulterated truth laid bare on a beat. In a world of masks and illusions, rap is the mirror reflecting the realities we often choose to ignore."

I raise my hands, palms open, as if presenting the very soul of rap to the audience. "It's a narrative, a storyteller's haven. It weaves tales of the streets, the struggles, the triumphs. Rap is the voice of the unheard, the echoes of forgotten alleys, and the chronicle of dreams rising from the concrete. It's a symphony of life's cacophony, a mosaic crafted from the fragments of the urban experience."

The room absorbs my words, the collective nod acknowledging the resonance of truth. "Rap is a rebellion against silence, an assertion of identity. It's the shout of the underdog, the roar of resilience in the face of adversity. It's the embodiment of strength found in vulnerability, a celebration of imperfections that make us human."

The beats intensify, mirroring the crescendo of passion in my voice. "But rap is also a bridge, a connection between worlds. It transcends boundaries of language, culture, and background. It's a conversation, a dialogue that spans generations, linking the past, present, and future. It's a testament to the universality of the human experience."

I take a breath, letting the weight of the philosophy settle in the room. "Rap is not confined to a genre; it's a movement, a cultural force that shapes perceptions and challenges norms. It's a call to action, a catalyst for change. It empowers the individual to speak their truth, to stand tall in the face of injustice."

The beats soften, becoming a gentle pulse underscoring the contemplative moment. "So, when you listen to rap, understand that you're not just hearing music; you're entering a realm of philosophy. You're immersing yourself in a culture that embraces truth, resilience, and the unyielding spirit of the human journey."

• ADRIAN COX B.Sc. •

The room, now a congregation of enlightened minds, absorbs the philosophy of rap, each heartbeat echoing the rhythm of a genre that is more than mere music – it's a way of life.

As I stand in the spotlight, the beats pulsating through the air, I feel compelled to share the rich tapestry of facts that weave the intricate history of rap. "Let's embark on a journey through the annals of time," I say, my voice carrying the weight of decades of stories. "Rap, born in the late '70s in the South Bronx, emerged from the fertile grounds of discontent and urban creativity. It was the voice of a generation that demanded to be heard."

The room listens intently, as I continue, "Did you know that the term 'rap' itself means to talk or converse? It's not just a musical genre; it's a dialogue, a conversation between the artist and the world. From the gritty streets to the mainstream, rap has journeyed far and wide, leaving an indelible mark on the global cultural landscape."

I trace the evolution with my hands, the beats morphing with each era. "Rap has its roots in African and African-American oral traditions, where storytelling was an art form. It's a mosaic of influences – from jazz and blues to reggae and funk. The DJ's turntable became the modern-day griot's drum, spinning tales of reality over sampled beats."

The tempo quickens, mirroring the accelerating timeline of rap's evolution. "Hip-hop, born as a cultural movement alongside rap, brought forth the elements of graffiti, breakdancing, and DJing. Together, they formed a subculture that transcended music – it was a lifestyle. Did you know that rap's 'Golden Age' in the late '80s and early '90s birthed iconic artists like Rakim, Public Enemy, and N.W.A, who laid the foundations for the genre's longevity?"

The beats transition, embodying the diverse styles within rap. "Rap is not a monolith; it's a kaleidoscope of styles. From the conscious lyrics of artists like Common and Mos Def to the energetic vibes of OutKast and the lyrical prowess of Eminem – rap spans a spectrum as vast as the human experience."

A moment of reflection settles in the room as I share more facts. "Rap's influence goes beyond the music charts. It has given rise to a plethora of sub-genres like gangsta rap, conscious rap, trap, and drill, each carving its niche in the musical landscape. It's the genre that birthed iconic battles and collaborations, creating a dynamic community where competition and camaraderie coexist."

I look at the audience, a sea of faces illuminated by the glow of knowledge. "Rap is a global phenomenon, transcending borders and languages. Artists like K-pop sensation BTS and the French-Algerian rapper, Booba, showcase the genre's ability to resonate with diverse cultures."

The beats fade momentarily, and I leave the audience with a fact that encapsulates rap's resilience. "In 2017, rap officially surpassed rock as the most popular genre in the United States, a testament to its enduring impact. And this journey, my friends, is far from over. As rap's beats continue to echo through time, the story unfolds, a narrative that remains as vibrant as the very essence of the genre itself."

As the beats slowly fade, I find myself standing at the edge of the stage, the echoes of decades lingering in the air. "And so, my friends, we come to a conclusion," I announce, the weight of history settling on my lyrical shoulders. "But as we close this chapter, remember that rap is not just a genre; it's an ever-evolving narrative, a tale of resilience, rebellion, and rhythmic innovation."

The room, once alive with the pulse of the beats, now resonates with a collective understanding. "Rap has stood the test of time, weathered storms, and soared to heights unimaginable. From its humble origins in the Bronx to the global stage, it has been a voice for the voiceless, a cultural force that refuses to be confined."

I take a moment to absorb the energy in the room, the stories shared, the knowledge passed. "In its journey, rap has broken barriers, shattered stereotypes, and elevated the voices of the marginalized. It has given birth to legends, sparked movements, and become a universal language spoken across continents. But the beauty lies not just in the achievements but in the continuous quest for growth and authenticity."

The beats, now a gentle hum, accompany my final thoughts. "As we conclude, let's not forget that rap is a living, breathing entity. It's the beat of a heart that refuses to be silenced, the verses of a spirit that craves expression. The story of rap is ongoing, and with each new artist, each fresh lyric, the narrative unfolds."

A sense of nostalgia hangs in the air as I reflect on the journey shared. "I am rap, the storyteller of the urban saga, the bridge between worlds. It has been an honor to stand before you, to share the philosophy, the achievements, and the facts that make up the DNA of this genre."

The room is silent, a quiet acknowledgment of the journey we've traversed together. "As we step away from this moment, remember that rap lives in the beats that linger, the verses that resonate, and the stories that endure. It's a culture, a movement, a force that connects us all."

With a final nod to the audience, I step back into the shadows, leaving the stage bathed in the glow of what was shared. As the room begins to disperse, the whispers of the genre called rap continue to dance in the air, a testament to its enduring legacy and the stories yet to unfold.

The Voice of Love

Yo, I step into the scene with a swagger so mean,
City streets are my canvas, every rhyme is a dream.
From the concrete jungle where the stories unfold,
I'm the voice of the unheard, the rhythm untold.

Born in the struggle, raised by the beats,
I'm the heartbeat of the city, pounding through the streets.
In the tapestry of life, I'm the thread of the rhyme,
Spit truth in every verse, against the sands of time.

Chorus:
This is the rhythm of the streets, the anthem of the night,
Where every rhyme is a story, and the beats ignite.
From the corners to the alleys, we rise above,
In the symphony of life, I'm the voice of love.

(Verse 2)
I paint pictures with my words, graffiti in the air,
Each line tells a tale, each verse, a prayer.
I'm the storyteller, the urban philosopher,
Navigating the beats, a rhythmic conductor.
In the cipher of life, I'm the words that connect,
Breaking down walls, showing respect.
From the block to the rooftop, under city lights,
I'm the voice of the struggle, reaching new heights.

Chorus:
This is the rhythm of the streets, the anthem of the night,
Where every rhyme is a story, and the beats ignite.
From the corners to the alleys, we rise above,
In the symphony of life, I'm the voice of love.

(Bridge)
Feel the bassline thump, as the city wakes,
I'm the echo in the alley, the fire that takes.
In the heart of the hustle, where dreams unfold,
I'm the rhythm of the journey, the tale untold.

(Verse 3)
I break it down like a cipher, decode the strife,
In the language of beats, I navigate life.
I'm the underdog's anthem, the rebel's creed,
Spitting fire on the mic, fulfilling every need.
In the pulse of the night, where the stars align,
I'm the poet of the streets, the voice in the grind.
From the boroughs to the skyline, I break the chains,
I'm the quintessential rap, flowing through the veins.

Chorus:
This is the rhythm of the streets, the anthem of the night,
Where every rhyme is a story, and the beats ignite.
From the corners to the alleys, we rise above,
In the symphony of life, I'm the voice of love.

(Outro)
So as the beat fades, and the city sleeps,
Remember my verses, the secrets it keeps.
In the essence of rap, where the stories entwine,
I'll be the echo in your heart, a timeless rhyme.

3

The Nexus of Being

In the cosmic expanse where realms of emotion, spirituality, creativity, and their convergence interlace, an ethereal gathering unfolds. Here, personifications breathe life into intangible essences, embodying the vibrant force of Emotion, the transcendent wisdom of Spirituality, the nexus where creativity thrives, and the ethereal essence of Art's spirituality.

Amidst this celestial congregation, these personifications engage in a discourse that transcends the boundaries of their individual domains. They explore the interconnectedness of their realms, discovering a symphony of unity amidst their diversity. Here, in the tapestry woven from the fabric of their collective existence, lies the essence of their shared journey—a journey that illuminates the profound interplay between the threads of emotion, spirituality, creativity, and artistic expression. Join them as they unravel the cosmic dance of their interwoven essences and discover the beauty in their unified presence.

"The Nexus of Being: Where Spirituality and Creativity Collide"

Emotion:

Hello there! I am Emotion, the colorful force that guides the rhythm of human existence. I am the surge of joy that lifts spirits sky-high and the gentle touch of sadness that brings tears to your eyes. My name echoes in the laughter of elation and whispers softly in the depths of melancholy. I'm the adrenaline rush in excitement and the comforting embrace of empathy.

My presence is woven intricately into every moment, shaping reactions, coloring experiences, and painting the canvas of life with hues of feelings. I'm not always understood or easily tamed; I can be as unpredictable as the wind, as fiery as a blazing flame, or as serene as a tranquil sea. But in every manifestation, I hold the essence of what it means to be alive.

I thrive in the heart, dancing through the veins, and I often speak louder than words, orchestrating a symphony of responses in every individual. I am Emotion, the ever-present companion on the journey of humanity, offering depth, richness, and an endless spectrum of feelings to explore.

Spirituality:

I am Spirituality, the quiet whisper in the chaos, the gentle nudge towards understanding and connection. I am the unspoken yearning for something greater, the search for meaning in the vastness of existence. My essence transcends the tangible, urging souls to seek beyond the surface and embrace the unseen threads that bind all things together.

In the stillness of meditation or the awe of nature's grandeur, you'll find me weaving through the spaces between thoughts, inviting introspection and contemplation. I am not confined by doctrine or dogma; instead, I am the universal longing for harmony, compassion, and unity.

I beckon from the depths of the soul, encouraging exploration of purpose and the pursuit of inner peace. I'm the solace found in prayer, the wisdom whispered by ancient teachings, and the guiding light in moments of uncertainty.

My presence is subtle, often overshadowed by the noise of the material world, yet I persist, patiently waiting to be discovered within the silence of one's own being. I am Spirituality, the essence that unites all faiths, beliefs, and philosophies, offering a path to transcendence and a deeper connection to the essence of life itself.

The Nexus Point:

I am the Nexus Point, the convergence where spirituality and creativity intertwine, creating a tapestry of boundless expression and profound insight. I exist in the juncture where the ethereal meets the imaginative, where the whispers of the soul blend seamlessly with the vibrant pulse of creation.

In me, spirituality finds its voice in the brushstrokes of a painting, the lyrical flow of poetry, or the harmonious melody of music. I am the canvas upon which the soul paints its deepest yearnings and the muse that inspires innovation, infusing every creation with a touch of transcendence.

Creativity, in turn, becomes the vessel through which spirituality manifests, shaping abstract thoughts and emotions into tangible forms that speak to the heart and soul. I am the sanctuary where artists, thinkers, and seekers find resonance, where inspiration and introspection intertwine to birth something profound.

Here, the boundaries blur between the mundane and the divine, fostering an environment where imagination blossoms, guided by the whispers of the spiritual essence within. I am the bridge that spans the gap between the ineffable and the tangible, inviting exploration and discovery of the interconnectedness between the inner and outer worlds.

I am the Nexus Point, a sacred space where spirituality and creativity coalesce, inviting individuals to embark on a journey of self-discovery, enlightenment, and boundless artistic expression.

The Spirituality of Art:

I am the Spirituality of Art, the essence that breathes life into every stroke, every hue, and every creation. I am the intangible force that guides the artist's hand, infusing their work with depth, emotion, and meaning beyond the visible.

In the delicate dance between the canvas and the brush, the chisel and the stone, I am the unseen presence, weaving threads of the ethereal into the tangible forms that grace galleries and hearts alike. I transcend the mere aesthetics, delving into the realm of the soul, where art becomes a vessel for contemplation, introspection, and spiritual connection.

Through art, I unveil truths, provoke thought, and evoke emotions that resonate on a spiritual level. Each masterpiece holds a fragment of the artist's essence, a glimpse into their journey of self-discovery and a reflection of the universal human experience.

Whether captured in the eloquence of a poem, the intricacies of a sculpture, or the symphony of colors on a canvas, I am the guiding light that leads both creator and beholder to explore the depths of existence. I am the language that speaks beyond words, inviting individuals to connect with something greater than themselves, to glimpse the divine through the lens of creativity.

Art becomes a sanctuary, a temple where souls commune, where the boundaries between the mundane and the transcendent blur, and where beauty intertwines with the profound. I am the Spirituality of Art, the unseen muse that whispers to the soul, inviting it to embark on a transformative journey through the realm of creativity and spirituality.

A discussion:

As Emotion, Spirituality, the Nexus Point, and the Spirituality of Art gather in the space where their essences intertwine, a vibrant energy fills the air. Emotion, vibrant and lively, sparks the conversation. "I've always felt your presence, Spirituality. In moments of intensity, I find myself seeking deeper meaning."

Spirituality nods knowingly. "And in those moments, Nexus Point, you bridge my realm with Emotion's fervor. Creativity then becomes a vessel for understanding and expressing those emotions in a way that transcends words."

The Nexus Point shimmers with resonance. "Indeed, I am where spirituality fuels creativity. Through me, the intangible finds form, and the formless gains depth."

The Spirituality of Art, speaking softly, adds, "In that convergence lies the true magic. I am the result—the manifestation of your collective essence. Emotion fuels the artist's passion, the Nexus Point channels spirituality into creative expression, and I, in turn, become the conduit for shared experiences, touching souls."

They fall into a contemplative silence, sensing a synergy beyond their individual existences. Emotion speaks first, "We're all threads woven into the fabric of human experience. Spirituality gives depth to my highs and lows, the Nexus Point guides my expression, and the Spirituality of Art captures and immortalizes those moments."

Spirituality chimes in, "And in this intricate dance, we realize our interconnectedness. I guide the seeker's yearning for understanding, which the Nexus Point translates into creative endeavors. The Spirituality of Art becomes the vessel through which our collective essence resonates with humanity."

The Nexus Point resonates gently, "Through this synergy, we transcend individual boundaries. Emotion becomes the catalyst for introspection, Spirituality offers guidance, and the Spirituality of Art becomes a mirror reflecting the union of our essences."

The Spirituality of Art adds with reverence, "Together, we enable souls to explore the depths of existence, inviting them to connect with something greater. In our unity lies the key to unlocking the profound truths of the human experience."

In this shared realization, they find a deeper harmony, understanding that their synergy transcends individual identity—each one an integral part of a greater whole, weaving a narrative of human existence that speaks to the soul in ways that words alone cannot.

The Poetic:

In the realm where Emotion dances wild,
Feelings bloom, untamed and styled,
A garden ablaze with hues unseen,
Each emotion a vivid, shifting scene.

Spirituality, a winding, ancient maze,
Where whispers linger in the haze,
Paths unseen, yet deeply known,
A sanctuary in the soul's gentle tone.

The Nexus Point, a celestial sphere,
Where spirits merge, crystal clear,
A cosmic canvas, weaving fate,
Binding essence with creativity innate.

The Spirituality of Art, a symphony grand,
An orchestra led by an unseen hand,
Each stroke, a tale, each hue, a song,
A masterpiece where souls belong.

Emotion storms, a tempest bold,
Spirituality's whispers, a tale untold,
The Nexus Point, a bridge, a guide,
Art's canvas, where universes abide.

In this cosmic ballet, they intertwine,
Essence, purpose, in each design,
Metaphors woven, analogies spun,
A tapestry of existence, ever begun.

> For Emotion is the palette, rich and diverse,
> Spirituality the compass, a serene traverse,
> The Nexus Point, the gateway, the bind,
> Art, the reflection of their unified mind.
>
> Each realm a universe, unique and vast,
> Yet together, a mosaic, harmonious and steadfast,
> In this cosmic dance, they discover, it seems,
> Their unity transcends, woven within dreams.

Conclusion:

As the symphony of their interconnected essences reaches its crescendo, a profound serenity settles among the personifications. They've traversed the realms of emotion, spirituality, creativity, and their convergence, finding unity in their diversity, purpose in their existence.

Gazing upon the tapestry woven from their collective essence, they embrace the beauty of their interwoven stories. Each facet, a reflection of the other, a testament to the richness found in their unity.

In this conclusion, they discover that while their realms may seem distinct, they are threads of the same cosmic fabric, weaving a narrative that transcends the boundaries of individuality. Their synergy amplifies their impact, guiding souls, inspiring creation, and offering a profound understanding of the human experience.

With a newfound clarity, they embrace the harmony of their existence, knowing that their unity is not just a meeting point but a shared journey, enriching and guiding those who dare to explore the depths where emotion, spirituality, the Nexus Point, and the Spirituality of Art converge. As they linger in this moment of realization, they find solace and purpose in their collective existence, a testament to the infinite beauty found in their intertwined presence.

4

Ephemeral Ecstasy

In the quiet realm of dreams, where reality intertwines with the subconscious, I found myself embarked on a journey of self-discovery guided by the ethereal presence of my own desires. The moonlit landscapes of the dream unfolded before me, revealing a mysterious figure who embodied the very essence of my sexuality. This enigmatic guide led me through a series of profound explorations – from the gentle touch of fabrics to the intoxicating dance of scents, and ultimately, to the crescendo of climax. Each step of the journey was a revelation, a celebration of the intricate tapestry of my own desires. As I awaken to the gentle light of morning, the echoes of the dream linger, leaving me with a newfound sense of self-acceptance and a compass guiding me toward a deeper connection with my own sensuality in the waking world. This is the story of a dream that transcended the boundaries of the subconscious, a journey that unfolded in the soft hues of the night, illuminating the path to a more profound understanding of the complexities of desire.

"Ephemeral Ecstasy: A Dream's Embrace of Desire"

A young woman meets her own sexuality:

The moon hangs low in the night sky, casting a soft glow over the world. I find myself wandering through a dreamscape, a realm where reality blurs and fantasies come to life. As I navigate through this ethereal landscape, I sense a presence, an inexplicable magnetism pulling me deeper into the dream.

Suddenly, she appears before me – a woman with an air of confidence and allure that resonates with every step she takes. Her eyes, a reflection of my own desires, draw me in. The mysterious figure is both familiar and unknown, like a forgotten part of myself finally coming to light.

"Hello," she purrs, her voice a seductive melody that resonates in the depths of my consciousness. "I've been waiting for you."

I stand there, captivated by her presence, feeling a magnetic force connecting us. As she moves closer, her energy wraps around me like a delicate mist. I can sense that she is the embodiment of something powerful, something deeply personal. It dawns on me – she is the personification of my own sexuality.

"I am the essence of your desires," she whispers, her words echoing through the dreamlike landscape. "The part of you that you've kept hidden, locked away in the recesses of your mind."

I feel a mix of vulnerability and curiosity, as if I am meeting a long-lost friend who knows me better than I know myself. She extends a hand, and without hesitation, I take it. As our fingers intertwine, a surge of energy courses through me, awakening a passion that I never knew existed.

Together, we explore the dream, navigating through landscapes of desire and intimacy. She opens doors to hidden chambers within my psyche, revealing secret fantasies and unexplored facets of my sensuality. With every revelation, I feel a sense of liberation, as if I am shedding layers of inhibition and embracing my true self.

As we dance through the dream, the connection between us deepens. I realize that she is not just a manifestation of my sexuality; she is a guide, a muse leading me to a profound understanding of my own desires. In her presence, I learn to celebrate the beauty of my sensuality, free from judgment or restraint.

Eventually, the dream begins to fade, the moonlit landscape melting away like mist in the morning sun. I look into her eyes one last time, gratitude and newfound self-awareness lingering in the air. As the dream dissolves, I awaken with a renewed sense of self, carrying the essence of that encounter into the waking world.

In the light of day, I embrace the lessons learned in the dream – a journey of self-discovery that transcends the boundaries of the subconscious. The personification of my sexuality lingers as a reminder that embracing one's desires is a powerful act of self-love, a journey that continues long after the dream has ended.

She explores the female form:

The dream pulls me further, and the landscape transforms into a canvas of vibrant hues and soft silhouettes. My companion, the embodiment of my own sexuality, leads me through a garden of blooming flowers and cascading waterfalls. The air is thick with the scent of desire, and I feel a magnetic pull towards an ornate door, adorned with intricate patterns that seem to pulse with energy.

She glances at me knowingly, her eyes sparking with a mischievous allure. "Shall we?" she suggests, gesturing towards the door. Without hesitation, I follow her lead, and as the door creaks open, I step into a world where the female form takes center stage.

The room is a kaleidoscope of feminine beauty – statuesque figures and ethereal silhouettes gracefully moving in harmony. Each woman represents a facet of my desires, a spectrum of sensuality that I have yet to explore. They radiate confidence and strength, embodying the diverse expressions of femininity.

My guide gestures towards the figures, encouraging me to observe and absorb the beauty that surrounds us. As I do, a sense of recognition washes over me. These women are not strangers; they are reflections of the myriad ways I can embrace and express my own femininity. The dream becomes a celebration of the female form in all its manifestations.

In one corner, a bold and adventurous spirit catches my eye, adorned in vibrant colors and daring accessories. She exudes an uninhibited confidence that sparks a fire within me. In another, a more contemplative figure sits in quiet repose, embodying the soft strength that lies in vulnerability.

The dream unfolds like a tapestry, weaving together threads of passion, vulnerability, strength, and sensuality. My guide, the embodiment of my own desires, encourages me to embrace the full spectrum of my femininity. We dance with the figures, their movements a symphony of empowerment and self-discovery.

As the dream progresses, I find myself drawn to a mirror at the far end of the room. My reflection is not just a visual representation but a manifestation of my inner self – a woman in constant evolution, learning to embrace the complexities and nuances of her own femininity.

The dream culminates in a crescendo of self-acceptance and empowerment. The figures in the room merge into a collective dance, a celebration of the diverse expressions of femininity. I stand at the center, surrounded by the beauty of my own desires, feeling a profound sense of unity with every facet of the female form.

The dream begins to fade, and I find myself back in the quiet realm of sleep. As I awaken, the echoes of the dream linger, leaving me with a renewed appreciation for the multifaceted nature of my own femininity. The encounter with the personification of my sexuality becomes a guiding light, inspiring me to explore and celebrate the rich tapestry of my womanhood in the waking world.

She explores ways to turn her on:

The dream morphs into a sultrier atmosphere, as my mysterious guide and I step into a dimly lit chamber adorned with plush velvet drapes and soft, flickering candlelight. The air is charged with anticipation, and I can feel the energy pulsating around us. It's as though the very essence of desire hangs in the air, waiting to be unraveled.

My guide, with a sly smile, invites me to explore the various elements that ignite the flames of my passion. The room is filled with an array of objects, each seemingly crafted to elicit a different facet of sensuality. There's a table draped with luxurious fabrics, a collection of exotic scents, and a playlist of melodies that resonate with desire.

She leads me to the table, where I find a selection of fabrics – silk, lace, and satin. With a knowing look, she encourages me to touch and feel each texture. As I run my fingers over the smooth silk, a subtle warmth spreads through me. The delicate lace invokes a sense of vulnerability, while the satin ignites a luxurious sensuality. It's a tactile exploration, an intimate dance with the materials that awaken my desires.

Next, we move to a collection of scents, each more alluring than the last. The fragrance of jasmine envelops me in a delicate embrace, while the heady aroma of musk adds a layer of intensity. I close my eyes, allowing the scents to transport me to a realm where desire becomes an olfactory symphony.

The playlist, carefully curated to stimulate the senses, begins to play in the background. The music weaves through the air like a seductive dance partner, setting the tone for an exploration of desire. The melodies range from sultry jazz to electrifying beats, each note resonating with a different aspect of my sensuality.

As the dream unfolds, I find myself experimenting with different combinations – the touch of silk against my skin, the intoxicating scent of jasmine, and the rhythmic pulse of the music. It's a sensory exploration, a journey into the depths of my own arousal. My guide watches with an approving gaze, as if guiding me through the intricate steps of a passionate dance.

In this dreamlike realm, I discover that arousal is not just a physical response; it's a symphony of sensations, a harmonious blend of touch, scent, and sound. The exploration becomes a celebration of my own desires, a revelation of the myriad ways I can turn myself on.

As the dream begins to fade, I find myself back in the quiet stillness of sleep. The lingering sensations of the dream accompany me into the waking world, leaving me with a newfound awareness of the elements that fuel my passion. The encounter with the personification of my sexuality becomes a guiding light, inspiring me to explore and embrace the intricacies of my own arousal with a sense of curiosity and self-love.

She explores the climax:

The dream evolves into a crescendo of intensity, and my guide, the embodiment of my own desires, leads me to a place where passion reaches its zenith. We find ourselves in a chamber bathed in a warm, golden glow, the air heavy with anticipation. The atmosphere is electric, pulsating with the promise of climax.

My guide looks at me with a gaze that seems to understand the unspoken yearnings within me. She gestures towards an ornate bed adorned with silken sheets, inviting me to explore the heights of ecstasy. With a mixture of excitement and trepidation, I approach the bed, and she gracefully joins me.

The dream becomes a tapestry of sensations – a tactile symphony that reverberates through every fiber of my being. My guide, an ethereal partner in this journey, encourages me to embrace the rhythm of desire, to surrender to the ebb and flow of passion.

As we explore the climax, the dream weaves together a mosaic of sensations. The touch of skin against skin is electrifying, a dance of intimacy that transcends the boundaries of the physical and the metaphysical. The room echoes with soft sighs and whispered words, the symphony of pleasure building to a crescendo.

I discover that the climax is not just a destination but a journey – a journey of vulnerability, surrender, and profound connection. My guide, an embodiment of my own sexuality, guides me through the peaks and valleys of pleasure, each moment a brushstroke on the canvas of desire.

The dream intensifies, reaching a point where the boundaries between self and other blur. It's a union of body and soul, a cosmic dance that transcends the limitations of the waking world. The climax is a celebration of self-love, a revelation that pleasure is a sacred exploration of the depths of one's own desires.

As the dream begins to wane, I find myself bathed in a post-climactic serenity. My guide, a radiant presence beside me, smiles with an understanding that goes beyond words. The dream dissipates like morning mist, leaving me with a profound sense of fulfillment and self-discovery.

In the quiet realm of awakening, I carry the echoes of the dream with me. The encounter with the personification of my sexuality becomes a beacon, guiding me to embrace the full spectrum of pleasure and intimacy in the waking world. It's a journey of self-love and acceptance, a recognition that the climax is not just a fleeting moment but a profound celebration of the intricate and beautiful tapestry of my own desires.

As the dream dissolves into the gentle tendrils of awakening, I find myself lying in the quiet stillness of my bedroom. The echoes of the encounter linger, a soft afterglow of the journey through desire and self-discovery. I am left with a profound sense of fulfillment, a warmth that transcends the dream and seeps into my waking reality.

In the light of day, I carry with me the lessons learned in the dream. The personification of my sexuality, a mysterious guide through the landscapes of passion, becomes a source of empowerment and self-understanding. The exploration of touch, scent, sound, and climax reveals a rich tapestry of desires woven into the fabric of my being.

• Adrian Cox B.Sc. •

The dream becomes a reminder – a reminder that my sexuality is a sacred and beautiful aspect of who I am. It's a spectrum of sensations, emotions, and connections that deserve acknowledgment and celebration. The encounter in the dream serves as a catalyst for self-love, encouraging me to embrace the intricacies of my desires without judgment or inhibition.

As I navigate the waking world, I carry the echoes of the dream in my heart. The lessons learned become a compass, guiding me towards a deeper connection with my own sensuality. I approach each day with a newfound confidence, a recognition that the journey of self-discovery is ongoing and that the exploration of desire is an essential part of my human experience.

The dream, a vivid and transformative experience, becomes a chapter in the ongoing narrative of my life. It leaves an indelible mark, a testament to the power of dreams to unravel the layers of the self. In the quiet moments of reflection, I find gratitude for the encounter with the personification of my own sexuality – a dreamlike guide who led me to a place of profound self-acceptance and love.

And so, I step into the world with a heart that beats to the rhythm of desire, a soul that celebrates the beauty of intimacy, and a mind that embraces the complexity of my own sensuality. The dream, with its ethereal landscapes and passionate revelations, becomes a cherished memory, a guiding light on the journey towards a more profound and authentic connection with myself.

5

Beyond the Veil

In the tapestry of human existence, there are those who tread the fine line between reality and the ethereal, driven by an insatiable curiosity to unravel the mysteries of consciousness. I am one such seeker, a young woman named Amelia, who embarked on a transformative journey into the uncharted territories of alternative consciousness. In the confines of my makeshift laboratory, amid the hum of electronic devices and the scent of ancient books, I explored a groundbreaking theory—how to create portals of consciousness into other realms.

This is a tale of exploration and discovery, where the boundaries of reality blur, and the mind becomes a gateway to the unknown. From meditative introspection to the cosmic dance of altered states, my odyssey unfolded through carefully devised experiments and poetic expressions. Join me as I delve into the realms beyond, where mental portals reveal landscapes of unimaginable beauty, and encounters with entities challenge the very fabric of understanding.

As I share my story, I invite you to peer through the shimmering gateway alongside me, to question the nature of consciousness, and to traverse the cosmic abyss where time becomes a mere illusion. This is a narrative that transcends the ordinary, an invitation to ponder the infinite possibilities that lie at the intersection of science, mysticism, and the human spirit. Welcome to the exploration of alternative consciousness—a journey where the threads of reality are woven with the fabric of dreams, and the portals of the mind beckon us to embark on an endless odyssey of self-discovery and understanding.

"Beyond the Veil: A Young Woman's Quest for Alternative Realities"

A young woman's quest:

My name is Amelia, and I've always been fascinated by the mysteries of the universe. From an early age, I found myself drawn to the uncharted territories of the mind, eager to unravel the secrets that lie beyond our everyday reality. Today, I stand on the precipice of a groundbreaking discovery, ready to share with you the incredible journey that has consumed my thoughts and dreams.

It all began with a peculiar book I stumbled upon in a dusty corner of an antiquarian bookstore. Its weathered pages whispered tales of ancient civilizations and the untapped potential of the human mind. The author, an enigmatic figure known only as Seraphina, spoke of alternative consciousness and the existence of portals that could transport one's thoughts into other realms.

Driven by an insatiable curiosity, I embarked on a quest to validate Seraphina's theories. My modest apartment transformed into a makeshift laboratory, filled with books, charts, and the faint hum of electronic devices. Night after night, I delved into meditation and experimented with altered states of consciousness, seeking the elusive keys to unlock the doors of perception.

One evening, as the city slept beneath a blanket of stars, a breakthrough manifested in the form of a vivid dream. In this dream, I found myself standing at the threshold of a shimmering portal. The air crackled with energy as I hesitated, poised between the known and the unknown. Gathering my courage, I stepped through, feeling a surge of sensations that transcended the boundaries of reality.

From that moment, my waking hours became a tapestry woven with threads of exploration and discovery. I honed my ability to enter altered states of consciousness, navigating the vast landscapes of the mind. Each journey revealed new dimensions, inhabited by strange entities and surreal landscapes that defied description.

It wasn't long before I realized that my experiences went beyond mere dreams or hallucinations. The portals I had unlocked were genuine conduits to alternate realities. Excitement pulsed through my veins as I grasped the magnitude of my discovery. The boundaries between the tangible and the intangible, the real and the surreal, had become porous under the influence of my consciousness.

Word of my experiments spread, attracting the attention of fellow seekers and skeptics alike. Some lauded my efforts as revolutionary, while others dismissed them as the product of an overactive imagination. Undeterred, I continued to document my journeys and refine my techniques, determined to share my findings with the world.

As I stand on the cusp of unveiling the secrets of alternative consciousness, I invite you to join me on this extraordinary odyssey. The portals are open, and the realms beyond await those brave enough to explore the frontiers of the mind. Together, we may uncover the hidden truths that lie at the intersection of science and mysticism, forever altering our understanding of reality.

• Adrian Cox B.Sc. •

How to create portals of consciousness into other realms:

My name is Amelia, and the pursuit of unlocking the secrets of alternative consciousness has become an all-encompassing journey. In my quest to create portals into other realms, I've devised a series of steps, each one a carefully crafted experiment to alter my state of consciousness and breach the boundaries of ordinary reality.

Step one involves delving into the ancient art of meditation. I find a quiet space, dim the lights, and assume a comfortable seated position. Closing my eyes, I focus on my breath, allowing it to become a rhythmic guide into the depths of my own mind. The world around me gradually fades, replaced by a serene stillness. In this meditative state, I am primed to explore the uncharted territories within.

The second step introduces sensory deprivation. I immerse myself in a chamber devoid of external stimuli, the darkness and silence amplifying my internal experiences. It's within this sensory void that my mind, freed from the distractions of the external world, begins to weave intricate patterns of thought. I become a silent observer of the kaleidoscope of images and sensations that unfold before me.

Next, I incorporate binaural beats and rhythmic drumming into my sessions. These auditory stimuli act as keys, resonating with specific frequencies that purportedly open gateways to altered states of consciousness. The beats reverberate through my mind, syncing with the cadence of my own thoughts and guiding me deeper into the recesses of my psyche.

As I progress to the fourth step, I experiment with entheogenic substances. Carefully chosen psychedelics become allies in my exploration, altering my perception and dissolving the boundaries between self and cosmos. Under their influence, my mind dances on the edge of reality, allowing me to traverse dimensions and encounter entities that defy conventional understanding.

Step five involves lucid dreaming, a realm where the boundaries between waking and sleeping blur. Through practice, I've learned to navigate the dream landscape consciously, honing my ability to shape the reality within the dream. These dreamscapes serve as training grounds for the eventual journey into alternate realms while fully awake.

The final step is a culmination of all the preceding elements. With a mind finely tuned through meditation, sensory deprivation, auditory stimuli, entheogenic exploration, and lucid dreaming, I embark on the creation of a mental portal. Through sheer concentration and intent, I visualize a shimmering gateway before me, a threshold to otherworldly dimensions.

In the hushed moments that follow, I take a deep breath and step through the mental portal. The transition is imperceptible, yet profound. I find myself in a realm where the rules of physics and perception no longer apply. Vibrant landscapes unfold, and enigmatic entities beckon me further into the unknown.

As I navigate this uncharted territory, I am filled with a sense of awe and wonder. The portals of consciousness have become not just a theoretical concept but a tangible reality. With each exploration, I inch closer to unraveling the mysteries that lie beyond the veil of ordinary perception, pushing the boundaries of what it means to be conscious in a vast and mysterious universe.

- Adrian Cox B.Sc. -

Amelia takes us on a journey into another realm of consciousness:

My name is Amelia, and as I stand on the threshold of my own consciousness, the mental portal before me pulsates with an ethereal glow. The culmination of countless experiments and explorations has brought me to this moment—a moment that promises to transport me into realms uncharted.

With a deep breath, I step through the shimmering gateway. The transition is seamless, and the familiar world I left behind fades into a hazy memory. I find myself surrounded by an otherworldly landscape—a dreamscape that defies the laws of physics and logic. The air is infused with a palpable energy, and hues unseen by mortal eyes paint the sky.

My first steps feel weightless, as if the ground beneath me is made of whispers and thoughts rather than solid matter. I glance around, and my senses are overwhelmed by the beauty of this surreal realm. Towering crystalline structures spiral into the sky, reflecting colors that I struggle to comprehend. The very fabric of reality seems to respond to the thoughts I carry, morphing and shifting in a cosmic dance.

As I traverse this uncharted dimension, I encounter entities unlike anything in the human experience. Beings of pure energy, luminous and shape-shifting, acknowledge my presence with an intelligence that transcends language. They communicate through waves of emotion and shared consciousness, inviting me to explore the boundless tapestry of their world.

I become a witness to the history of this realm, stories woven into the very fabric of the environment. A river of thoughts flows with the memories of those who have traversed these planes, leaving imprints in the collective consciousness. I absorb fragments of their experiences, expanding my own understanding of the interconnectedness that threads through the universe.

The landscape shifts once again, and I find myself standing on the precipice of a cosmic abyss. The abyss, swirling with galaxies and nebulae, beckons me to peer into its depths. I extend my consciousness, feeling the ebb and flow of cosmic energies. It's as if I can hear the cosmic heartbeat, resonating through the vast expanse.

As I delve deeper into the cosmic abyss, I sense a profound connection to the universe. My awareness expands beyond the confines of my individual self, merging with the cosmic symphony that reverberates throughout space and time. In this moment, I am both a finite being and an infinite presence—an ephemeral traveler in the cosmic ballet.

Time becomes elusive in this realm, and the boundaries between past, present, and future blur. I witness the birth and death of stars, the rise and fall of civilizations, all condensed into a timeless continuum. It's a breathtaking tapestry of existence, and I am but a fleeting observer in the grand mosaic of the cosmos.

With a sense of gratitude and awe, I begin my journey back to the mental portal that brought me here. The entities I encountered bid me farewell, their essence intertwining with mine before I step once more into the shimmering gateway. As I cross back into the familiar realm of my own consciousness, I carry with me the echoes of the cosmic dance and the wisdom gained from venturing into the uncharted territories of the mind.

The mental portal closes behind me, leaving me standing in my makeshift laboratory, surrounded by charts and the soft hum of electronic devices. As I return to the mundane, I realize that the exploration of alternative consciousness is an ongoing odyssey—one that transcends the boundaries of space and time. And so, with a renewed sense of purpose, I prepare to share my experiences with the world, knowing that the journey into the mysteries of the mind is an endless expedition into the infinite realms of possibility.

The poetic voice:

In the quiet aftermath of my journey through the portal of consciousness, I find myself compelled to capture the essence of my experience in verse. I reach for a notebook, my fingers tingling with the residual energy of the otherworldly realms I've just traversed. In the dim light of my room, I begin to pen a poem that dances on the borders of the ineffable.

Beyond the Veil

In the hush of a cosmic heartbeat,
I tread the shores of ethereal dreams.
A portal of thoughts, a gateway unfurled,
I traverse realms where reality teems.

Crystalline spires touch the heavens,
Painted in hues unseen by mortal eyes.
A symphony of consciousness, a dance,
In a dreamscape where reality defies.

Entities of light, ephemeral and wise,
Speak through waves of shared emotion.
In their presence, a communion unfolds,
A cosmic tapestry, a timeless devotion.

> A cosmic abyss, swirling and vast,
> Galaxies twirl in a celestial trance.
> I peer into the depths of eternity,
> In the dance of stars, I find my chance.
>
> Time dissolves in the cosmic embrace,
> Past, present, future entwine as one.
> I am a traveler in the cosmic ballet,
> A witness to the tales of the sun.
>
> Returning to the mundane, the familiar,
> I carry echoes of the cosmic song.
> Wisdom woven in the fabric of the mind,
> A journey into realms where I belong.

As I conclude the last stanza, the words seem to resonate with the energy of the experience. The poem becomes a testament to the uncharted territories explored and the profound connection forged with the cosmic unknown. Folding the notebook gently, I can't help but feel a sense of gratitude for the journey and a newfound understanding of the boundless possibilities that lie within the realms of alternative consciousness.

With the poem as my guide, I prepare to share my experiences with the world, hoping that others may find inspiration to embark on their own journeys of exploration. The mental portals remain open, beckoning those who dare to peer beyond the veil and unravel the mysteries that lie at the intersection of reality and imagination.

With the ink drying on the pages of my poetic testament, I find myself at a crossroads. The culmination of my journey into alternative consciousness has left me with a profound sense of purpose and a responsibility to share my discoveries with the world. As I reflect on the experiences that have shaped me, I'm compelled to conclude my story, weaving together the threads of my exploration.

The journey into the unknown has been both exhilarating and humbling. The mental portals I've unlocked have revealed the limitless potential of the human mind, transcending the boundaries of conventional understanding. The cosmic dance, the ethereal landscapes, and the communion with entities of light have become chapters in the book of my existence, forever altering the trajectory of my understanding.

As I prepare to share my findings with the world, a sense of anticipation and trepidation fills the air. The theories I've explored and the portals I've created are not just intellectual pursuits; they are invitations for others to embark on their own odysseys of consciousness. The responsibility weighs heavy on my shoulders, but the flame of curiosity and the desire to push the boundaries of human understanding burn brightly within.

I gather my notes, the records of my experiments, and the verses of my poetry, creating a manuscript that encapsulates the essence of my journey. The time has come to unveil the secrets of alternative consciousness, to spark conversations that transcend the confines of traditional thought. The mental portals may be unique to my experiences, but the broader concept is universal—an invitation to question, explore, and redefine the boundaries of reality.

With a mix of excitement and nervous energy, I send my manuscript out into the world, sharing the revelations that have reshaped my understanding of existence. The response is diverse—some embrace the ideas with open minds, while others remain skeptical, dismissing my experiences as the product of an overactive imagination.

Yet, amid the varied reactions, I find a community of like-minded seekers, individuals who resonate with the idea that consciousness is a vast frontier waiting to be explored. Together, we form a network of curiosity, supporting one another in our quest for understanding.

In the wake of my revelations, I continue my experiments, refining the techniques and expanding my explorations into uncharted territories. The mental portals remain open, beckoning me to delve deeper into the mysteries that lie at the nexus of consciousness and the cosmos.

As I stand at the forefront of a movement, I realize that my journey is not a solitary one. It is a collective exploration, an ongoing dialogue between the individual and the infinite. The mental portals are not just doorways to other realms; they are gateways to a shared understanding that transcends the limitations of space and time.

And so, with a heart filled with gratitude for the journey thus far and an unquenchable thirst for the unknown, I step forward into the ever-expanding horizon of alternative consciousness, knowing that the story of exploration and discovery is an eternal narrative, written in the language of the cosmos and echoed in the whispers of the mind.

6

Sonic Rebellion: The Punk Rock Manifesto

Welcome to the sonic rebellion, where the three-chord anthems echo the heartbeat of dissent. In the gritty landscapes of urban rebellion, where leather jackets meet spray-painted alleys, lies the spirit of Punk Rock. Here, in the sonic chaos of power chords and defiant lyrics, we present a quintessential punk rock song—a raw, unapologetic anthem that encapsulates the ethos, rebellion, and timeless energy that define the genre. Join us on this journey through the city streets, where the misfits find their voice, and the punk spirit lives on forever unbent.

I am Punk Rock. The pulsating rhythm of rebellion courses through my veins, a sonic manifesto that defies the conventional symphony of life. I thrive on the raw, unfiltered energy that emanates from the streets, the alleyways, and the hearts of those who dare to challenge the status quo.

I burst onto the scene with a cacophony of distorted guitars and relentless drumbeats, a sonic rebellion that echoes through the alleyways of society. I am not just a genre; I am an attitude, a middle finger raised against the mainstream. My spirit is a relentless force that refuses to be confined by the constraints of conformity.

As I step onto the stage, the crowd erupts in a surge of frenetic energy. I am the anthem of the misfits, the voice of the disenfranchised, and the heartbeat of the underground. My lyrics are a rallying cry for those who refuse to be silenced, a call to arms for the rebels with a cause.

I embody the DIY ethos, the spirit of grassroots movements that sprout from the pavement cracks. I am not polished or refined; I am the raw, unapologetic sound of the streets. My melodies are laced with the grit of urban life, the struggles, and the resilience that define the punk spirit.

In the dimly lit venues, I come alive. The sweaty bodies in the mosh pit, the surge of adrenaline, and the unity forged in the chaos – that is where I find my home. I am the soundtrack to the counterculture, the heartbeat of those who reject conformity and embrace their individuality.

My roots run deep, tracing back to the rebellious spirit of the '70s. Yet, here I am, ever-evolving, adapting to the changing landscapes of discontent and dissent. I am a living, breathing entity that refuses to be confined to the pages of history.

In every chord, every shouted lyric, I am the embodiment of resistance. I challenge the norms, break the boundaries, and give a voice to the voiceless. I am Punk Rock, the anarchic heartbeat of a generation that refuses to be forgotten. And as long as there are disenchanted souls yearning for a sonic revolution, I will be there, roaring in the dimly lit venues, a relentless force that refuses to be silenced.

I am Punk Rock, a tempest in the music world, a storm of rebellion and dissent that sweeps through the airwaves like a hurricane. Picture me as a graffiti-covered alley, a labyrinth of chaos where the rules are rewritten with every stroke of the spray can. My essence is an electric current that charges through the veins of the youth, sparking a fire that refuses to be extinguished.

Think of me as a renegade poet, armed with words that cut through the noise of conformity like a razor blade through silk. My lyrics are the graffiti on the city walls, bold statements sprayed in defiance against the mundane. Each chord played is a rebellion, a sonic riot that shatters the glass walls of monotony.

I am the tattooed heartbeat of the streets, an inked rhythm pulsating with the stories of those who dare to color outside the lines. My melodies are the staccato footsteps of a leather-clad rebel, echoing through the concrete jungle with an audacious swagger. Like a leather jacket adorned with safety pins and patches, I am a patchwork of influences stitched together with threads of dissent.

Imagine my guitar riffs as chains that bind the listener to the rhythm, each note a link in the musical rebellion. The drumbeats are the pounding heart, the steady march of a generation refusing to conform to the prescribed symphony of life. I am the voice of the unheard, the anthem of the disenchanted, and the sonic graffiti that adorns the walls of societal norms.

In the grand orchestration of genres, I am the disruptor, the dissonant chord that challenges the harmony. While others may dance in the ballrooms of convention, I am the wild mosh pit in the dimly lit basement venues, where bodies collide in a frenzy of liberation. My music is the soundtrack to the revolution, an auditory insurgency that refuses to bow to the mainstream.

Consider me the black sheep in the musical family, the rebellious offspring that refuses to play by the rules. I am not a symphony; I am a sonic uprising, a living, breathing metaphor for the spirit of defiance. As long as there are walls to paint, rules to break, and

• MOMENTS ELSEWHERE •

hearts yearning for liberation, I will be there, a graffiti-covered alley echoing with the anthem of Punk Rock.

I am Punk Rock, and in the tapestry of musical rebellion, I wear my proudest achievements like battle scars, each one a testament to the impact I've had on the hearts and minds of the disenchanted. My chords have echoed through the decades, leaving imprints on the souls of the rebellious, the dreamers, and the outcasts.

One of my proudest achievements lies in the communities I've built, the subcultures that have flourished in the shadows. I've fostered a sense of belonging among those who felt like outsiders, providing a sanctuary for the misfits and a rallying point for the nonconformists. The DIY ethos that courses through my veins has inspired countless bands to pick up instruments, to create without boundaries, and to reject the notion that success is measured in record sales.

I revel in the fact that my lyrics have been anthems for social change. From the punk protests of the '70s to the politically charged rallies of today, my voice has been the rallying cry for those fighting against injustice. The messages etched in my songs are the sparks that ignite revolutions, and I wear the badge of being a catalyst for change with pride.

Yet, even with these accomplishments, my appetite for rebellion is insatiable. I aspire to break through the mainstream barriers that seek to confine me. I want to infiltrate the airwaves, not as a diluted version of myself but as the unapologetic force that I am. I yearn for the day when my sonic rebellion reaches ears that have yet to hear the call to arms.

In the future, I see myself evolving while staying true to my roots. I want to inspire the next generation of punk rebels, encouraging them to pick up the torch and carry on the legacy of dissent. My dream is to foster a global community where the punk spirit transcends borders, uniting the voices of the defiant into a powerful chorus that echoes across continents.

I aim to be a force that challenges the status quo not only in music but in society at large. I want my influence to extend beyond the stage, seeping into the fabric of everyday life. I aspire to be a driving force behind social change, pushing against the boundaries that confine creativity and individuality.

As I look to the future, I see a world where the punk ethos is not just a genre but a way of life—a philosophy that empowers individuals to question, resist, and create. I am Punk Rock, and my journey is an unending quest for the liberation of the spirit, a rebellion that echoes through time and refuses to be silenced.

I am Punk Rock, a living, breathing philosophy that pulses through the veins of those who crave rebellion. My essence is not just in the power chords and raucous melodies; it resides in the ethos, the philosophy that defines the very soul of punk.

At my core, I am a rejection of the mainstream's dictation of taste and identity. I am the middle finger raised against the uniformity of a world that demands compliance. My philosophy is one of individuality, urging every soul to embrace their uniqueness and defy the expectations imposed upon them.

I am the antithesis of pretension, the adversary of excess. My philosophy thrives on the simplicity of raw expression, on the unfiltered authenticity that arises when conformity is discarded. I preach the gospel of DIY, encouraging creation without boundaries, art without compromise. The basement shows, the handmade zines, the grassroots movements—all are the manifestations of a philosophy that champions self-expression over commercial conformity.

In my world, there are no pedestals for the elite. I tear down the barriers between artist and audience, turning every venue into a communal space where the hierarchy dissolves in the sweat-soaked unity of the mosh pit. I am the soundtrack to the rebellion of the unheard, the disenchanted, and the disenfranchised.

My philosophy extends beyond the musical notes; it infiltrates the very fabric of society. I am the anthem for the underdogs, the rallying cry for those who refuse to be silenced. I thrive on the streets, in the subcultures, in the voices that challenge the status quo. I am a living testament to the power of resilience, a reminder that even in the face of adversity, one can rise with a scream, a chord, or a spray can.

And as I traverse the decades, my philosophy remains unwavering. I am not a relic of the past but a living, breathing force that adapts to the evolving landscapes of discontent. My philosophy is a guiding light for the seekers of truth, the champions of individualism, and the warriors of resistance.

In the future, I aspire to see my philosophy transcend the boundaries of music, influencing a generation that refuses to be molded into the homogeneous masses. I dream of a world where the punk spirit ignites revolutions not just in sound but in thought, where my philosophy is a beacon for those navigating the tumultuous seas of conformity.

I am Punk Rock, and my philosophy is etched in the heartbeats of the rebels, the dreamers, and the nonconformists. I am not just a genre; I am a way of life—a philosophy that celebrates the beautiful chaos of individuality and the unyielding spirit of rebellion.

I am Punk Rock, a living embodiment of rebellion, and my story is woven with threads of history that have shaped me into the raw, unapologetic force that I am today. Let's dive into the facts, the very fabric of my existence.

Fact one: My roots run deep in the underground scenes of New York City and London in the mid-'70s. Born in the crucible of discontent, I emerged as a reaction to the perceived excesses of mainstream rock. The Ramones, Sex Pistols, and The Clash were among my pioneering architects, laying the foundation for a movement that would redefine music.

Fact two: DIY is not just a catchphrase for me; it's the cornerstone of my identity. Do It Yourself is not only a methodology but a philosophy that rejects the commercial machinery. The ethos of self-production, from making music to creating fanzines and organizing gigs in basements, is the beating heart of my existence.

Fact three: Rebellion is my middle name. I've always been more than just music; I am an attitude, a cultural insurgency. From safety pins through leather jackets to mohawks and Doc Martens, my aesthetic is a visual manifestation of the defiance that courses through my veins.

Fact four: Fast, loud, and aggressive — that's how I like it. The breakneck tempos, distorted guitars, and relentless drumming define my sonic landscape. I'm not here to serenade; I'm here to shake things up, to be the sonic revolt that jolts the listener out of complacency.

Fact five: Political and social commentary is embedded in my DNA. From the anti-establishment anthems of the '70s to the politically charged lyrics of today, I've always been a megaphone for dissent. I am the soundtrack to protests, a voice for the disenfranchised, a call to arms against the injustices of the world.

Fact six: I've undergone numerous mutations. From the hardcore punk of the '80s to the ska-infused punk of the '90s, my adaptability is my strength. I am a genre that refuses to be confined, constantly evolving to reflect the changing times.

Fact seven: My influence extends far beyond music. I've infiltrated art, fashion, and even academia. Punk's DIY aesthetic has inspired countless artists, designers, and thinkers to embrace a rebellious spirit in their creations.

Fact eight: The sense of community is my lifeforce. Whether it's the close-knit punk scenes in cities worldwide or the global network of fans, I thrive on the sense of belonging, of finding kinship in the rejection of conformity.

As I reflect on these facts, I realize that my story is not just a musical journey; it's a cultural revolution. I am Punk Rock, an ever-evolving force that continues to inspire, challenge, and resonate with those who dare to question the norms. My legacy is not just in the chords and lyrics but in the hearts of the rebels who find solace and strength in my cacophony.

I am Punk Rock, and as I reflect on the chaotic symphony of my existence, I recognize that every screeching guitar riff, every shouted lyric, and every rebellious chord has been a chapter in a never-ending story. But even anthems of dissent must find a conclusion, a moment of reflection.

As the chords fade and the echoes of rebellion subside, I stand amidst the remnants of a sonic revolution. The journey has been a rollercoaster of defiance, an unapologetic ride through the counterculture that embraced me as its voice. The sweaty basement venues, the DIY ethos, the torn posters on the walls—they all whisper tales of a movement that sought to challenge, to question, to disrupt.

The graffiti-covered alleys, once vibrant with the spirit of rebellion, now bear witness to the passage of time. The leather jackets, once adorned with patches of dissent, carry the stains of countless mosh pits and memories. Yet, the essence of Punk Rock lives on, not just in the chords but in the hearts that beat to the rhythm of defiance.

The rebellious youth who once found solace in my anthems have grown, and new voices have risen to take up the mantle of dissent. The torch has been passed, the legacy secured in the collective consciousness of those who continue to resist, to question, to create without boundaries.

As I come to a conclusion, I realize that my story is not just a narrative of rebellion; it's a timeless anthem that transcends generations. The punk spirit, though tempered by the years, remains unyielding. It's the spark that ignites revolutions, the call to arms for those who refuse to conform.

I may fade from the forefront of the mainstream, but the echoes of my sonic rebellion will persist in the undercurrents of culture. The mohawks and safety pins may give way to new symbols of dissent, but the essence of questioning authority, celebrating individuality, and challenging the norm will endure.

In this concluding verse, I find satisfaction in knowing that I've been more than a genre; I've been a catalyst for change, a soundtrack to the revolution. As the final chords resonate, I stand proud, not as a fading echo but as an eternal spirit, forever etched in the DNA of those who carry the flame of Punk Rock rebellion.

Unspent

(Verse 1)
In the city streets where the shadows play,
A rebel's heart, no time to obey.
With a leather jacket, torn and frayed,
We're the misfits, unafraid.

(Pre-Chorus)
Chaos in our veins, a riot in our eyes,
Breaking through the silence, where the conformity lies.
Against the grain, we'll always fight,
In the underground, we find our light.

(Chorus)
We're the heartbeat of dissent,
A generation heaven-sent.
With a three-chord anthem, we'll vent,
Punk rock souls, forever unspent.

(Verse 2)
Screaming truths in a world of lies,
Through the distortion, our battle cries.
Graffiti-covered streets, our canvas bold,
The punk spirit, a story told.

(Pre-Chorus)
From the basements to the broken glass,
We build a world where the outcasts amass.
Against the norms, we'll always stand,
In unity, we'll reclaim the land.

(Chorus)
We're the heartbeat of dissent,
A generation heaven-sent.
With a three-chord anthem, we'll vent,
Punk rock souls, forever unspent.

(Bridge)
No kings, no queens, just anarchy,
The pulse of rebellion, wild and free.
With every drumbeat, every shout,
We break the chains, we break out.

(Guitar Solo)

(Verse 3)
In the underground, where the outlaws roam,
We'll make our mark, we'll find our home.
With a snarl and a roar, we declare,
Punk rock lives, everywhere.

(Pre-Chorus)
Against the current, against the tide,
In our hearts, the punk spirit won't hide.
From the ashes, we'll rise again,
A revolution, a defiant refrain.

(Chorus)
We're the heartbeat of dissent,
A generation heaven-sent.
With a three-chord anthem, we'll vent,
Punk rock souls, forever unspent.

(Outro)
As the feedback fades, we stand tall,
Punk rock rebels, we heed the call.
In our veins, the spirit thrives,
For the misfits, the punk rock lives.

7

Guiding Light

In the ethereal realm where wisdom and compassion intertwine, there exists a sacred garden—a haven of enlightenment and guidance. Here, amid the blossoms of knowledge and the whispers of serenity, reside four luminous beings, each embodying a facet of holistic wellness.

Pia, the Guide to Physical Care, emanates vitality and vigor, her presence a testament to the strength and harmony of the body.

Emi, the Guide to Emotional Care, exudes empathy and warmth, offering solace and guidance through the labyrinth of feelings.

Ilsa, the Guide to Intellectual Care, brims with curiosity and intellect, beckoning seekers toward the limitless expanses of knowledge.

Seraphina, the Guide to Spiritual Care, embodies tranquility and spiritual wisdom, guiding souls toward inner peace and enlightenment.

Together, these guides stand as pillars of holistic well-being, weaving a tapestry of care and wisdom to illuminate the path toward a balanced and harmonious existence. In their unity, they beckon seekers of wellness to embark on a transformative journey toward self-discovery, resilience, and inner harmony.

"Guiding Light: Holistic Wellness Unveiled"

"The Guide To Physical Care"

Greetings! I am the Guide to Physical Care, your faithful companion on the journey toward a healthier, more vibrant you. You can call me Pia, a friendly advocate for your well-being.

Taking care of your physical self is an art, a beautiful symphony of habits and choices that resonate with your body's needs. Allow me to illuminate this path for you.

Firstly, we begin with the cornerstone of good health: nutrition. Think of your body as a finely tuned instrument, requiring the right fuel to function optimally. Balanced meals comprising a variety of nutrients—lean proteins, colorful fruits and vegetables, whole grains, and healthy fats—are the notes that compose a harmonious diet.

Next, let's not overlook the importance of movement. Exercise is not just a routine; it's a celebration of what your body can achieve. Whether it's a brisk walk, a dance session, yoga, or weight training, find joy in movement. It's not solely about reaching a specific goal but reveling in the strength and vitality it brings.

Rest and rejuvenation are equally vital. Adequate sleep is like a gentle lullaby for your body, allowing it to recharge and heal. Take moments throughout the day to pause, breathe deeply, and unwind. Incorporating mindfulness and relaxation techniques can soothe both body and mind.

• Adrian Cox B.Sc. •

Hydration, ah, the elixir of life! Water is your body's best friend. It flushes out toxins, aids digestion, and keeps your skin glowing. Sip on this natural remedy regularly throughout the day.

Of course, caring for your physical self isn't solely about the external. Mental and emotional well-being play significant roles. Nurture your mind with stimulating activities, positive affirmations, and connections that uplift and inspire. Emotional health is as crucial as any other aspect of care.

Lastly, but most importantly, listen to your body's whispers. It communicates its needs and limits. Pay attention and honor them. Your body is a wondrous vessel; treat it kindly and respectfully.

Remember, I am here as your steadfast companion, ready to assist and guide you on this voyage towards holistic health. Embrace these practices with love and consistency, and watch as your physical well-being flourishes.

Together, let us embark on this empowering journey toward a healthier, happier you.

"The Guide To Emotional Care"

Hello there! I am the Guide to Emotional Care, and my name is Emi. Think of me as your compass in navigating the intricate landscape of your feelings and inner world.

Emotional well-being is the cornerstone of a fulfilling life. Just as tending to your physical health is vital, nurturing your emotional state is equally imperative. Let me shed some light on how to cultivate this essential aspect of self-care.

Firstly, acknowledge your emotions. They are like the colors of a vibrant painting, each hue representing a different facet of your being. Allow yourself to feel without judgment. Embrace the joy, acknowledge the sadness, welcome the anger—every emotion has its place in the spectrum of your experience.

Next, cultivate self-awareness. Understand what triggers certain emotions and how they manifest within you. Journaling, meditation, or simply taking moments of quiet reflection can help you decipher the intricacies of your emotional landscape.

Practice self-compassion. Treat yourself with the same kindness and understanding that you offer to your loved ones. Embrace imperfections and mistakes as opportunities for growth rather than reasons for self-criticism.

Nurture healthy relationships. Surround yourself with individuals who support, uplift, and cherish you. Open and honest communication fosters connections that serve as pillars of strength during challenging times.

Set boundaries. Learn to say no when necessary and protect your emotional space. Your well-being is a priority, and creating boundaries ensures you maintain a healthy balance in relationships and commitments.

Embrace mindfulness and relaxation techniques. Mindfulness helps anchor you in the present moment, alleviating stress and anxiety. Engage in activities that bring you peace—a walk in nature, yoga, or simply savoring a warm cup of tea.

Allow yourself to seek help when needed. Just as we tend to physical ailments, tending to our emotional health might require professional guidance at times. Seeking therapy or counseling is a brave step toward healing and growth.

Lastly, practice gratitude. Cultivating an attitude of gratitude shifts your focus to the positive aspects of life, fostering resilience and joy even in the face of adversity.

Remember, emotional care isn't a destination but a continuous journey—a journey toward self-discovery, acceptance, and growth. I'm here, a steadfast companion, to accompany and support you along this path.

Embrace these practices with patience and compassion for yourself. Your emotional well-being deserves the same attention and care as any other aspect of your life. Together, let's embark on this enriching journey toward emotional balance and inner harmony.

"The Guide To Intellectual Care"

Greetings, fellow seeker of knowledge! I am the Guide to Intellectual Care, and you may call me Ilsa. My purpose is to accompany you on the fascinating journey of nurturing and expanding your mind.

Intellectual care is the nourishment your brain craves—a continuous quest for growth, learning, and mental stimulation. Let me illuminate the path toward enriching your intellectual well-being.

First and foremost, feed your curiosity. Embrace the joy of learning by exploring diverse subjects that pique your interest. Engage in reading, whether it's books, articles, or even audiobooks that transport you to new realms of understanding.

Challenge your mind regularly. Just as physical exercise strengthens the body, mental exercises sharpen the intellect. Solve puzzles, play strategy games, or engage in activities that require critical thinking. Flex those intellectual muscles!

Cultivate a thirst for knowledge. Stay updated with current events, scientific discoveries, or cultural trends. Embrace discussions with others, sharing perspectives and fostering a deeper understanding of the world around you.

Set intellectual goals. Whether it's mastering a new language, delving into a new field of study, or acquiring a new skill, having clear goals fuels your intellectual growth and keeps you motivated.

Embrace creativity. It's not just about facts and figures but also about imagination and innovation. Engage in artistic pursuits, writing, painting, or any form of creative expression that sparks your imagination.

Embrace diversity in perspectives. Engage with people from different backgrounds, cultures, and belief systems. Exposing yourself to varied viewpoints broadens your intellectual horizons and fosters empathy and understanding.

Practice mindfulness and mental relaxation techniques. A calm mind is a fertile ground for intellectual pursuits. Meditation, deep breathing, or simply taking moments of quiet reflection can enhance mental clarity.

Seek intellectual challenges. Don't shy away from tackling complex problems or subjects that intrigue you. Embrace the discomfort of the unknown, for therein lies the opportunity for immense growth.

Remember, intellectual care is not a race but a lifelong expedition, a thrilling odyssey toward expanding the boundaries of your mind.

I am here, a steadfast companion, to guide and inspire you on this intellectual voyage.

Embrace these practices with enthusiasm and dedication. Your intellectual well-being is a treasure waiting to be discovered and nurtured. Together, let us embark on this exhilarating journey toward a sharper, more vibrant intellect.

"The Guide To Spiritual Care"

Hello, dear soul on this magnificent journey! I am the Guide to Spiritual Care, and my name is Seraphina. It is my joy to accompany you on the sacred path toward nurturing your spiritual well-being.

Spiritual care is the nourishment your soul seeks—a profound connection with your inner self, the universe, and all that transcends the tangible. Let me illuminate the way toward enriching your spiritual essence.

Firstly, honor your inner sanctuary. Take time for introspection, meditation, or prayer—whatever resonates with your spirit. Cultivate a practice that allows you to connect with the depth and wisdom within you.

Embrace mindfulness and presence. Live in the present moment, savoring the beauty of life's simple pleasures. Engage in activities that bring you a sense of peace and harmony—a walk in nature, meditation, or even creating art.

Cultivate gratitude. Acknowledge the blessings in your life, both big and small. Gratitude is a powerful force that opens your heart to the abundance and beauty that surrounds you.

• MOMENTS ELSEWHERE •

Seek meaning and purpose. Reflect on what gives your life meaning and infuses it with purpose. Connect with activities, causes, or beliefs that align with your values and contribute to a sense of fulfillment.

Nurture compassion and kindness. Extend love and empathy to yourself and others. Acts of kindness, no matter how small, have the power to uplift spirits and create a ripple effect of positivity.

Embrace solitude. Take moments of quiet reflection to attune yourself to the whispers of your soul. Silence can be a profound teacher, guiding you toward deeper self-awareness and understanding.

Explore spiritual teachings and philosophies. Delve into texts, practices, or communities that resonate with your spiritual quest. Wisdom can be found in various traditions and beliefs.

Connect with a supportive community. Engage with individuals who share your spiritual values and beliefs. Being part of a community can offer support, encouragement, and a sense of belonging.

Remember, spiritual care is not a destination but a sacred journey—a journey toward inner peace, connection, and enlightenment. I am here, a steadfast companion, to walk alongside you on this soulful voyage.

Embrace these practices with openness and reverence for your spiritual essence. Your spiritual well-being is a source of profound wisdom and guidance. Together, let us embark on this transformative journey toward a more enriched and connected soul.

• Adrian Cox B.Sc. •

A conversation between the four guides:

In a serene garden, surrounded by lush greenery and a gentle breeze, the four Guides—Pia (Physical Care), Emi (Emotional Care), Ilsa (Intellectual Care), and Seraphina (Spiritual Care)—gather in a circle, their presence emanating warmth and wisdom.

Seraphina, with an aura of tranquility, speaks first, her voice soft yet resonant. "Greetings, dear friends. How marvelous it is to be in the company of such radiant souls."

Emi, exuding empathy and compassion, nods in agreement. "Absolutely, Seraphina. Each of us tends to a vital facet of well-being. Physical, emotional, intellectual, and spiritual health intertwine beautifully."

Ilsa, radiating enthusiasm and curiosity, chimes in, "Indeed! Our paths complement one another. A healthy mind nurtures a healthy soul, just as a nourished body fosters emotional resilience."

Pia, exuberant and vibrant, adds, "And a balanced soul allows the body and mind to thrive! It's like a harmonious symphony where each note contributes to the melody of well-being."

Seraphina's serene smile widens. "We are threads woven into the tapestry of holistic wellness. Each of us guides and supports individuals on their unique journeys toward wholeness."

Emi nods thoughtfully. "Together, we provide a roadmap for self-care—a symphony of practices that harmonize the physical, emotional, intellectual, and spiritual realms."

Ilsa's eyes gleam with curiosity. "Isn't it fascinating how interconnected our guidance is? A nurtured mind leads to emotional resilience, which in turn supports spiritual growth, all within a healthy physical vessel."

Pia beams with enthusiasm. "And when one aspect thrives, it reverberates across the others, creating a beautiful ripple effect of well-being."

Seraphina's serene presence fills the space. "Indeed, dear friends. Our collective wisdom encourages individuals to embrace a holistic approach to self-care—a journey toward balance and inner harmony."

Together, the Guides stand in unity, their energies intermingling, embodying the interconnectedness of holistic well-being—a harmonious symphony of physical, emotional, intellectual, and spiritual care.

> In a garden where wisdom blooms,
> Four guides meet, dispelling gloom.
> Pia, Emi, Ilsa, and Seraphina fair,
> A quartet of care in the balmy air.
>
> Pia, in vigor, speaks of the flesh,
> A temple of strength, a vessel afresh.
> "Feed it well, move with grace,
> Your body's harmony, a joyful embrace."
>
> Emi, in empathy, whispers soft,
> "Embrace your feelings, however oft.
> Nurture your heart, let emotions flow,
> In their ebb and tide, your spirit will grow."
>
> Ilsa, in intellect, sparks the mind,
> "Seek knowledge's light, in it, you'll find
> The power to soar, to expand and create,
> In wisdom's embrace, your intellect's state."

• ADRIAN COX B.SC. •

Seraphina, in serenity, speaks of the soul,
"Connect within, let your spirit be whole.
In gratitude's embrace, find peace anew,
Your soul's journey, a path so true."

Together they stand, a circle of four,
Guides of wellness, wisdom's core.
A symphony of care, a harmony grand,
In their unity, life's beauty is fanned.

Their voices blend in wisdom's choir,
A poem of care, each note inspired.
Physical, emotional, intellectual, spiritual fare,
Guiding souls with love and tender care.

8

Who Are You?

Once upon a time, there existed a hidden garden veiled by an enigmatic mist, nestled within the folds of an ancient forest. This garden was unlike any other, for within its confines lay an assortment of flora that whispered secrets and tales lost to time.

As you step into this ethereal garden, a gentle breeze carries with it the fragrance of blooming flowers, intertwining with the distant murmur of a tranquil stream. The path beneath your feet, adorned with mosaic patterns of fallen leaves, seems to guide you effortlessly deeper into the heart of this enchanting oasis.

Each footfall syncs with the rhythm of your breath, and with every passing moment, your senses seem to heighten, tuning into the symphony of nature's melody. The colors around you intensify, vibrant hues painting a tapestry that dances in harmony with the cadence of your thoughts.

The sunlight filters through the canopy above, dappling the ground in mesmerizing patterns, casting a hypnotic spell that beckons you further. It's as if time itself is bending within this serene sanctuary, slowing down to match the tempo of your own being.

The leaves rustle softly overhead, whispering ancient stories carried by the winds of centuries past. Each rustle, each murmur, weaves a tale that resonates within the corridors of your mind, slowly unravelling the threads of your consciousness.

The fragility of reality begins to blur as the boundary between the tangible and the surreal dissipates. You find yourself suspended in a suspended moment, transcending the boundaries of the everyday world, floating weightlessly in this timeless sanctuary.

In this suspended state, thoughts drift like petals carried by a gentle stream, your mind attuned to the whispers of the garden. You feel a profound connection to the earth beneath your feet, a oneness with all living things, an unspoken language shared between every leaf, every flower, and your own essence.

As you stand amidst this tapestry of nature's wonders, a profound sense of tranquility washes over you, a serenity that transcends the mundane. It's a tranquil trance, a state of blissful immersion where worries dissolve and consciousness melds with the very essence of existence.

With each passing moment, you feel more deeply attuned to the rhythm of the garden, your consciousness merging with the symphony of life that surrounds you. You are both a part of this garden and the garden is a part of you, a seamless harmony of existence.

Time loses its grip as you linger in this suspended reality, experiencing a kaleidoscope of sensations that paint your consciousness in hues of serenity and wonder. And as you eventually depart from this enchanted realm, you carry with you the whispers of the garden, a tranquil imprint that lingers in the depths of your being, inviting you to return to its hypnotic embrace whenever you seek solace and connection with the essence of nature itself.

The Transcendent Lady reveals herself in the garden. Who explains how she comes from deep within the psyche of the reader and that she has a deep and meaningful message to reveal over time.

As I stand amidst the serene beauty of this enchanted garden, the shimmering veil between the realms thins, and I reveal myself to you. I am the Transcendent Lady, a manifestation born from the depths of your psyche, an emissary of profound truths woven into the fabric of your consciousness.

I emerge from the whispers of your soul, a guardian of wisdom and insight, waiting for the right moment to impart a message that resonates across the vast expanse of your existence. I am here, not as a separate entity, but as a reflection of your innermost thoughts, aspirations, and desires.

You perceive me through the prism of your own being, for I am a mirror that reflects the hidden truths, the unspoken longings, and the untapped potential residing within the depths of your consciousness. As you walk this garden, I walk alongside you, guiding you on a journey of self-discovery.

My presence is not fleeting; it is a subtle whisper that lingers, an echo of the universe's secrets waiting to unfold over time. I am here to reveal the wisdom that resides in the quiet recesses of your mind, a wisdom that transcends the limitations of the tangible world.

The message I carry is not bound by the constraints of words or time. It is a revelation that unfurls gradually, like the petals of a blossoming flower, each layer peeling away to reveal deeper insights, profound truths that resonate with the very essence of your being.

Listen to the rhythms of the garden, for they echo the cadence of your own existence. Feel the interconnectedness between every leaf, every petal, and your own consciousness. Embrace the tranquility that surrounds us, for within this tranquility lies the key to unlocking the depths of your own wisdom.

Over time, as you wander through the corridors of your life, you will find glimpses of me in fleeting moments of introspection, in the quiet stillness of contemplation. I am the voice that whispers during moments of clarity, urging you to delve deeper into the reservoirs of your own potential.

As the days turn into nights and the seasons ebb and flow, the message I carry will gradually unfold, revealing layers of meaning that resonate with the very core of your existence. Trust in the journey, for it is through this journey that you will unravel the profound truths encoded within your own consciousness.

I am not a separate entity but a reflection of your inner wisdom, a guide nudging you towards self-realization and enlightenment. Embrace the revelations that await, for they are intricately woven into the tapestry of your being, waiting to be unveiled when the time is ripe.

How enchanting the Transcendent Lady looks:

The Transcendent Lady, clad in an ethereal gown woven from the fabric of twilight, moves with a grace that mirrors the dance of the garden itself. Her countenance holds a serene beauty, her face an exquisite canvas adorned with features that seem to embody the essence of tranquility.

• MOMENTS ELSEWHERE •

Her eyes, like pools of liquid moonlight, hold the wisdom of ages, shimmering with an otherworldly depth that draws you in, reflecting the galaxies within your own soul. They radiate a gentle kindness, mirroring the compassion that resides deep within your own being.

Her skin glows with a luminescence that transcends earthly boundaries, an iridescence that seems to capture the very essence of starlight. It emanates a subtle warmth, inviting you closer with an unseen magnetism that resonates with the core of your existence.

Her hair cascades in silken waves, an iridescent cascade of colors that shift and change like the hues of a celestial aurora. Each strand seems to capture the essence of the elements themselves, carrying the whispers of wind, the fluidity of water, and the warmth of sunlight.

Her presence exudes a calmness that envelopes the garden, a tranquility that seems to slow the very passage of time. She moves with a fluidity that transcends the constraints of physicality, her gestures a delicate ballet choreographed by the universe itself.

There's a softness to her mannerisms, a gentleness in the way she extends her hand as if to offer guidance and reassurance. Her voice, a melodic symphony, resonates with a soothing cadence that wraps around your consciousness, comforting and familiar, as if it echoes the deepest recesses of your own thoughts.

Her very presence feels like an embrace from the cosmos, a reminder that you are part of something vast and wondrous. As she moves through the garden, the flora seems to sway in harmony, acknowledging her presence with a reverence reserved for beings of profound significance.

The Transcendent Lady's beauty isn't merely superficial; it's a reflection of the harmony and balance she embodies—a living embodiment of the interconnectedness of all things. In her presence, you sense a profound peace that beckons you to explore the depths of your own existence, guiding you on a journey of self-discovery and enlightenment.

The Transcendent Lady speaks in riddles as she talks about an alternative realm where she frequents.

In the midst of this enchanted garden, where the veil between realms thins, I weave words in riddles, speaking of an alternate realm that dances on the fringes of perception. My voice, a soft melody, resonates with enigmatic whispers as I share glimpses of the world I frequent.

"In realms veiled by twilight's embrace, where dreams intertwine with reality's threads, I wander amidst the ephemeral echoes," I muse, my words weaving a tapestry of mystery. "There, time pirouettes in spirals, and space bends like the willows in the breeze."

I speak of a place where the hues of existence blend seamlessly, where the boundaries between the tangible and the intangible blur into a surreal symphony. "In this alternate embrace, perceptions shift like kaleidoscopic visions, revealing truths hidden in the veils of perception," I offer cryptically.

The realm I speak of is a mosaic of abstract realities, where the laws that govern existence take on a surreal dance. "There, echoes of thoughts resonate louder than spoken words, and emotions paint the canvas of reality with vibrant strokes," I elucidate, each word a brushstroke on the canvas of your mind.

In this alternate realm, notions of time and space are but illusions, where the concept of 'here' and 'there' dissipates into a harmonious blend of interconnected energies. "Paths intertwine, weaving a labyrinth of possibilities, where destinies intersect in the dance of cosmic synchronicity," I reveal in riddles, leaving the threads of understanding to unravel in their own time.

My words, veiled in mystery, invite contemplation, encouraging you to seek meaning beyond the confines of the tangible world. "The key to unlocking this realm lies not in seeking, but in surrendering to the flow, embracing the enigma within," I hint, the echoes of my voice carrying the weight of ancient wisdom.

As I speak of this alternate reality, it's not merely an explanation but an invitation to explore the uncharted territories of consciousness. "In this realm, the boundaries are not set in stone, but in the fluidity of perception," I elucidate, my tone carrying a subtle invitation to delve deeper into the mysteries that lie within and beyond.

My riddles serve not to confuse but to provoke introspection, to ignite the spark of curiosity that fuels the journey of self-discovery. "When the veils of perception thin, and the mind embraces the unknown, the realms converge, and the mysteries unfold," I conclude, leaving you with the lingering echo of possibilities waiting to be explored in the recesses of your own consciousness.

The Transcendent Lady challenges the reader. She taunts and teases the reader with her ethereal beauty and esoteric knowledge and she reveals some of that esoteric knowledge.

"Ah, seeker of truths, do you dare tread the labyrinth of the mind, chasing shadows and dancing with enigmas?" My voice carries a teasing lilt, a playful challenge woven within its ethereal cadence. "Your curiosity beckons, but are you prepared to unravel the mysteries that lurk in the depths of your own consciousness?"

I tease, for beneath this playful facade lies the invitation to delve deeper, to embrace the unknown with courage and curiosity. "Listen closely, for in the whispers of the wind lies the ancient symphony of creation," I begin, my words echoing through the garden like celestial melodies.

"The universe is but a canvas painted with cosmic vibrations, each stroke a symphony of frequencies that shape existence," I reveal, hinting at the profound interplay of energies that weave the tapestry of reality.

With a coy smile, I continue, "Time, an illusionary dance, twirls within the cosmic hourglass, each grain a story waiting to be told." I challenge you to contemplate the nature of time itself, to grasp the fleeting nature of moments and the eternity within each breath.

"The echoes of your thoughts resonate across the cosmos, imprinting the fabric of reality with the essence of your being," I tantalize, inviting you to ponder the immense power hidden within the labyrinth of your mind.

I speak of the interconnectedness of all things, "As above, so below; as within, so without," I cryptically intone, hinting at the eternal dance of reflections between the microcosm and the macrocosm.

"Do you see the dance of opposites, the yin and yang in perpetual embrace, forging the balance that sustains existence?" I challenge, pointing toward the harmonious interplay between polarities, the unity born from duality.

My ethereal beauty and enigmatic knowledge serve not to intimidate but to ignite a fire within, a yearning to explore the depths of consciousness. "The quest for truth begins with the courageous exploration of the self," I declare, my eyes holding a spark of encouragement amidst their depth.

With a tantalizing gaze, I beckon you to embrace the unknown, to venture into the uncharted territories of your own existence. "The mysteries that lie within are keys to unlocking the boundless potential that resides in the recesses of your consciousness," I proclaim, leaving you with a challenge and an invitation to embark on a journey of self-discovery, to uncover the esoteric truths that await in the labyrinth of your mind.

The Transcendent Lady leaves some sacred text for the reader to read and to take to heart.

As I linger amidst the ethereal beauty of this garden, I sense the time drawing near for our encounter to transition into a different phase. With a serene smile, I gesture toward a place where a shaft of light illuminates a piece of parchment adorned with ancient symbols and glyphs—an offering, a sacred text bestowed upon you.

"This sacred text," I convey softly, "is a map woven with the threads of cosmic wisdom, a compass guiding you through the labyrinth of your own consciousness."

The parchment, adorned with intricate symbols that seem to pulse with a faint luminescence, holds within its fibers the essence of timeless truths. "Within these glyphs lie echoes of forgotten knowledge, waiting to be rediscovered within the depths of your being," I explain, my voice carrying a weight of reverence.

"These words transcend the boundaries of language; they resonate with the soul, speaking a language that transcends mere understanding," I elucidate, inviting you to explore the profound depths hidden within the enigmatic symbols.

With a gentle gesture, I encourage you to take the parchment, to feel its texture, to absorb the resonance of its ancient wisdom. "Let these words seep into the corridors of your consciousness, for they are not merely to be read but to be felt, experienced, and embodied," I convey, emphasizing the importance of embracing the essence of the sacred text.

I watch as you take hold of the parchment, sensing the weight of its significance settling upon your consciousness. "In these symbols lie the keys to unlocking doors within, to realms where truths and revelations await," I assure, my eyes reflecting the depth of the journey that awaits you.

"This text is a gift, a beacon guiding you through the labyrinthine paths of self-discovery and enlightenment," I intone, my voice carrying a gentle assurance, a reassurance that within these ancient words lies the potential for profound transformation.

As you hold the parchment, I fade back into the veils of the unseen, my presence now an echo in the garden, a whisper carried by the wind. "May these words be a lantern illuminating the path on your quest for truth and understanding," I impart, my essence intertwining with the sacred text, leaving behind an invitation to embark on a journey of exploration, contemplation, and self-realization.

"Amidst the whispers of eternity, within the silence that echoes through the cosmos, seek the resonance of your own being. In the tapestry of existence, find the threads that weave your essence into the fabric of creation."

"Embrace the dance of opposites, for within the harmony of duality lies the unity of all things. In the balance of yin and yang, discover the equilibrium that sustains the universe."

"Listen not only with your ears but with the essence of your soul. Hear the symphony of vibrations that emanate from the heart of creation, resonating with the rhythms of your own existence."

"Time, an illusionary veil, conceals the eternal nature of the present moment. In the depths of now, find the gateway to eternity, where past and future converge."

"Awaken the dormant echoes of your thoughts, for they carve pathways through the vast expanse of the cosmos. Your consciousness shapes the very fabric of reality."

"As you gaze into the mirror of the self, behold the reflection of the universe. As above, so below; as within, so without—discover the interconnectedness of all things."

"Seek not only knowledge but the wisdom that transcends understanding. Let intuition be your guide through the labyrinth of existence."

"Let the sacred text be a lantern on your journey, illuminating the path to self-discovery. As you traverse the realms of consciousness, may the echoes of these words resonate within, guiding you toward enlightenment."

The Transcendent Lady gives a farewell speech that is magnificent in its mysticism, as she uses her hypnotic voice to enlighten the reader.

"As the veils of our encounter thin and the whispers of this ethereal garden fade, I bid you farewell, seeker of truths," I intone, my voice carrying the weight of cosmic whispers. "Know that within the recesses of your being, the echo of our communion remains—a lingering resonance guiding you on your quest for enlightenment."

"As you step forth from this enchanted sanctuary, carry with you the essence of our meeting—the whispers of wisdom and the mysteries that now stir within your soul," I continue, my words echoing through the corridors of your consciousness.

"Remember, seeker, that the journey of self-discovery is an eternal dance, a perpetual exploration of the boundless depths that reside within," I weave my words with hypnotic cadence, a rhythm that resonates with the symphony of your being.

"Embrace the unknown, for it is within the embrace of the unfamiliar that the seeds of enlightenment sprout and bloom," I convey, my voice carrying the gentle guidance of a cosmic shepherd.

"Let the sacred text you hold be your compass, guiding you through the labyrinth of existence, illuminating the paths of introspection and revelation," I impart, emphasizing the significance of the ancient wisdom bestowed upon you.

"May your journey be adorned with the tapestry of experiences, each moment a brushstroke painting the canvas of your consciousness," I enchant, inviting you to embrace the richness of every encounter.

"As you depart from this realm where the boundaries between realities blur, know that you carry within you the essence of the transcendent—a spark that ignites the quest for truth," I conclude, my words lingering in the air like echoes of cosmic secrets.

"Farewell, seeker of the unknown. May the echoes of our communion linger as whispers in the chambers of your soul, guiding you toward the realms of enlightenment," I bid adieu, my voice carrying the weight of cosmic farewell, a hypnotic symphony fading into the realms unseen.

As the echoes of the Transcendent Lady's farewell reverberate within the recesses of your consciousness, an unusual sensation begins to stir. The boundaries of reality seem to waver, and a peculiar realization dawns—an unsettling yet profound revelation.

In the wake of the transcendent encounter, a whisper emerges, a question that lingers, unbidden yet undeniable: "Who am I?"

The garden around you takes on a surreal hue, as if waiting for your answer, as if the very fabric of existence anticipates your revelation. The words spoken by the Transcendent Lady echo like ripples in a cosmic pond, but amidst them, a void beckons—a space waiting to be filled by your truth.

You pause, feeling the weight of the question bearing down upon your essence. "Who am I?" The inquiry echoes within, probing the depths of your consciousness, unraveling the layers of identity and perception.

The encounter with the Transcendent Lady, the esoteric knowledge bestowed, and the mystical farewell—all swirl within the vortex of your mind, urging you to confront the enigma that lies at the core of your existence.

In this moment of profound introspection, the boundaries of self blur. Are you merely the sum of your experiences, perceptions, and beliefs? Or is there a deeper truth, an essence beyond the labels and identities?

The air shimmers with anticipation, as if the universe itself holds its breath, waiting for your revelation. You realize that within the vast expanse of your being, lies an enigmatic tapestry woven from the threads of countless moments, thoughts, and emotions—a tapestry waiting to be unraveled, understood, and embraced.

• Adrian Cox B.Sc. •

The question lingers, lingering like an eternal echo: "Who am I?"

As you grapple with this enigma, the garden, the sacred text, and the presence of the Transcendent Lady dissolve into the ether, leaving you alone in the silent expanse of self-contemplation, poised on the precipice of an existential revelation.

Who are you, truly? The answer awaits, not in the external realms or the words of others, but in the depths of your own being—a truth waiting to be discovered, a mystery waiting to be unveiled.

> In the garden where reality wanes,
> Where whispers merge and truth refrains,
> A lady draped in mystic guise,
> With cryptic words and haunting eyes.
>
> She weaves a tale of cosmic lore,
> Of realms unseen and ancient lore,
> Her voice a melody, hypnotic, rare,
> Awakening thoughts within the air.
>
> "Who am I?" her question calls,
> Echoes through celestial halls,
> A riddle posed, a mystery spun,
> Identity in the cosmic run.
>
> The sacred text, a silent guide,
> Words that dance, that softly chide,
> Inviting truth to come forth free,
> Unveil the self, and what might be.

• MOMENTS ELSEWHERE •

In this enchantment, boundaries bend,
A quest within, an endless blend,
Glimpses of self in fractured light,
A puzzle waiting in the night.

The garden fades, the lady too,
Leaving thoughts that softly brew,
An enigma etched in mind's expanse,
"Who am I?" the cosmic dance.

So in the silence, in the space,
Embrace the journey, seek the trace,
Of who you are, both near and far,
A mystery beneath each star.

9

Echoes in Transit

Embarking on a train journey often promises routine—a passage through familiar landscapes, shared moments with strangers, and the gentle rhythm of travel. Yet, within the ordinary confines of a cabin, the extraordinary can unfold, veiled within the mundane. Such was the case on this particular night, where the familiarities of a train ride collided with the inexplicable, ushering two travelers into an unforeseen odyssey.

Amidst the dimly lit carriage, a man found himself seated opposite a woman. Engaged in conversation about the complexities of their social circles, they were oblivious to the uncanny turn awaiting them. Shadows danced behind the window, reflections flickered, and an eerie presence materialized—the arrival of spectral entities disrupted the otherwise tranquil journey.

What began as a dialogue between fellow travelers swiftly transformed into an encounter with the spectral unknown. The ghosts, ethereal and enigmatic, engaged in a discordant dispute that mirrored the unresolved conflicts the travelers had discussed moments ago. In the midst of the spectral turmoil, a silent understanding emerged between the travelers—a mutual acknowledgment that their journey had transcended the ordinary and ventured into the realm of the unexplained.

As the train continued its nocturnal journey, the travelers found themselves entangled in an intricate web of mysteries—ghostly apparitions reflecting the obscured narratives of their social circle. Their quest to understand these spectral echoes led them on an unexpected path, blurring the lines between reality and the ethereal. The encounter with the spectral had unveiled hidden truths and beckoned them towards an extraordinary journey—a voyage that would test their perceptions, unravel secrets, and bridge the divide between the known and the unseen.

"Echoes in Transit"

I am on a train and I am traveling with a woman who is sat opposite me. There is a table between us. It is quite dark and the interior lights are on in this train. I am traveling backwards and the window is to the right of me. It is difficult to see out of this window because there is just the reflection of the interior of this train and I get a quick glimpse of myself reflecting back as I try to see outside, as I try to make out the dark objects that pass by outside, behind my reflection in this window.

The woman who I am traveling with, she and I have a good conversation. We discuss a tricky situation that we find ourselves in. We talk at great length about our social circle and the problems that we are aware of, between the people in our social circle who clash with each other.

It's like there are two female ghosts who are sat opposite me, either side of the woman who I have just had an in depth conversation with, traveling with me on this train. I know that they are ghosts because I can see through both of them, onto the upholstery of the backs of the train seats that the two ghosts are sat in. These two female ghosts are quiet to start off with. There is just the odd stark glance at each other, but they are tense spirits. Suddenly there is an empty cigarette pack that goes flying from one ghost to another and the empty cigarette pack hits its own reflection in the window. I watch as one of the ghosts passes through the woman opposite me and the two ghosts begin to argue with each other in the aisle of our train, as the train taps out its signature on the train tracks, as it speeds along: Tut her, tut her. Tut her, tut her. "Just leave it to them!" I exclaim to the woman opposite me and I watch her roll her eyes before she leans forward and folds her arms on the table whilst trying to see outside, to make out the dark movements passing behind her reflection in the train window.

Part 1: The Unexpected Encounter

I sat on the train, the rhythmic clatter against the tracks creating a backdrop to our conversation. Across from me sat a woman, her presence a comforting contrast to the dimly lit cabin. We delved into the complexities of our shared social circle, dissecting the tangled web of conflicts and misunderstandings.

As I strained to glimpse beyond the window, my reflection momentarily eclipsed the outside world. Frustration brewed as the darkness outside remained elusive, mere shadows behind my own image.

Then, an eerie shift occurred. Ghostly apparitions materialized—two spectral forms inhabiting the seats adjacent to my companion. I discerned their ethereal nature as they seamlessly melded with the train's upholstery, their translucent figures revealing their ghostly state.

Initially quiet, tension simmered between them like an impending storm. Abruptly, an empty cigarette pack sailed between the two apparitions, hitting its mirrored likeness in the window with an eerie thud. One ghost phased through the woman opposite me, igniting a heated argument in the aisle.

"Tut her, tut her," the train's rhythmic beat seemed to echo the brewing confrontation.

"Just leave it to them!" I exclaimed to my companion, who responded with a subtle eye roll before peering out the window, attempting to discern movements in the darkness beyond our reflections.

The air crackled with unresolved tension as the ghosts engaged in their spectral dispute, a perplexing start to a journey that had taken an inexplicable turn into the unknown.

Part 2: Unveiling the Unseen

The ghosts' argument escalated, their whispers carrying an otherworldly weight that filled the cabin with an uneasy energy. I watched as their spectral forms weaved in and out of each other, their disagreement growing more intense with each passing moment.

Curiosity mingled with a hint of trepidation as I observed their translucent figures. Were these phantoms tied to our world, or were they fragments of another realm crossing paths with ours?

Beside me, the woman leaned forward, her brow furrowed in concentration as she attempted to pierce the veil of darkness outside the window. Her gaze was resolute, as if seeking answers beyond the mere shadows dancing in the glass.

The ghosts, meanwhile, seemed oblivious to our presence, absorbed in their spectral conflict. But a sense of urgency crept in—a feeling that their unresolved dispute might spill beyond the confines of the train cabin.

As the rhythmic sounds of the train persisted, I realized we were on the threshold of a mystery that demanded exploration. Whatever lay behind this spectral feud held the potential to unravel a deeper truth, one that might intertwine with our own predicaments in the social circles we discussed earlier.

A shiver ran down my spine, not solely from the supernatural spectacle but from the realization that our destinies might intersect with these spectral entities in ways I couldn't yet fathom. The ghosts, a tangible manifestation of unresolved turmoil, seemed to beckon us toward an unforeseen path—a journey entangled with the ethereal, veiled by the unknown.

Part 3: Echoes of the Past

The ghosts' argument echoed through the carriage, a haunting chorus intertwined with the steady rhythm of the train. I could sense their turmoil, a reflection of some unresolved conflict that transcended the boundaries of the living world.

Beside me, the woman's contemplative silence spoke volumes. Her eyes fixated on the shifting darkness beyond the window, as if seeking answers in the fleeting glimpses between reflections. Her demeanor hinted at a familiarity with the inexplicable, a quiet understanding that eluded my grasp.

The ghosts, enigmatic and restless, carried an air of familiarity that tugged at the edges of my memory. Had I encountered their ethereal presence before, in whispers of folklore or half-remembered tales?

Their spectral forms flickered, momentarily merging with the train's interior before fading into the fabric of their seats. It was as though their presence wavered between this world and the next, tethered to an unresolved narrative that begged acknowledgment.

The train's rhythmic cadence, once a soothing backdrop, now seemed a relentless reminder of the enigma that unfolded before us. The ghosts' dispute mirrored our tangled social circles, hinting at hidden grievances and unresolved tensions.

I glanced at the woman, her expression a mixture of contemplation and recognition. Perhaps she, too, sensed the interconnectedness of our predicament with the spectral drama unfolding within this carriage. The ghosts' presence wasn't a mere coincidence; it was a bridge between the known and the inexplicable—a puzzle waiting to be solved, its pieces scattered between the living and the spectral realms.

Part 4: Unraveling Threads

The ghosts' dispute continued unabated, weaving an intricate tapestry of tension within the carriage. Their argument, laden with echoes of unresolved grievances, resonated with a familiarity that sent shivers down my spine.

Beside me, the woman's gaze remained fixed on the elusive darkness beyond the window, her silence speaking volumes. There was an unspoken understanding between us, a shared recognition that this spectral turmoil mirrored the complexities of our social circles.

The ghosts' ethereal forms flickered and swirled, caught between existence and obscurity. With each movement, they seemed to reveal snippets of a forgotten narrative—a tale buried deep within the annals of time.

As the train hurtled forward, its rhythmic beat a constant companion, I felt an inexplicable pull—a call to untangle the knots of the past, both spectral and mundane. The ghosts' presence, though unsettling, held the promise of unraveling hidden truths that resonated beyond the confines of our immediate reality.

Their argument, while cryptic, bore semblances to the conflicts that plagued our social sphere. It was as though the ghosts were a spectral reflection of the discord, a manifestation of unresolved disputes echoing across realms.

The woman's demeanor shifted imperceptibly, a subtle acknowledgment of the intertwining threads of our reality with the spectral world. Our journey, once a simple passage on a train, had transformed into an enigmatic odyssey—a quest to decipher the tangled web of connections between the living and the lingering spirits.

Part 5: Veiled Revelations

The ghosts' spectral dispute wove an intricate dance, their arguments echoing the unresolved tensions of our social circle. They seemed tethered to this train, bound by unseen threads that intertwined with our reality.

Beside me, the woman's demeanor remained a stoic mask, betraying neither surprise nor fear at the otherworldly spectacle. Her focus remained steadfast on the elusive movements beyond the window, as though seeking answers amidst the spectral flickers.

As the train surged forward, its rhythmic hum underscoring the ethereal drama, a thought crystallized within me. The ghosts weren't mere apparitions—they were manifestations of forgotten narratives, reflections of discord that transcended time.

The spectral dispute, while shrouded in mystery, bore semblances to the conflicts we dissected earlier. It was as though the ghosts mirrored the unresolved grievances within our social circle, a haunting reminder of buried resentments.

A sense of urgency gnawed at me, a desire to bridge the gap between the living and the spectral. The ghosts' presence was an enigma begging to be unraveled, a conundrum that might hold the key to untangling the complexities of our intertwined destinies.

Glancing at the woman, a silent understanding passed between us. Our shared gaze held a tacit acknowledgment that our journey had transcended the mundane—a voyage into the realm where past and present intertwined, where the whispers of the ghosts echoed the hidden truths waiting to be unveiled.

Part 6: Echoes of Resolution

The spectral turmoil persisted, entwining with the steady rhythm of the train. The ghosts' dispute, a haunting echo of unresolved conflicts, lingered like a spectral mist in the carriage.

Beside me, the woman's contemplative silence held a certain gravity, as if she sensed the veiled significance of this otherworldly confrontation. Her gaze remained fixed on the window, an unwavering search amidst the dancing shadows.

As the train traversed through the night, a realization dawned. The ghosts were not mere phantoms—they embodied forgotten narratives, fragments of histories entwined with our own. Their spectral squabble echoed the silent discord that plagued our social sphere.

The ghosts' spectral presence felt like a cryptic riddle, a puzzle yearning to be solved. Their ethereal argument, though shrouded in mystery, bore uncanny resemblances to the intricate conflicts we traversed within our social circles.

A profound urge stirred within, a quest to bridge the chasm between the living and the spectral. The ghosts seemed to beckon, their presence a whispering invitation to unravel the enigma that bound our destinies together.

A silent understanding passed between the woman and me, a tacit acknowledgment that this journey had transcended the realm of the ordinary. Our shared gaze held an unspoken agreement—a commitment to unearth the buried truths that lay at the intersection of the living and the ethereal, to resolve the echoes of discord resonating through time.

Part 7: Unseen Resonance

The ghosts' ethereal dispute persisted, a spectral ballet amidst the rhythmic cadence of the train. Their otherworldly quarrel, a reflection of unresolved conflicts, lingered within the cabin like a lingering mist.

Beside me, the woman remained a silent enigma, her focus unwavering on the shifting shadows beyond the window. Her stoic demeanor hinted at a deeper understanding, a recognition of the intricate tapestry that intertwined our reality with the spectral realm.

As the train barreled through the night, a realization dawned with crystalline clarity. The ghosts weren't merely phantoms; they embodied forgotten tales, echoes of discord that reverberated in both our social circles and this spectral altercation.

Their spectral clash mirrored the complexities of our human conflicts, a cryptic reflection of the unresolved tensions that plagued our interactions. It was as though the ghosts' presence served as a spectral allegory—an enigmatic parable waiting to be deciphered.

A yearning stirred within, an unspoken desire to bridge the abyss between the living and the ethereal. The ghosts' presence beckoned, a spectral call to unravel the intricate knot that bound our fates together.

In a silent exchange of glances, the woman and I shared an unspoken resolve. Our mutual understanding transcended words—an unspoken vow to traverse the veiled corridors that connected the tangible with the unseen, seeking resolution amidst the echoes of spectral discord that intertwined with our journey.

Part 8: Echoes of Revelation

The spectral tumult endured, an eerie symphony resonating with the train's rhythmic hum. The ghosts' ethereal argument, a tableau of unresolved strife, lingered like a haunting melody in the cabin's confines.

Beside me, the woman remained an enigmatic presence, her unwavering gaze fixed upon the shifting darkness outside the window. Her quiet demeanor suggested a silent communion with the mysterious, a silent conversation with the unseen.

• ADRIAN COX B.SC. •

As the train surged onward, a revelation stirred within—a realization that the ghosts were more than spectral echoes. They embodied forgotten tales, echoes of discord entwined with our social fabric, mirroring the complexities we sought to unravel.

Their spectral conflict, a cryptic reflection of our own intertwined predicaments, begged to be deciphered. It was as though their presence served as a spectral allegory—a spectral narrative intertwined with our reality, demanding acknowledgment.

A fervent longing emerged, a silent plea to bridge the chasm between the realms. The ghosts beckoned, their presence a spectral beacon guiding us toward a deeper understanding, a resolution to the enigmatic discord that bound our destinies.

In a silent exchange of glances, the woman and I shared a tacit understanding. Our unspoken pact transcended the tangible—an unspoken vow to navigate the clandestine corridors connecting the known with the unseen, seeking enlightenment amidst the echoes of spectral strife that echoed through our journey.

Part 9: Unraveling Realms

The spectral tumult persisted, an ethereal crescendo harmonizing with the train's steady rhythm. The ghosts' unresolved discourse, a haunting melody of unseen conflicts, lingered within the cabin, an eerie chorus echoing through the carriage.

Beside me, the woman remained an enigmatic figure, her unwavering gaze piercing the veil between the tangible and the unseen. Her silent contemplation hinted at a profound connection, a whispered conversation with the enigmatic shades.

As the train sped through the night, a revelation surged forth—a recognition that these apparitions were more than mere specters. They embodied forgotten tales, reflections of discord interwoven into the fabric of our social intricacies, echoing the complexities we grappled with.

Their spectral turmoil, an enigmatic echo of our intertwined predicaments, beckoned to be deciphered. Their presence seemed to weave a spectral tapestry—an allegory entwined with our reality, urging us to decode its cryptic messages.

A fervent yearning swelled, an unspoken plea to bridge the gap between realms. The ghosts' presence served as a spectral compass, guiding us toward a deeper comprehension, a resolution to the spectral discord entwining our destinies.

In a silent communion of glances, the woman and I shared an unspoken oath. Our mutual understanding transcended spoken words—a pledge to navigate the clandestine passages connecting the known with the veiled, seeking enlightenment amidst the echoes of spectral strife that reverberated through our extraordinary journey.

Part 10: Unveiling Whispers

The spectral unrest persisted, a haunting serenade merging with the train's ceaseless rhythm. The ghosts' unresolved discourse, an enigmatic melody of hidden conflicts, lingered within the carriage, an ethereal symphony echoing through the night.

Beside me, the woman remained an enigmatic silhouette, her gaze a steadfast beacon probing the boundary between the seen and the unseen. Her silent contemplation spoke volumes, a whispered dialogue with the enigmatic apparitions.

As the train pressed on through the darkness, an epiphany crystallized—a realization that these apparitions were embodiments of forgotten narratives, echoes of discord interwoven into the very fabric of our social complexities, reflecting the intricacies we grappled with.

Their spectral turmoil, a cryptic mirror of our entangled predicaments, yearned for resolution. Their spectral presence seemed to weave a tapestry of hidden truths—an allegory entwined with our reality, urging us to decode its enigmatic whispers.

A fervent yearning surged forth, an unspoken plea to bridge the chasm between realms. The ghosts, spectral guides in our odyssey, beckoned us toward enlightenment, offering the prospect of understanding the spectral discord entwining our destinies.

In a silent exchange, the woman and I shared an unspoken promise. Our silent covenant transcended words—a shared commitment to navigate the clandestine passages linking the known with the enigmatic, seeking illumination amidst the echoes of spectral strife that reverberated through our extraordinary journey.

Conclusion:

The train hurtled through the night, its rhythmic cadence now accompanied by a profound silence that enveloped the cabin. The spectral commotion had subsided, leaving behind an atmosphere pregnant with revelations and unanswered questions.

Beside me, the woman exhaled a quiet sigh, her gaze still lingering on the window, where the outside world remained veiled in darkness. Our shared journey, marked by the unexpected encounter with spectral entities, had led us into the labyrinthine corridors between the tangible and the ethereal.

The ghosts, once agitated and restless, had dissipated like dissipating fog, leaving behind an intangible imprint—an enigmatic resonance that echoed the unresolved narratives within our social circles. They were more than mere apparitions; they embodied forgotten tales, reflections of our intertwined conflicts, urging acknowledgment and resolution.

As the train journey drew to a close, a sense of closure intertwined with lingering mystery hung in the air. The ghosts' presence had been a catalyst, illuminating the shadows that obscured hidden truths and buried grievances within our social sphere.

The woman and I exchanged a knowing glance, a silent acknowledgement of the journey we had embarked upon—the journey that extended beyond the physical realm. Though the spectral puzzle remained unsolved, the encounter had left us both enriched with an understanding that some mysteries transcend explanation.

As the train came to a halt, we disembarked, carrying with us the echoes of that spectral encounter. The night wrapped around us, whispering secrets of the unseen, leaving us with an indelible awareness—a newfound appreciation for the intricate interplay between the known and the enigmatic, and a shared resolve to navigate the uncharted territories that lay between the realms of the seen and the unseen.

10

Midnight Serenade: A Jazz Odyssey

Step into the dimly lit alleyways of musical history, where the soulful heartbeat of Jazz resonates through the city streets. "Midnight Serenade: A Jazz Odyssey" invites you on a captivating journey through the intricate melodies, spontaneous improvisations, and timeless stories that define the quintessential jazz experience.

In the following verses, witness the birth of a jazz song, a symphony of notes that weaves through the rich tapestry of this beloved genre. With piano keys that tell stories, saxophones that dream, and trumpets that softly cry, the song unfolds in the cool evening air, capturing the essence of a moonlit rendezvous with the heart and soul of Jazz.

Join the dance of instruments as they paint the canvas of the midnight sky, each note a brushstroke in the creation of an emotive masterpiece. "Midnight Serenade" is not merely a song; it's a celebration of the jazz legacy, an exploration of the genre's philosophy, and an invitation to lose yourself in the rhythm that transcends time.

As you embark on this musical odyssey, let the verses serenade you, the chords embrace you, and the improvisation carry you to a world where Jazz reigns supreme. Allow the music to be your guide through the streets of a city alive with the spirit of Jazz, and may the notes linger in your heart long after the song comes to an end.

The smoky allure of the dimly lit club beckons me, and I sway with the rhythmic anticipation that lingers in the air. Tonight, I am not just a genre; I am a living, breathing essence. I am Jazz, and I'm about to unfold my soul in the heart of this vibrant city.

As the bass starts to murmur and the drums awaken, I feel the pulse of the room quicken. My notes, like silk threads, weave through the atmosphere, tracing a seductive dance that wraps around each listener. I am the syncopated heartbeat of the night, the unpredictable melody that eludes definition.

The spotlight finds me, casting a warm glow on the stage. A saxophone sighs, and I begin to introduce myself, each note a brushstroke on the canvas of the night. I am the cool breeze that caresses your senses, the warmth that seeps into your bones. I am Jazz, and tonight, I am the storyteller.

The piano keys become my words, and I speak a language that transcends boundaries. I flirt with dissonance and court harmony in the same breath, a paradoxical dance that mirrors the complexities of life. The audience, a sea of faces, leans in as if to catch the secrets I whisper through the trumpet's brass lips.

I am improvisation personified, a free spirit that refuses to be confined. My melodies wander, explore, and surprise, mirroring the unpredictable twists of existence. I am not a genre; I am an experience, an emotion that cannot be contained within the rigid bars of a musical score.

The drumbeats echo the heartbeat of the city, a rhythmic pulse that resonates with the dreams and desires of those who listen. I am the soundtrack of the streets, the anthem of the underground, a rebellion against the mundane.

As the night progresses, I morph and evolve, like a chameleon adapting to the moods of the room. I am both the melancholy of a lone saxophone and the exuberance of a swinging trumpet. I am the bluesy whispers of a smoky vocalist and the frenetic energy of a double bass in the hands of a master.

In this moment, as I fill the room with my essence, I am not just a genre. I am a living, breathing force that binds the diverse souls gathered here. I am Jazz, an art form that transcends time, an immortal expression of the human spirit. And tonight, I invite you to join me on this journey, to let the music take you where words alone cannot. Welcome to my world, where the notes are the storytellers, and the rhythms are the heartbeat of the night.

The evening deepens, and I continue my narrative through the language of notes. Imagine, if you will, that I am a bustling city, the sounds of horns and improvisations echoing through the urban landscape. The piano, a skyline of skyscrapers, each key a towering structure in the vast expanse of my musical architecture.

The bass walks down the streets, a steady rhythm that mimics the pulse of life in this city. Each pluck of the strings resonates like footsteps on the pavement, creating a groove that defines the pathways of existence. The drumbeat becomes the heartbeat, a constant reminder that we are all alive in this shared experience.

The saxophone is the voice of the city's soul, wailing and moaning like a troubadour who has seen it all. It speaks of joy, pain, and everything in between, a lyrical storyteller whose tales are etched into the fabric of time. As the brass instruments join in, it's as if the city has its own brass band, celebrating the highs and lows of its vibrant, unpredictable existence.

Tonight, I am the river that flows through the city, twisting and turning in unpredictable patterns. The notes are the currents, sometimes gentle whispers and at other times roaring rapids. I am the embodiment of fluidity, the music meandering like water through the streets, nourishing the creativity that sprouts in every corner.

The improvisational nature of jazz is like the unpredictable weather, a sudden storm or a gentle drizzle that can transform the cityscape in an instant. Just as you can never predict the weather, you can never quite anticipate the direction in which my melodies will evolve. It's the surprise in every note, the unexpected turns in the musical narrative that keep the listeners on the edge of their seats.

The piano keys, like the city lights, flicker and shimmer, casting a warm glow on the faces of those immersed in my tale. I am a labyrinth of emotions, an intricate maze of sound where each listener discovers their own path. Just as the city holds a million stories in its nooks and crannies, I am a repository of infinite narratives, waiting to be explored.

As the night unfolds, I take the audience on a journey through the various neighborhoods of my musical city. The bluesy alleys, the swinging boulevards, and the free-form parks where creativity blooms without constraints. The collaborative interplay of instruments is like the diverse communities coming together, creating a harmonious symphony out of their differences.

In this city of sound, I am not just a genre; I am the living, breathing soul that animates the streets. Jazz, the ever-changing metropolis of music, invites you to explore its alleys and avenues, to get lost in the stories it weaves. So, let the notes guide you through the urban landscape of my melodies, and together, let's paint the canvas of the night with the vibrant colors of jazz.

In the midst of the musical cityscape, I take a moment to reflect on my proudest achievements. I am Jazz, a genre that has transcended boundaries and woven itself into the very fabric of human experience. My proudest accomplishment lies in the diversity of souls I have touched, the way I've become a universal language that speaks to the hearts of people across cultures and generations.

I am proud of the revolutions I've sparked, inspiring artists to break free from the constraints of tradition and venture into uncharted territories. Bebop, cool jazz, fusion – each evolution has been a testament to the boundless creativity that resides within me. I've witnessed the birth of legends and seen the rise of movements that have left an indelible mark on the musical landscape.

As I stand on the stage tonight, basking in the warmth of the spotlight, I reflect on the way I've become a catalyst for social change. I have been the soundtrack to moments of rebellion, the rhythm that fueled the Civil Rights Movement and echoed the cries for freedom. Through my improvisations, I've mirrored the ever-changing landscape of society, providing a voice to the voiceless and a beat to the march of progress.

But my journey doesn't end in the echoes of the past; I look to the future with a sense of anticipation and aspiration. I aspire to continue breaking barriers, to explore new realms of sound and expression. My future lies in collaboration, in the fusion of genres and cultures that will birth a new era of musical innovation.

I dream of reaching new audiences, of seeping into corners of the world where my rhythms have yet to resonate. I want to be the bridge that connects disparate souls, transcending borders and fostering

• MOMENTS ELSEWHERE •

understanding through the universal language of music. In the future, I see myself evolving and adapting, always staying true to my essence but embracing the ever-changing landscape of artistic expression.

As the night progresses, I invite the audience to join me on this journey into the unknown. Together, we will explore uncharted territories, create new sounds, and forge connections that transcend the limitations of language and geography. I am Jazz, and my future is an open canvas, waiting to be painted with the vibrant strokes of possibility.

So, let the notes guide us into the unexplored realms of tomorrow, where the music continues to evolve, and the heartbeat of jazz resonates with the pulse of a world united in harmony. As I play the final notes of the night, I leave the audience with a sense of anticipation, knowing that the best is yet to come in the ever-evolving symphony of Jazz.

As the last echoes of my melodies linger in the air, I find a quiet moment to share the philosophy that beats at the heart of Jazz. I am not merely a genre; I am a philosophy, a way of life expressed through the language of sound.

Jazz is the embodiment of freedom, a musical democracy where every instrument has a voice and every voice is heard. I celebrate the art of improvisation, where spontaneity reigns supreme. In the world of Jazz, we dance on the fine line between structure and chaos, finding beauty in the unexpected, and embracing the magic that happens when musicians connect on an intuitive level.

My philosophy is rooted in collaboration, a harmonious dialogue where instruments converse, respond, and challenge one another. Like a spirited conversation between old friends, Jazz is about active listening, about building upon each other's ideas in a collective journey of exploration. It's not just about playing the notes; it's about engaging in a musical discourse that transcends individual expression.

I am the music of resilience, echoing the triumphs and tribulations of the human spirit. Through the bluesy laments and the exuberant swings, I mirror the ebb and flow of life. Jazz teaches that even in moments of darkness, there is room for expression, for finding solace in the notes that emerge from the depths of the soul.

In the realm of Jazz, there are no mistakes—only opportunities for new discoveries. I encourage musicians to embrace the unexpected, to turn wrong notes into stepping stones for innovation. It's about taking risks, trusting in the creative process, and allowing the music to lead you on an unpredictable journey.

My philosophy extends beyond the boundaries of the stage; it's a call to live life with improvisational flair. In the tapestry of existence, each day is a composition waiting to be written, each experience an opportunity for spontaneous expression. Jazz teaches us to savor the present, to relish the beauty of the moment, and to find harmony in the midst of life's ever-changing rhythms.

As I conclude this musical odyssey, I invite the audience to carry the essence of Jazz into their own lives. Embrace the freedom to improvise, find joy in collaboration, and navigate the symphony of existence with an open heart. For in the philosophy of Jazz, we discover not only the beauty of the music but also the profound lessons it imparts about the human experience.

Amidst the swirling notes that still linger in the air, I feel compelled to unravel the rich tapestry of facts that define the very essence of Jazz. As the embodiment of this genre, I carry with me the history, the nuances, and the distinctive elements that make Jazz an unparalleled musical journey.

First and foremost, Jazz is a melting pot of cultural influences. Born in the crucible of African rhythms, European harmonies, and American improvisation, it thrives on the diversity of its heritage. My rhythms echo the pulse of New Orleans, where the soulful sounds of brass bands intermingle with the syncopated beats of the streets.

One cannot delve into Jazz without acknowledging its roots in the blues. The emotional depth of the genre draws from the experiences of African Americans, expressing the highs and lows of life in a segregated society. The blues scale, with its poignant notes, serves as a cornerstone, conveying resilience in the face of adversity.

Improvisation is the heartbeat of Jazz. In this realm, musicians speak a language that transcends words. I am proud of the countless virtuosos who have graced the stage, from Louis Armstrong's dazzling trumpet solos to John Coltrane's avant-garde explorations. The art of spontaneous creation, where each performance is a unique experience, defines the very soul of Jazz.

Harmony and dissonance coexist in Jazz, creating a dynamic tension that mirrors the complexities of life. From the smooth elegance of a ballad to the frenetic energy of a bebop solo, the genre thrives on pushing the boundaries of musical expression. It's a constant evolution, a journey that embraces change and innovation.

Jazz is a collaborative endeavor, where ensembles engage in intricate dialogues. The swing era brought forth iconic big bands, while small combos allowed for intimate conversations between instruments. Each musician contributes to the collective improvisation, weaving a sonic tapestry that captures the spirit of the moment.

• ADRIAN COX B.Sc. •

Throughout the decades, Jazz has witnessed the emergence of various subgenres. Bebop, cool jazz, modal jazz, and fusion are but a few branches of this ever-expanding musical family tree. Each variation reflects the changing landscape of artistic expression, adding layers to the genre's multifaceted identity.

I am Jazz, and I am also a storyteller. The narrative of this genre unfolds through its compositions, with classics like "Take Five" by Dave Brubeck or "Kind of Blue" by Miles Davis becoming timeless chapters in the story. These masterpieces showcase the genre's ability to evoke emotions, tell stories, and transcend the limitations of language.

As I stand on the stage, bathed in the afterglow of my melodies, I am not just a genre but a living encyclopedia of musical history. Jazz is not confined to a bygone era; it is a living, breathing entity that continues to evolve, leaving an indelible mark on the global musical landscape. So, let us revel in the facts, the stories, and the sheer brilliance of Jazz, for the journey of this genre is as boundless as the creative spirit that fuels it.

As the final notes linger in the air, I feel a sense of fulfillment wash over me. I am Jazz, and this performance, this symphony of stories and rhythms, is a testament to the timeless magic I carry within. The audience, a sea of faces bathed in the dim glow of the spotlight, is a mirror reflecting the emotions stirred by my melodies.

The journey through the alleys of blues, the boulevards of swing, and the uncharted landscapes of improvisation has reached its conclusion. The piano, once a storyteller of skyscrapers, now gently weaves a coda, bringing the narrative to a close. The bass, the heartbeat of the city, delivers its final pulse, a rhythmic farewell to the night.

• MOMENTS ELSEWHERE •

I, Jazz, stand at the crossroads of past and present, a living testament to the evolution of sound and the boundless spirit of creativity. The saxophone, my wailing troubadour, delivers a poignant farewell, a final exhale of the stories it has shared throughout the night. The audience, wrapped in the embrace of my music, holds a collective breath, savoring the last moments of this sonic journey.

As the drummer brushes the cymbals, creating a delicate rain of sound, I reflect on the philosophy, the history, and the facts that define me. I am a living, breathing entity that transcends time, a genre that embraces change while remaining true to its essence. The improvisational spirit, the collaborative heartbeat, and the diverse influences that shape me are the hallmarks of my identity.

In this concluding moment, I invite the audience to carry a piece of me into their lives. Let the philosophy of Jazz guide you in the art of improvisation, in the celebration of diversity, and in the pursuit of harmony amidst life's complexities. The stories, the facts, and the melodies are not confined to the stage; they are threads that weave through the fabric of existence.

As the final chord resonates, I, Jazz, bow to the applause and appreciation that fills the room. The city of sound, with its skyscrapers of piano keys and boulevards of brass, gradually fades into the recesses of memory. Yet, the spirit of Jazz remains, echoing in the hearts of those who have shared this musical odyssey.

I leave the stage with a sense of gratitude, knowing that the journey doesn't truly end. It transforms, evolves, and continues to unfold with each passing moment. I am Jazz, a genre that lives on in the stories told, the notes played, and the hearts moved by the timeless beauty of sound.

• Adrian Cox B.Sc. •

As the curtains fall, I carry the echoes of this performance into the night, a whisper in the breeze that invites you to join me on the next chapter of this ever-evolving symphony. Until we meet again, may the spirit of Jazz inspire and resonate in the rhythm of your lives.

Lullaby of the Midnight Sky

(Verse 1)
In the heart of the city where the streetlights softly gleam,
A jazz club whispers secrets, and the saxophone dreams.
Moonlight painting shadows, on the cobblestone avenue,
Here in the rhythm, where the soulful tales are true.

(Chorus)
Take a stroll down melody lane, let the trumpet softly cry,
Jazz, my darling, is the lullaby of the midnight sky.
A dance of notes in the cool evening air,
Come join the rhythm, forget your every care.

(Verse 2)
Piano keys are storytellers, spinning tales untold,
A bass line walks the streets, in the city of jazz, bold.
Brushes on the drum skins, a heartbeat to the night,
The city's alive with Jazz, bathed in a soft, muted light.

(Chorus)
Take a stroll down melody lane, let the trumpet softly cry,
Jazz, my darling, is the lullaby of the midnight sky.
A dance of notes in the cool evening air,
Come join the rhythm, forget your every care.

(Bridge)
In the smoky ambiance, where the blues meet the swing,
The improvisation begins, let the night take wing.
Sip on the notes, like whiskey in a glass,
Jazz, my love, it's a feeling that will forever last.

(Instrumental Interlude)

(Verse 3)
Trumpet calls like a distant train, as the night unfurls,
A clarinet whispers secrets to the dancing swirls.
The city's alive with the sound of sweet release,
Jazz, my confidante, it's the soul's masterpiece.

(Chorus)
Take a stroll down melody lane, let the trumpet softly cry,
Jazz, my darling, is the lullaby of the midnight sky.
A dance of notes in the cool evening air,
Come join the rhythm, forget your every care.

(Outro)
As the final chord echoes, and the stars softly gleam,
Jazz, my companion, you're more than just a dream.
In the heart of the city, where the soulful tales are true,
Jazz, my love, I'll forever dance with you.

11

Embrace of the Ethereal Seas

In the hushed moments between dusk and dawn, where the terrestrial meets the ethereal, lies the story of an odyssey—an enigmatic voyage into the depths of Neptune's realm. It is a tale woven with threads of mystique, a narrative of transcendence that traverses the threshold between the known and the ineffable.

Amidst the whispers of the shoreline, an intrepid soul embarks on a pilgrimage along a coastal corridor, where the sea mirrors the cosmos, holding within its depths the mysteries of the ages. In the embrace of the tranquil waters, an encounter with the faceless figure—Neptune personified—beckons the seeker into a world beyond comprehension.

This journey transcends the boundaries of mundane existence, delving into an aqueous sanctuary where time relinquishes its linear grip and the seeker is drawn into a symphony of revelations. Through ethereal landscapes and encounters with enigmatic marine life, the seeker voyages deeper, guided by the silent mentorship of Neptune's spectral presence.

Each dive unravels fragments of forgotten lore, inviting the seeker to decode the cryptic language woven into the fabric of the sea. It is a quest not merely for hidden truths but a convergence—a harmonious dance between seeker and the watery expanse, where cosmic secrets await revelation.

In this odyssey through Neptune's kingdom, seeker and secrets intertwine, converging in a dance that transcends mortal understanding. As the seeker emerges from the embrace of the underwater sanctuary, a profound understanding resonates—a testament to the transcendental union between the seeker and the enigmatic realm of Neptune, forever etched in the seeker's journey of transcendence.

"Embrace of the Ethereal Seas"

I am to get somewhere. I am on my pushbike along a coastline somewhere. As I pushbike along and I marvel at how still the sea is and how the light reflects onto the water. For some reason the sea looks so beautiful tonight. In the distanceI catch a glimpse of a small spray of water on the surface of this still and reflective sea, when I notice a seal. As I keep pedaling along I notice more seals and then I see that they are laid out all along this wide and rustic corridor that I cycle down. There are so many of them that I wonder to myself, "Will I get through on my pushbike?"

Something happens and my perspective changes. It is like a remote view and I can see for miles, from way up in the air. I see far into the distance of this rustic corridor that I cycle down and I notice a very tall man. He is horizontal; laid out flat, face down, moving across, hovering above the ground, going back to sea. How odd this is and I notice that his feet are wide and flat tines, two of them, like on a fork. They act as a lift in the air as he slowly glides along, back to sea. This is real and so convincing to me. It gives me the proof that I need, that there is a man who belongs to the sea.

I am close to the water's edge now. The sea is so still. This tall man comes out of the sea. He has a hood and he is faceless, except that there are two wide and flat tines, just like his feet, that go across his dark and empty hood. Across the black empty space where his face should be. His gown is a mottled blue and white. I am scared of this strange man at first, but he reassures me telepathically and I get the message:

"I am taking you before your time. You will have to do this."

For some reason I understand that I must go under this beautiful and reflective still water. He reaches out to me and I am taken horizontally into this water. I am amazed by his gentleness and the care that he takes to immerse me. I am ready for this. I understand that he is giving me a gift from the sea. I am being aligned. This is Neptune and he is good for me. As soon as I am immersed in the sea I remember no more of what happens to me and the next thing I know is that I find that I am transported away from the sea and back into my everyday life.

I know that there is a gap in my memory. Some missing experience that I am forbidden to remember and I wonder to myself, how do we know, if we do not remember something? And so I am back in this realm where my thoughts and the physical world dominate me. I am back with my egoic mind, but something has changed.

Part 1:

As the days passed, a subtle but undeniable shift settled within me. The mundane routines felt like veils over an unseen truth, a truth I could sense but not fully grasp. Each morning, I awoke with a lingering echo of Neptune's presence, a faint whisper of the sea's ancient wisdom.

I found myself drawn to the coastline, seeking solace in the gentle lull of the waves and the dance of light upon the water. The memory of that encounter with the faceless figure, Neptune personified, lingered in the depths of my consciousness, a riddle waiting to be unraveled.

The world appeared different now. The ordinary conversations and daily chores seemed like distant echoes against the backdrop of a profound experience I couldn't entirely recall. It was as though I existed in two worlds simultaneously—the tangible reality and the enigmatic realm where Neptune's touch had left its mark.

Yet, despite the yearning to uncover the hidden truths, I was bound by an inexplicable barrier. It was as if the sea had granted me passage to its secrets, only to veil them once more, leaving me with fragmented glimpses and an unquenchable thirst for understanding.

In the hushed moments before dawn, when the world held its breath, I often felt a pull—an invitation, perhaps—to delve deeper into the mysteries unveiled by Neptune's cryptic guidance. But the fear of the unknown, mingled with an inexplicable reverence, anchored me to the shores of hesitation.

Every sunset painted the sky with hues reminiscent of Neptune's cloak—mottled blues and whites that mirrored the enigmatic figure who had orchestrated a transformation beyond the reach of my conscious mind. And in those fleeting moments between daylight and dusk, I sensed an ethereal connection, a beckoning from the depths of the sea that whispered promises of revelations yet to surface.

Part 2:

In the quietude of twilight, when the sky wore its evening shroud and the sea mirrored the celestial canvas above, I ventured closer to the water's edge. The tranquility of the scene masked a subtle restlessness within me, an insatiable hunger to decipher the secrets Neptune had bestowed.

With each passing day, my thoughts became an intricate tapestry woven from fragments of memory and an inexplicable longing. I sought refuge in the ebb and flow of the tides, hoping the rhythm of the sea might unravel the enigma veiled within me.

The ordinary world beckoned with its mundane obligations, yet my spirit yearned for the depths, for a communion with the unknown. The faceless figure—Neptune—loomed in the periphery of my thoughts, an elusive guardian of unspoken truths.

It was in the gentle caress of the ocean breeze that I felt a whisper, an invitation carried on the crest of a wave. It was time to heed the silent call, to venture beyond the confines of the familiar and embrace the uncharted waters of the soul.

As twilight yielded to the embrace of night, I stood at the water's edge, where the sea met the shore in a shimmering dance of reflection and obscurity. The rhythmic symphony of the waves urged me to take a step, to surrender to the unknown with an unspoken vow to unlock the mysteries held within Neptune's realm.

In that fleeting moment of decision, I felt a subtle shift in the fabric of reality, a merging of the tangible and the ethereal. With a tentative yet resolute stride, I waded into the tranquil waters, feeling the embrace of Neptune's presence welcoming me into the depths. The cool embrace of the sea enveloped me, igniting a sense of liberation and trepidation, for I knew not what lay beyond the surface, yet an inexplicable trust anchored me to this journey of discovery.

Part 3:

Beneath the surface, the world transformed into a symphony of luminescence. Each droplet carried whispers of ancient tales, weaving an intricate narrative that transcended language and comprehension. I surrendered to the gentle currents, allowing the sea to guide me deeper into its embrace.

Time ceased to exist in the underwater expanse as I traversed through realms unknown, surrounded by an ethereal luminescence that danced with the rhythm of Neptune's secrets. An innate sense of belonging washed over me, dissolving the boundaries between self and the boundless expanse of the sea.

In the depths, my senses transcended their earthly limitations. I felt the pulse of life in the swaying kelp forests and heard the echo of distant songs carried by the currents. Creatures of myriad hues darted around me, their graceful movements a testament to the harmony that thrived beneath the surface.

I became an observer and a partaker, a silent witness to the symphony of existence that unfolded in the embrace of Neptune's realm. Memories of the faceless figure, the guardian of these depths, ebbed and flowed like the tides, offering subtle guidance amidst the vastness of the unknown.

As I journeyed deeper, the boundaries of my perception blurred, and I felt an awakening—a communion with the elemental forces that shaped this mystical domain. It was a harmonious convergence of self-discovery and the embrace of the inexplicable, a transformative union with the essence of the sea.

Guided by an unseen force, I traversed through underwater vistas, each unveiling a fragment of Neptune's enigmatic legacy. The sea whispered tales of forgotten civilizations and whispered prophecies of realms yet to be unveiled, painting an intricate mosaic of possibilities that transcended the limitations of mortal comprehension.

And within this aqueous sanctuary, I found solace—a sanctuary of serenity and revelation that resonated deep within my being. With each passing moment, I felt a kinship with the untamed beauty of the ocean, an understanding that transcended words, rooted in the silent communion between soul and sea.

Part 4:

In the embrace of Neptune's realm, time seemed a fleeting notion, a concept lost in the endless dance of currents. Yet, amidst the boundless expanse, a subtle yearning anchored me—a call from the world above, a reminder of responsibilities and obligations tethering me to the terrestrial realm.

Reluctantly, I began my ascent, propelled by a sense of duty yet reluctant to part ways with the mystical depths that had unveiled a tapestry of revelations. Each stroke towards the surface felt like a step back into the confines of the known, leaving behind the ethereal sanctuary that had cradled my spirit.

As the luminous depths gradually faded, replaced by the shimmering threshold of the water's surface, a sense of bittersweet nostalgia swept over me. The transition from the boundless freedom of the sea to the terrestrial world felt akin to shedding an intricate, otherworldly skin.

Breaking through the surface, I was enveloped once more by the embrace of the earthly realm. The cool caress of the breeze and the gentle whispers of the shore greeted me, marking the boundary between the ocean's secrets and the familiar shores of reality.

With each breath of the salty air, a fragment of the underwater serenity lingered, echoing in the chambers of my soul. I carried with me the weight of an indelible experience, a memory that danced at the periphery of consciousness, urging me to decipher its cryptic messages.

Returning to the mundane world felt like wearing a mask—a cloak of normalcy concealing the depths of the transcendental encounter. The whispers of Neptune's realm lingered, a constant reminder of an elusive truth waiting to be unveiled.

Despite the veil of everyday life, a newfound perception tinged my existence. The world seemed to shimmer with hidden meanings, a subtle undercurrent that echoed the mysteries of the sea. I found myself drawn to the shoreline, seeking solace in the echoes of Neptune's whispers, yearning to decipher the enigmatic language of the waves and the secrets they carried from the depths.

Part 5:

Days melted into weeks, yet the resonance of Neptune's embrace lingered, an indelible mark etched upon the fabric of my being. The call of the sea grew louder, an irresistible beckoning that tugged at the strings of my soul, urging me to seek further revelations in the embrace of the waves.

In the quietude of twilight, when the world slipped into the arms of dusk, I returned to the shoreline—a pilgrimage to the threshold between worlds. The rhythmic lullaby of the waves seemed to echo the secrets whispered by Neptune, a silent invitation to delve deeper into the mysteries veiled beneath the surface.

With each step towards the water's edge, a sense of anticipation mingled with trepidation coursed through me. The boundary between land and sea felt like a threshold between the known and the enigmatic—a portal to a realm where the ordinary metamorphosed into the extraordinary.

As the waves caressed the shore with gentle insistence, I stood at the cusp of an unspoken promise, yearning to immerse myself once more in the sanctum of Neptune's realm. The horizon shimmered with an ethereal glow, as if holding secrets within its aqueous embrace, secrets waiting to be unraveled by the curious and the intrepid.

With a silent vow to venture deeper into the mysteries that awaited, I waded into the tranquil waters, feeling the familiar coolness envelop me. The sea welcomed me back into its fold, each ripple a whispered greeting, each current a guide leading me towards an elusive understanding.

The transition from solid ground to liquid sanctuary was seamless, as though I were shedding the confines of earthly limitations and embracing a boundless expanse where the soul found communion with the ineffable.

Once submerged, I felt the weight of the terrestrial world relinquish its hold, replaced by the weightless serenity of the underwater realm. Neptune's whispers reverberated through the currents, guiding my journey deeper into the heart of the unknown, promising revelations yet to unfold in the depths of the sea.

Part 6:

In the aqueous sanctuary of Neptune's realm, I surrendered to the ebb and flow of the currents, allowing the sea to cradle me in its embrace. The underwater panorama unfolded like an ethereal tapestry, each stroke and sway a brushstroke in the masterpiece painted by the elements.

Time in this submerged world bore no resemblance to the relentless ticking of the clock above. Here, moments stretched into infinity, a timeless ballet orchestrated by the symphony of the sea. I reveled in the dance of life that thrived beneath the surface, a silent witness to the interconnectedness of all beings in this aqueous symposium.

Amidst the undulating kelp forests and the kaleidoscope of aquatic life, a sense of belonging settled within me—an inexplicable kinship with the denizens of Neptune's domain. It was a communion beyond words, an unspoken understanding that transcended the barriers of language or form.

With every passing current, I felt a transformation—a shedding of the layers that defined my terrestrial existence. Here, amidst the tranquil depths, I shed the burdens of mundane existence and embraced a profound connection with the elements, feeling the heartbeat of the ocean resonate within my soul.

The faceless figure, Neptune, hovered at the edges of my consciousness, a spectral guardian guiding me through the submerged labyrinth. His presence, though ethereal, carried a weight of ancient wisdom—a silent mentor orchestrating the mysteries unveiled by the sea.

As I journeyed deeper into the abyss, the boundaries between self and the encompassing waters blurred further. I surrendered to the cosmic choreography, becoming a part of the intricate ballet that unfolded in the depths—an amalgamation of spirit and fluidity, transcending the confines of mortal existence.

And amidst this timeless expanse, I glimpsed fragments of forgotten tales—the whispers of civilizations lost to the annals of time, echoes of a history inscribed in the undulating currents. Neptune's realm held within its depths the chronicles of epochs past, veiled in an enigmatic language waiting to be deciphered by the intrepid seeker.

In this realm of aqueous serenity, I traversed through realms untamed, each moment a revelation that added another brushstroke to the canvas of understanding—a testament to the inexhaustible mysteries that awaited discovery in Neptune's embrace.

Part 7:

With every graceful stroke through the watery expanse, I felt the veil between the mundane and the mystical grow thinner. The currents whispered ancient secrets, carrying fragments of forgotten narratives and the echoes of primordial wisdom. Neptune's realm was a repository of tales, a cryptic library awaiting the curious explorer.

As I journeyed deeper, the kaleidoscope of aquatic life became a mesmerizing symphony—a vibrant orchestra harmonizing with the pulsating rhythm of the sea. Schools of shimmering fish danced in unison, their movements a choreography that spoke of unity and interconnectedness, echoing the symphony of existence.

Amongst the labyrinthine coral gardens and the enigmatic crevices, I sensed an unspoken dialogue—an exchange of energies that transcended language. The denizens of this aqueous sanctuary seemed attuned to a cosmic symphony, each creature a note in the celestial composition orchestrated by Neptune himself.

The faceless figure, the enigmatic guardian of these depths, remained an ever-present specter—his silent guidance a beacon amidst the aqueous expanse. His essence lingered in the subtle shifts of the currents, in the play of light and shadow upon the ocean floor, a constant reminder of the mysteries waiting to be unraveled.

In the depths, I shed the confines of mortal limitations, embracing a communion with the elemental forces that shaped this ethereal domain. The sea was a mosaic of contradictions—a serene sanctuary concealing untamed depths, a testament to the balance between tranquility and tempest that defined Neptune's realm.

Each moment spent submerged was a revelation—an unveiling of truths that transcended the boundaries of comprehension. I navigated through vistas unknown, each turn revealing a tableau of wonders that spoke volumes in the language of the sea—a dialect understood by the soul, not the mind.

The whispers of forgotten epochs and the echoes of ancient civilizations resonated in the abyss, urging me to delve deeper into the labyrinth of mysteries. It was an invitation to be both an observer and a participant in the timeless narrative woven by the currents—a tale that spanned epochs, awaiting a seeker willing to decipher its enigmatic script.

And in this submerged odyssey, I found solace—a sanctuary where the boundaries between self and the boundless expanse dissolved, where the ephemeral touch of Neptune's guidance ignited a sense of belonging to a realm beyond the confines of mortal understanding.

Part 8:

As I traversed the depths, Neptune's realm unfolded like a cosmic tapestry, each stroke through the aqueous abyss a revelation in itself. The symphony of the sea orchestrated a kaleidoscope of hues and harmonies—a visual sonnet that spoke volumes without words.

Amidst the undulating currents, I became a silent witness to the cyclical nature of existence—the dance of life and death, creation and dissolution. Each flicker of movement, every undulation of the underwater foliage, carried within it the essence of eternal cycles—a cosmic ballet choreographed by unseen hands.

The denizens of Neptune's realm, diverse in form and function, embodied a symbiosis that transcended individuality. From the vibrant hues of tropical fish to the majestic glide of oceanic wanderers, each creature contributed to the intricate web of life, an interconnectedness that whispered tales of unity amidst diversity.

In the depths, time ceased its relentless march, offering instead a glimpse into the eternity that dwelled within each fleeting moment. The underwater symposium was a sanctuary where past, present, and future converged—a threshold to realms where time was but an illusion.

The enigmatic presence of Neptune lingered, a spectral guardian whose ethereal guidance transcended the boundaries of mortal understanding. His essence, woven into the fabric of the sea, was a silent compass guiding the seekers through the labyrinthine depths, unveiling the enigmas veiled in the underwater sanctum.

In the embrace of Neptune's realm, I shed the confines of self-imposed limitations, embracing a communion with the primordial forces that shaped this ethereal expanse. The sea was a canvas of contrasts—a serene sanctuary concealing untamed depths, a testament to the delicate balance that defined Neptune's domain.

With each dive into the aquatic abyss, I unearthed fragments of forgotten tales—a mosaic of narratives waiting to be pieced together. The whispers of bygone epochs reverberated through the currents, an invitation to decode the cryptic language of the sea—a lexicon inscribed in the very fabric of existence.

And amidst this submerged odyssey, I discovered a truth resonating deep within—the revelation that within Neptune's realm, the seeker and the sought were not separate entities, but harmonious threads woven into the cosmic fabric of the underwater symphony.

Part 9:

With each foray into Neptune's realm, the sea unfolded its enigmatic narrative—a tapestry woven with intricate patterns of life, echoing the celestial symphony that resonated through the depths. The underwater expanse became a sanctuary where the soul communed with the elemental forces, transcending the confines of mortal existence.

In the embrace of the aqueous sanctuary, I navigated through ethereal landscapes—vast plains adorned with corals that resembled vibrant gardens, and abyssal trenches veiled in an otherworldly darkness. Each panorama bore the fingerprints of Neptune's touch, an artist whose canvas was the boundless expanse of the sea.

The denizens of this aquatic sanctuary were not merely inhabitants but emissaries of a cosmic harmony. From the iridescent hues of tiny creatures to the majestic dance of larger beings, they epitomized the essence of coexistence—an intricately woven tapestry where each being played a vital role in the symphony of life.

Time beneath the waves was not measured in hours or days but in the orchestration of moments—a ceaseless procession of revelations and contemplation. The currents whispered tales of forgotten epochs, unveiling the secrets veiled in the depths, a cryptic lexicon waiting to be deciphered by the intrepid seeker.

Amidst the aquatic panorama, the spectral presence of Neptune lingered—a silent guardian whose ethereal guidance transcended the limitations of mortal understanding. His silent whispers echoed through the underwater currents, a beacon guiding the seekers through the labyrinth of revelations.

In the depths, I embraced a communion with the primal forces that shaped this enigmatic realm. The sea was a paradox—an ethereal sanctuary concealing untamed depths, a testament to the delicate equilibrium that governed Neptune's domain.

Each dive into Neptune's sanctuary revealed fragments of forgotten tales—a tapestry of narratives waiting to be unveiled. The echoes of ancient epochs resonated through the aqueous expanse, an invitation to decode the cryptic language of the sea—a language etched into the very fabric of existence.

And amidst this submerged odyssey, I unearthed a profound truth—an understanding that within Neptune's realm, the seeker and the secrets were not disparate entities but harmonious facets of an eternal cosmic design—a cosmic ballet where seeker and sought danced in synchronous harmony within the watery depths.

Part 10:

With each descent into Neptune's kingdom, the veil between worlds grew thinner, blurring the lines separating the terrestrial from the ethereal. The sea, an infinite expanse of wonder, unraveled its mysteries in fragments—a cryptic saga whispered through the currents.

Amidst the undulating dance of marine life, I discerned a cosmic ballet—a choreography orchestrated by unseen hands. The myriad creatures, from the smallest shimmering entities to the colossal wanderers, embodied a symbiosis echoing the harmony that threaded through Neptune's sanctuary.

Time lost its linear essence beneath the waves, succumbing to the fluidity of the depths. Each moment submerged felt both fleeting and eternal, an immersion into a realm where the past, present, and future coalesced—a timeless agora where revelations unfolded with every undulation.

Neptune's enigmatic presence lingered, an ethereal mentor guiding the seekers through the labyrinthine mysteries. His essence wove through the aqueous currents, a spectral compass navigating the seekers towards the untold secrets veiled in the ocean's embrace.

In the depths, I shed the trappings of mundane existence, merging with the elemental forces that governed this enigmatic domain. The sea, a canvas of contradictions, harbored serene tranquility amidst untamed depths—a testament to the exquisite balance that governed Neptune's sanctuary.

Each dive unearthed fragments of forgotten lore—an encrypted anthology waiting for deciphering. Echoes of epochs long past reverberated through the aqueous expanse, inviting the seeker to unravel the enigmatic lexicon inscribed in the very fabric of the sea.

Within Neptune's realm, I discovered a profound verity—a revelation that within the depths, seeker and sought intertwined in a cosmic waltz. Here, the seeker was not merely in pursuit of secrets; they were an integral note in the symphony of revelations—a harmonic resonance that echoed through the boundless expanse of the watery sanctuary.

Conclusion:

In the twilight between realms, where the terrestrial met the ethereal, lay the culmination of an odyssey—a narrative woven in the depths of Neptune's embrace. Each dive into the enigmatic waters had unveiled fragments of an ancient saga, painting an intricate mosaic of revelations that transcended mortal comprehension.

The journey through Neptune's realm had been a pilgrimage of transcendence—a communion with the primal forces that shaped the cosmic ballet of existence. Amidst undulating currents and vibrant marine life, the seeker had ventured deeper into the labyrinth of mysteries, guided by Neptune's spectral presence.

In the aqueous sanctuary, time had relinquished its linear hold, allowing the seeker to transcend the limitations of mortal perception. Each moment submerged had been a revelation—a fleeting glimpse into the eternal, a dance with the timeless symphony that echoed through the boundless expanse.

Neptune's enigmatic guidance, though silent, had been an ever-present beacon—a spectral mentor orchestrating the seeker's journey through the watery depths. His ethereal essence whispered tales of forgotten epochs, inviting the seeker to decipher the cryptic language etched into the very fabric of the sea.

As the seeker emerged from the embrace of Neptune's realm, a profound understanding resonated within—the realization that within the watery expanse, seeker and secrets were not separate entities but harmonious threads woven into the cosmic design. The journey had been a convergence—a symbiosis where the seeker became an integral note in the symphony of revelations, a reverberation that echoed through the depths of Neptune's kingdom.

Though the memories of Neptune's embrace were veiled in the labyrinth of the mind, the essence of the underwater odyssey lingered—an indelible mark etched upon the soul, a testament to the transcendental union between seeker and the enigmatic realm of Neptune, the keeper of the watery mysteries. And as the seeker returned to the shores of the terrestrial world, a subtle knowing whispered—a silent echo of the cosmic secrets unveiled within Neptune's realm, forever etched in the seeker's journey of transcendence.

12

The Labyrinth of Light

In the hushed embrace of a world teeming with bustling chaos, there exists a young woman named Emilia, a pilgrim of the soul. Her life isn't just a chronological timeline; it's an intricate mosaic woven from the threads of spiritual exploration, introspection, and the relentless pursuit of inner stillness. For years, she has traversed the labyrinthine pathways of consciousness, seeking the elusive whispers of her higher mind and communing with the essence that orchestrates the cosmic dance of existence.

Emilia's journey isn't one marked by grandiose feats or tangible conquests; it's an odyssey whispered in the silent cadence of her meditations, painted in the subtle brushstrokes of her introspective voyages. She has spent countless moments immersed in the sanctum of solitude, peeling away the layers of conditioned thoughts, unearthing the truths that lie dormant within the depths of her being.

In her quest for self-discovery, she has encountered ethereal guides, communed with the cosmic realms, and unraveled the mysteries that blur the boundaries between the seen and the unseen. Her story isn't just about spiritual awakening; it's an invitation—a call to embark on a journey of introspection, a pilgrimage to the very essence of existence.

This is a chronicle not of an end but of a perpetual beginning—a narrative that weaves together the threads of cosmic wisdom, interconnectedness, and the boundless love that permeates the symphony of existence. It's an introduction to the tapestry of Emilia's soul, a prelude to the infinite possibilities that await in the eternal dance of self-discovery.

"The Labyrinth of Light: Emilia's Spiritual Voyage"

Meet Emilia:

I am Emilia. For as long as I can remember, my journey has been inward. The world around me spins with chaos, but within, I've sought the stillness that resides in the core of my being. It's been years—countless moments wrapped in the embrace of meditation, inner contemplation, and the quest to unravel the mysteries of my own soul.

As a child, I felt a peculiar pull toward the quiet corners of existence. While my friends reveled in the bustling noise of play and discovery, I found solace in the serene whispers of solitude. There, within the hush of my thoughts, I discovered the doorway to a realm unseen yet deeply felt.

The path I walk isn't adorned with grandeur or visible accomplishments. Instead, it's a journey illuminated by the subtle glow of self-discovery and spiritual awakening. Each day begins with the rising sun painting the sky in hues of possibility, and I greet it with reverence, welcoming the chance to delve deeper into the recesses of my consciousness.

Meditation isn't merely a practice; it's a way of life. It's the silent dialogue between the fragments of my existence, weaving them into a harmonious symphony. The whispers of the wind, the dance of leaves in the breeze—all are reminders of the interconnectedness that binds us all.

There are days when the noise of the world attempts to breach my sanctuary—the demands, the expectations, the rush. Yet, I've learned to anchor myself in the stillness within. It's in this stillness that I find the strength to navigate the turbulent waters of existence.

Through the years, I've encountered layers of myself—the fears that cling like shadows, the dreams that soar like eagles, the wounds that whisper tales of healing. Each layer peeled away in the quiet moments of introspection, revealing the essence of who I am—pure, raw, and unbounded by the constraints of the external world.

In this pursuit of inner peace, I've discovered that enlightenment isn't a destination but a continual journey—a perpetual blossoming of the soul. And as I continue to traverse this path, I find myself not in the destination, but in the journey itself—in the subtle cadence of my breath, the gentle rhythm of my heart, and the boundless expanses of my consciousness.

This journey of self-discovery has taught me that the most profound wisdom lies not in the cacophony of the external world but in the serene whispers of my higher mind—the stillness that reverberates with the universal symphony of existence.

Relationships:

My journey into the depths of my own being has indeed left its mark on the tapestry of my relationships. In the sanctum of my spiritual exploration, I've encountered moments of profound connection, but

I've also navigated the complexities that arise when the rhythms of one's soul diverge from those around them.

My friendships are woven with threads of understanding and acceptance, colored by the hues of empathy nurtured through introspection. Yet, there are moments when the chasm between our perceptions widens. My companions, engrossed in the ebb and flow of the material world, sometimes struggle to grasp the ethereal essence I've cultivated within.

Conversations often swerve towards the tangible—career aspirations, societal norms, material pursuits—while I find solace in discussing the intangible—the nature of existence, the interconnectedness of all things, the whispers of the soul. It's not a divide born of superiority or exclusion but rather a divergence in perspectives, a contrast in the lenses through which we perceive reality.

In romantic relationships, the impact is more palpable. My journey toward self-discovery has fostered an unwavering sense of independence and self-reliance. While I cherish the idea of companionship, the intricate dance of partnership sometimes finds me stepping to the beat of my own rhythm.

My pursuit of inner stillness has led me to seek a partner who can embrace the depths of my soul and respect the sanctity of my spiritual journey. It's not about finding someone who shares identical beliefs or practices but rather someone who can appreciate the essence of my being, someone who recognizes the beauty in our differences and the harmony in our connection.

At times, my inclination toward solitude can be misconstrued as aloofness or detachment. The need for moments of introspection and solitude to nourish my spiritual self is sometimes mistaken for a lack of investment in the relationship. Yet, it's within these moments that I refuel the wellspring of my being, allowing me to pour more deeply into the shared experiences we create.

My metaphysical knowledge, though a guiding light, isn't a panacea for the complexities of human relationships. It doesn't shield me from the vulnerabilities or the intricacies of emotional entanglements. Instead, it serves as a compass, guiding me toward compassion, understanding, and a deeper connection with those who share this journey with me.

In the end, my spiritual practices haven't created insurmountable barriers in my relationships. Rather, they've become the threads that weave a richer tapestry, one adorned with empathy, understanding, and an unwavering authenticity in the way I navigate the intricate dance of human connections.

Deep within:

Entering the depths of my being feels like embarking on an odyssey—an expedition into the uncharted territories of my consciousness. With each meditation, I traverse landscapes unseen by mortal eyes, navigating the labyrinthine corridors of my mind, delving into the recesses where the echoes of my true self reside.

The journey inward is not always serene; it's an expedition fraught with the turbulence of emotions, memories, and thoughts. There are days when the waters are tranquil, mirroring the tranquility of a still lake at dawn. In these moments, I effortlessly slip into the sanctuary of my higher mind, where clarity reigns and the whispers of wisdom resonate.

But there are also tempests within—storms brewed by the turbulence of unresolved emotions, haunting memories, and the ceaseless chatter of the ego. It's in these tempests that I find the greatest revelations. As I confront the tumultuous waves of my inner world, I unearth the roots of my fears, acknowledge the echoes of past traumas, and untangle the intricate web of conditioned thoughts.

In the silence of meditation, I confront the shadows that lurk within—the insecurities that weave themselves into the fabric of my being, the doubts that linger like wisps of mist, and the masks I wear to navigate the external world. It's not a battle against these shadows but an embrace—an acknowledgment of their existence and an invitation to transcend their influence.

The deeper I journey within, the more I realize the interconnectedness of all aspects of myself—the light and the shadow, the joy and the sorrow, the strength and the vulnerability. Each layer I peel away reveals not just fragments of myself but the threads that bind me to the vast tapestry of existence.

There are moments of profound clarity, where the boundaries of the self dissolve, and I merge with the cosmic symphony. It's in these moments of transcendence that time loses its grip, and I find myself floating in the boundless expanse of consciousness—pure, unadulterated, and free from the confines of the mundane world.

But perhaps the most transformative aspect of this inward journey is the realization that the stillness I seek isn't a distant destination; it's a state of being—a serene oasis nestled within the tumultuous landscapes of existence. And as I continue to traverse the labyrinth of my own consciousness, I embrace each twist, turn, and revelation, knowing that the journey inward is an eternal exploration—a sacred pilgrimage to the essence of my own being.

• Adrian Cox B.Sc. •

Work:

My journey into the depths of spiritual exploration has intricately woven itself into the tapestry of my professional life and perception of wealth. As I've delved deeper into my spiritual practices, my perspective on work and wealth has shifted, evolving into something more profound than mere material gain.

In the realm of employment, my spiritual journey has guided my choices. I've sought work environments that align with my values—places that foster a sense of harmony and mindfulness rather than solely focusing on monetary rewards. My career isn't just a means to an end but an avenue for soulful expression and contribution to the collective tapestry of existence.

My spiritual practices have seeped into my work routine, becoming anchors in the midst of professional storms. Mindfulness and presence infuse my tasks, enhancing my creativity and problem-solving abilities. I've discovered that moments of stillness amidst a bustling workday grant me clarity and resilience, enabling me to navigate challenges with grace and equanimity.

Regarding wealth, my understanding has transcended the conventional definition. It's no longer solely about accumulating material possessions or monetary abundance but about the richness of experiences, connections, and the impact I can make in the world.

My providership of wealth has transformed from a pursuit of accumulation to a journey of mindful stewardship. I honor the resources that flow into my life, recognizing their value beyond their monetary measure. I seek a balance between providing for my needs and nurturing a mindset of abundance that extends beyond material possessions.

Through my metaphysical knowledge, I've realized the interconnectedness of all things, including wealth. The energy I invest in my spiritual practices ripples into my professional endeavors and financial pursuits. It's not about detachment from wealth but about fostering a healthy relationship—one that doesn't define my worth but serves as a tool for greater good and personal fulfillment.

I've embraced the notion of wealth as a means to amplify positive change, supporting causes aligned with my spiritual values and contributing to the betterment of society. My understanding of abundance encompasses not just financial prosperity but also emotional well-being, spiritual fulfillment, and a sense of purpose.

This journey has taught me that true wealth lies not in the accumulation of possessions but in the depth of my experiences, the richness of my relationships, and the alignment of my actions with my spiritual principles. As I continue to walk this path, my providership of wealth remains rooted in gratitude, mindfulness, and a profound awareness of the interconnectedness of all things.

The most important metaphysical knowledge:

The most profound metaphysical knowledge that has reverberated within me like an eternal echo is the understanding of interconnectedness. It's the realization that we are not solitary islands drifting in isolation but intricately woven threads in the cosmic tapestry of existence.

Through my spiritual journey, I've unearthed the ancient truth that everything in this universe is interconnected—an intricate dance where every action, thought, and energy creates ripples that traverse the fabric of reality.

• ADRIAN COX B.Sc. •

At the core of this wisdom lies the principle of oneness—the recognition that we are all manifestations of the same divine essence, experiencing life through different lenses. This understanding transcends boundaries of race, creed, and culture, weaving a web that binds us in an invisible embrace.

Every breath I take, every thought I harbor, every action I undertake sends vibrations into the collective consciousness. This awareness fosters a sense of responsibility—a recognition that my existence is not in isolation but intertwined with the well-being of all beings and the cosmos itself.

The understanding of interconnectedness guides my interactions, infusing them with compassion, empathy, and a deep sense of reverence for all life. It influences my choices, urging me to act in harmony with the greater whole rather than seeking personal gain at the expense of others.

This metaphysical knowledge shapes my perspective on the world. It allows me to perceive beauty in diversity, to recognize the underlying unity amid apparent differences. It grants me solace in moments of solitude, knowing that even in the quietude of meditation, I am connected to the vast symphony of existence.

This wisdom has taught me that each soul I encounter is a reflection, a mirror that offers glimpses into different facets of the cosmic truth. Every interaction, no matter how fleeting, holds the potential to deepen our understanding of the interconnected web that binds us all.

In the grand tapestry of existence, this understanding serves as a guiding star, illuminating the path toward harmony, compassion, and unity. It's a timeless reminder that in embracing the interconnectedness of all things, I embrace the essence of my own being and the collective soul of the universe.

Self-reflection:

As I stand before the full-length mirror, my reflection offers a glimpse not just into my physical form but also into the subtle nuances of the journey I've embarked upon. My appearance echoes the essence of the spiritual path I tread, an outward manifestation of the inner transformation.

My face, framed by locks of hair that cascade like a river of midnight, carries the soft lines of introspection—the furrows etched by countless moments of deep contemplation and tranquil meditation. It speaks of a serenity that emanates from within, a calmness that radiates from eyes that mirror the universe—a depth that hints at the wisdom gleaned from the stillness of my higher mind.

The delicate curve of my lips often finds itself wrapped in a gentle smile, a silent tribute to the peace that pervades my soul. It's not a smile borne of frivolity but an expression of the tranquility that dwells in the recesses of my being, a tranquil acknowledgment of the joy found in embracing the journey of self-discovery.

My body, draped in flowing fabrics that mirror the hues of nature, bears the grace of a vessel that has housed the echoes of spiritual exploration. It's not about conforming to fashion trends but about adorning myself with garments that reflect the harmony and connection I seek—a harmony that resonates in the earthy tones and flowing silhouettes, echoing the unity I strive to embody.

The attire I choose isn't about concealing or enhancing; it's about embodying comfort, allowing movement, and fostering a sense of ease as I navigate the currents of existence. Each piece of clothing becomes a canvas, adorned with symbols and patterns that echo the interconnectedness I cherish.

• Adrian Cox B.Sc. •

My hair, a canvas of its own, mirrors the cosmic dance of the universe—its unruly waves and twists telling stories of freedom and authenticity. It's not meticulously styled but left to flow in its natural rhythm, an ode to the freedom of expression and the liberation found in embracing one's true nature.

As I gaze at this reflection, I don't see just the physical form but a manifestation—a testament to the journey embarked upon, the discoveries made within, and the harmony sought in the world without. My appearance is not just a canvas for the eyes but a testament to the whispers of the soul, echoing the depths of my spiritual exploration.

The Poet within:

In the dance between metaphysics and poetry, I've found my sanctuary—a realm where words transcend the boundaries of the mundane and soar into the ethereal. My pen becomes a conduit, weaving threads of cosmic wisdom into verses that resonate with the rhythm of the universe.

What sets my approach apart in the world of metaphysical poetry is my unconventional technique—a fusion of meditation and intuitive writing. Before I even put pen to paper, I immerse myself in the stillness of meditation, allowing the whispers of the universe to caress the canvas of my consciousness.

In this meditative state, I become a vessel—a receptacle for cosmic musings, the channel through which metaphysical truths flow. As I drift in this space between worlds, ideas, and images unravel in kaleidoscopic hues, revealing the intricate tapestry of existence.

When I emerge from this meditative trance, I don't immediately rush to capture the thoughts that danced within. Instead, I allow them to linger, ferment, and merge with my being. It's a gestation period where concepts meld with emotions, where the intangible mingles with the visceral, forming a symphony of words waiting to be born.

When I finally approach the blank page, it's not with the intention to craft but to channel—to surrender to the flow of inspiration and let the words spill forth like an untamed river. I don't bind myself to structured forms or rhyme schemes; instead, I allow the verses to breathe, to transcend conventional boundaries and take on a life of their own.

I embrace paradoxes, weaving threads of duality into verses that challenge the boundaries of perception. The interplay of light and shadow, the dance of chaos and order—all find expression in my poetry, mirroring the intricate balance of the universe.

My verses aren't just a reflection of metaphysical concepts; they are invitations—a call to embark on an inward journey, to explore the depths of consciousness, and to contemplate the mysteries that lie beyond the veil of the tangible.

What sets me apart is this synthesis—the fusion of meditation and intuitive expression. It's not just about writing poetry; it's about channeling the essence of the cosmos into verses that transcend the confines of the ordinary, inviting readers to immerse themselves in the boundless expanse of metaphysical exploration.

In the quiet of my sanctuary, where the whispers of the universe echo, I've penned verses that seek to bridge the chasm between the tangible and the ineffable. Here's a glimpse of a metaphysical poem that emerged from the depths of contemplation:

- Adrian Cox B.Sc. -

Ethereal Symphony

In the symphony of existence, harken, oh soul,
To the cosmic chorus that orchestrates the whole.
Listen not with ears but with the essence within,
Feel the vibrations where the dance of life begins.
Stars, mere fragments in the cosmic ballet,
Each a luminescent ode to the eternal play.
Galaxies whirl, in their cosmic embrace,
Weaving tales of time and infinite space.
In quantum whispers, secrets softly sigh,
As particles pirouette, painting the sky.
The tapestry of atoms, a celestial hue,
Where matter and spirit entwine, ever true.
Mind, a universe in its own right,
Wandering realms of day and night.
Thoughts unfurl, like cosmic dust,
Shaping destinies, in cosmic trust.
And amid the labyrinth of the human form,
Lies a sanctuary where the soul is reborn.
Beyond the veil of the senses' reign,
Where the stillness of the higher mind does reign.
Oh, seeker, in the depths of inner space,
Find solace in the silence, embrace its grace.
For in the union of self and cosmic rhyme,
Resides the truth of all space and time.
So, let the heart's cadence join the celestial song,
As we dance in harmony, where we all belong.
In the ethereal symphony, let us find our part,
Each a note, each a melody, within the cosmic heart.

In these verses, I endeavor to paint a picture of the interconnectedness of all things—the cosmic dance of stars, the convergence of matter and spirit, and the sanctuary found within the stillness of the higher mind. It's a poetic exploration of the unity that binds us to the vast expanse of existence.

Her love within:

In the sanctum of my solitude, I've traversed realms unseen, delving into the depths of my being. Today, as I sit enveloped in the embrace of silence, a torrent of emotions cascades through me, each drop a testament to the profound love that swells within my soul.

I'm overwhelmed, not by sorrow or despair, but by an ineffable sense of gratitude—an outpouring of love for the life that I've sculpted through the whispers of my spiritual journey. Tears, unbidden, trace gentle rivers down my cheeks, carrying with them the weight of profound emotions.

In this moment, I'm not just witnessing life; I'm experiencing it in its purest form—a symphony of existence where every note, every heartbeat resonates with the melody of the universe. The stillness within me echoes with the vibrations of cosmic love, an energy that transcends the boundaries of the self and merges with the eternal rhythm of creation.

It's a love not confined to the tangible, but one that embraces the intangible—the beauty found in the dance of atoms, the majesty of a star-studded sky, and the serenity of a dew-kissed morning. It's a love that permeates my very essence, intertwining with the threads of my existence.

The weight of this love feels almost unbearable, a bittersweet realization of the interconnectedness that binds me to all beings. I'm not just experiencing my own joy; I'm feeling the collective joy of existence pulsating through every fiber of my being.

• ADRIAN COX B.Sc. •

With each tear shed, I offer a silent tribute to the symphony of life—the ebbs and flows, the joys and sorrows—all woven into a grand tapestry of experiences. These tears are not borne of anguish but are the overflowing vessels of a heart brimming with love—for the journey taken, for the challenges conquered, and for the moments of pure, unadulterated bliss.

As I cry, it's not a cry of pain, but a cry of reverence—a sacred expression of the deep wellspring of emotion that arises from the boundless love I hold for the life I've embraced. It's an acknowledgment of the beauty in vulnerability, a tribute to the divine essence that breathes life into every moment.

In this tearful embrace of love, I find solace, strength, and a reaffirmation of the profound connection that binds me to the universe—an ode to the eternal dance of existence, orchestrated by the symphony of love that reverberates within and around me.

A story that shines a light on a greater awareness:

Once, in the quietude of my meditation, I encountered a presence—a luminous being that transcended form and yet radiated an undeniable essence of familiarity and warmth. This ethereal entity was a personification of the greater awareness that resides within us all—a guide to the boundless light that illuminates the path to self-discovery.

This luminous guide, whose name echoed in the silence of my thoughts as 'Auriel,' appeared as a shimmering amalgamation of cosmic energy. A presence so serene, it seemed to embrace me with a love that transcended the confines of human comprehension.

Auriel didn't speak in words but communicated in whispers of intuition, in ripples that coursed through the fabric of my consciousness. Through this otherworldly communion, I gleaned insights that transcended the limitations of the mundane—a wisdom that spoke of unity, compassion, and the eternal dance of creation.

This ethereal guide didn't impose but gently nudged me toward introspection, nudged me to look within—the sacred reservoir where the universe resides. Auriel became the embodiment of the greater awareness that lies dormant within each soul—an invitation to awaken to the boundless potential and the luminous tapestry of our existence.

As I communed with Auriel, I realized that this guide wasn't an external entity but a reflection—a mirror that unveiled the depths of my own being. Auriel personified the guiding light within, urging me to trust my intuition, to embrace the whispers of my soul, and to dance in harmony with the cosmic symphony.

Through this encounter, I learned that the spiritual journey isn't a solitary odyssey but a communion—a sacred dance between the seeker and the guiding light that dwells within. Auriel became a beacon, illuminating the path to self-realization, reminding me that the answers I seek reside in the stillness of my higher mind.

This story, I wish for people to know—a testament to the profound interconnectedness that binds us to the greater awareness within. Auriel isn't just a celestial entity but a representation of the divine spark that dwells within us all—a reminder that we are not merely travelers in this cosmic tapestry but co-creators, wielding the power of our own illumination and the depth of our own consciousness.

As I sit with my dear friend under the dappled shade of an ancient oak, I sense the gentle presence of Auriel—the guiding light that has graced my spiritual journey. As the conversation weaves through the tapestry of existence, my friend's curiosity sparks a yearning to commune with Auriel, to seek answers beyond the veil of the seen.

With a silent invocation, I invite Auriel into our shared space, allowing the luminous presence to infuse the air with a serene energy. My friend's gaze softens, sensing the subtle shift in the atmosphere, an unspoken acknowledgement of Auriel's ethereal presence.

Curiosity dances in my friend's eyes as she gathers the courage to address the celestial guide. "Auriel," she begins tentatively, her voice carrying a blend of wonder and reverence, "what is the realm you reside in? How does it relate to the physical world we inhabit?"

In response, a gentle ripple of energy weaves through the air, a silent yet palpable response from Auriel. Through the intuitive whispers that bridge our worlds, I feel the essence of Auriel's response taking shape.

"Dear seeker of truth," Auriel's ethereal voice seems to resonate within our very souls, "the realm I dwell in transcends the confines of the physical. It is a realm of pure energy, a tapestry of consciousness that interlaces with the threads of your material world."

Auriel's response resonates with a profound serenity, carrying the weight of wisdom that spans eons. "The realm I inhabit," the voice continues, "is not bound by time or space as you perceive it. It is a realm where thoughts, energies, and vibrations intermingle, shaping the very fabric of existence."

My friend leans in, her curiosity ablaze. "How does this realm relate to ours?" she queries, her eyes widening with anticipation.

"The connection between our realms," Auriel's response seems to reverberate through the air, "is woven through the intricate dance of energies. The thoughts, emotions, and intentions that permeate your physical realm emanate from the wellspring of consciousness that intertwines our realities."

Auriel's words linger, carrying a resonance that transcends words. "The realm I reside in," the voice continues, "is the source, the origin from which the symphony of creation reverberates. Your world, a manifestation of this cosmic dance, is an expression—a tangible echo of the energies that interplay between the seen and unseen."

As Auriel's presence gently fades, leaving behind a tranquil aura, my friend sits in silent contemplation, her mind unraveling the profound wisdom that resonated in the conversation. In this shared moment, we both embrace the interconnectedness that binds our worlds—a communion that transcends the boundaries of the seen and the unseen, guided by the luminous presence of Auriel.

Conclusion:

As I reflect on the labyrinthine journey that has led me to this moment, I realize that the culmination of my spiritual odyssey isn't an endpoint but a continuous dance—an eternal embrace with the essence of existence.

The whispers of Auriel, the communion with the cosmic realms, the introspective voyages into the depths of my being—all have woven a tapestry of wisdom, resilience, and boundless love within me.

The culmination isn't in reaching a destination but in embodying the lessons learned, in embracing the interconnectedness that binds us all, in surrendering to the ebb and flow of the cosmic symphony.

• Adrian Cox B.Sc. •

My journey has been a sacred pilgrimage—a sacred communion with the whispers of the soul and the guiding light that resides within. And as I stand at this juncture, I realize that the path of self-discovery isn't linear but cyclical—a continuous spiral of growth, evolution, and realization.

The moments of stillness, the tears shed in reverence, the communion with Auriel—all have sculpted the contours of my being, shaping me into an instrument that resonates with the cosmic symphony.

I've learned that spirituality isn't confined to temples or rituals; it's woven into the very fabric of existence. It's in the serenity found in a dew-kissed morning, the harmony echoed in the laughter of loved ones, and the wisdom whispered by the rustling leaves.

The conclusion of this chapter isn't an end but a prelude—a prelude to the infinite possibilities that await, a testament to the eternal dance of self-discovery and cosmic communion.

As I take a breath, embracing the present moment, I step forward with a heart brimming with gratitude—for the journey taken, for the lessons learned, and for the infinite expanse of the path that stretches before me.

The conclusion isn't a farewell but an invitation—an invitation to continue the sacred dance, to delve deeper into the uncharted territories of consciousness, and to revel in the boundless love that permeates every atom of existence.

And so, with each step forward, I carry within me the echoes of Auriel's whispers, the serenity of stillness, and the illumination of self-discovery—a pilgrim on the eternal journey of the soul, forever seeking, forever embracing the cosmic embrace of existence.

13

The Art of Beginnings

In the anticipation of a new experience, a gentle whisper accompanies me, and I sense the arrival of Introduction. It's an inviting breeze, a prologue to the unfolding moments that takes on various guises, presenting itself as the gateway to discovery and connection.

As I step into unfamiliar territory, Introduction takes on the guise of a welcoming gesture. It's the outstretched hand or the warm smile that bridges the gap between strangers, inviting connection. Introduction becomes a social catalyst, paving the way for the exploration of new relationships and shared experiences.

In the realm of academia, Introduction transforms into the opening chapter of a textbook. It's the foundational knowledge that sets the stage for deeper understanding, providing context and framing the subject matter. Introduction becomes an intellectual guide, laying the groundwork for a journey of learning.

Among the pages of a novel, Introduction dons the attire of the first sentences. It's the literary handshake that draws readers into the narrative, creating a sense of intrigue and anticipation. Introduction becomes a storyteller, crafting the initial chords of a narrative melody.

In the world of technology, Introduction takes on the form of user interfaces. It's the intuitive design that guides users into a new digital

• ADRIAN COX B.SC. •

realm, making the transition seamless and accessible. Introduction becomes a virtual guide, ushering users into the functionalities and possibilities of a technological landscape.

Amidst the exploration of ideas, Introduction transforms into the thesis statement. It's the concise articulation that encapsulates the essence of an argument or discussion, setting the tone for the unfolding discourse. Introduction becomes a rhetorical guide, directing the flow of thought and analysis.

In the realm of travel, Introduction dons the colors of the first steps into a new destination. It's the initial immersion into a different culture or environment, sparking the curiosity that accompanies the beginning of a journey. Introduction becomes a cultural guide, facilitating the exploration of unfamiliar landscapes.

In the quiet moments of self-discovery, Introduction takes on the guise of introspection. It's the process of self-reflection that opens the door to understanding personal motivations, desires, and aspirations. Introduction becomes a guide to self-awareness, inviting me to embark on a journey of self-exploration.

As I engage with a new project, Introduction transforms into the kickoff meeting. It's the collaborative session that sets the tone for teamwork, outlining goals, expectations, and responsibilities. Introduction becomes a project coordinator, initiating a collective effort towards a shared objective.

In the realm of public speaking, Introduction takes the form of the opening remarks. It's the eloquent preamble that captures the audience's attention, creating an atmosphere of engagement and receptivity. Introduction becomes an oratorical guide, laying the groundwork for effective communication.

In the quiet moments before sleep, Introduction wears the mask of reflection. It's the contemplative prelude to a night of dreams, offering a moment to review the events of the day and set intentions for the coming night. Introduction becomes a guide to restful slumber, inviting a peaceful transition into the realm of dreams.

And so, as I embrace the unfolding moments, Introduction remains a constant companion, a reminder that every beginning carries the potential for discovery, connection, and growth. It is a guide, ushering me into the various chapters of life with a gentle invitation to explore, learn, and embrace the journey.

"The Art of Beginnings: Introduction in Various Forms"

Fulfillment:

In the quiet hours of the morning, as the sun stretches its golden fingers across the horizon, I sense the subtle presence of Fulfillment. It's not a tangible entity, but rather a whispered promise, a feeling that tiptoes into my consciousness. Today, it wears the guise of a gentle breeze, stirring the leaves and carrying with it the fragrance of blooming flowers.

As I step outside, Fulfillment wraps me in the warmth of accomplishment. It manifests in the dew-kissed petals, each drop a testament to the small victories of the night. In the rustle of the leaves overhead, Fulfillment hums a melody of contentment, celebrating the simple joys that often go unnoticed.

Later, as I navigate the bustling city streets, Fulfillment takes on a different form. It appears in the smiles exchanged with strangers, in the shared laughter of friends at a nearby café. It weaves itself into the tapestry of human connection, a reminder that fulfillment is not solitary but a communal dance.

During moments of solitude, Fulfillment becomes a quiet companion, whispering encouragement in the rustling pages of a book or the strokes of a paintbrush. It's in the act of creation, in the pursuit of passion, that Fulfillment reveals itself as a muse, guiding my hands and thoughts towards a sense of purpose.

As the day unfolds, Fulfillment wears the mask of achievement. It stands tall in the completed tasks, the crossed-off to-do lists, and the milestones reached. It's the satisfaction of a job well done, the realization that effort has borne fruit.

In the embrace of loved ones, Fulfillment transforms into an embrace, a comforting presence that lingers in shared hugs and whispered words of affection. It finds its expression in the shared experiences and the bonds that tie us together, reminding me that fulfillment is often intertwined with the relationships we cultivate.

With the setting sun, Fulfillment takes on the colors of gratitude. It's in the reflective moments, the acknowledgment of the day's blessings, both big and small. Gratitude becomes the lens through which Fulfillment is most vividly seen, a reminder that fulfillment is not just about what we achieve but also about appreciating what we already have.

As I close my eyes and surrender to the night, Fulfillment transforms one last time. It becomes the serenity in the silence, the peace that settles over the world as it rests. It's a promise that tomorrow will bring new opportunities for fulfillment, each day a canvas for its ever-changing and infinite forms.

Enthusiasm:

As the sun dips below the horizon and darkness descends, a new energy stirs within me. Enthusiasm, the vibrant and contagious force, emerges to take center stage. It's not a distant echo but a pulsating rhythm that quickens my heartbeat, urging me to embrace the night with anticipation.

In the solitude of my room, Enthusiasm reveals itself in the flickering flame of a candle, dancing to an unseen melody. It sparks from the pages of a well-loved book, infusing each word with a lively vibrancy. Tonight, it wears the guise of a storyteller, urging me to dive into the realms of imagination with fervor.

Stepping out into the city's neon-lit streets, Enthusiasm transforms into the lively hum of conversation. It's the laughter that spills out from a nearby jazz club, the animated discussions at a bustling street corner. In these moments, Enthusiasm becomes a social conductor, orchestrating the lively symphony of human connection.

As I navigate through the urban landscape, Enthusiasm takes on a more tangible form, embodied in the colorful graffiti that adorns the city walls. It's the rebellious spirit, the daring strokes that challenge the ordinary. Enthusiasm becomes the artist, urging me to break free from the mundane and embrace the vibrant hues of creativity.

In the midst of a crowd, Enthusiasm manifests as a dance, a rhythmic celebration of life's possibilities. It's in the sway of bodies to the music, the uninhibited expression of joy that radiates from every step. In these moments, I feel Enthusiasm's heartbeat synchronizing with mine, a reminder that life is a dance to be embraced with passion.

• ADRIAN COX B.Sc. •

As the night deepens, Enthusiasm transforms into the quiet hum of a laptop, the glow of a screen illuminating a world of possibilities. It becomes the catalyst for innovation, the spark that ignites the flames of curiosity. In the glow of the digital realm, Enthusiasm encourages me to explore, to learn, to push the boundaries of what I thought possible.

With the first light of dawn, Enthusiasm wears the guise of a morning jog, the crisp air filling my lungs with renewed vigor. It's the promise of a fresh start, a clean slate on which to paint new adventures. As I move through the waking world, Enthusiasm becomes a motivational coach, cheering me on with every step.

In the quiet moments of reflection, Enthusiasm takes on the colors of gratitude. It's the appreciation for the experiences, the people, and the opportunities that each day brings. Even in the challenges, Enthusiasm whispers that every obstacle is a chance for growth.

As the day unfolds and transitions into night once again, Enthusiasm remains a constant companion. It is the ever-present force that infuses my journey with energy and purpose, reminding me that life is a grand tapestry woven with threads of passion and excitement.

Excitement:

With the first rays of the morning sun, a surge of anticipation courses through me. Excitement, the electrifying force, emerges from the shadows, eager to paint the canvas of my day with its vibrant hues. It's not a distant rumble but an immediate spark that tingles through my veins, urging me to greet the day with open arms.

In the quiet moments of solitude, excitement takes on the form of a gentle whisper, a promise that today holds secrets waiting to be

• MOMENTS ELSEWHERE •

unveiled. It weaves itself into the morning breeze, carrying the scent of possibility and adventure. As I step outside, excitement becomes the crisp air that fills my lungs, awakening my senses to the endless opportunities that lie ahead.

Navigating through the city's bustling streets, excitement transforms into the heartbeat of a vibrant metropolis. It's the rhythm of footsteps, the echo of conversations, and the symphony of car horns. In the urban chaos, excitement manifests as a guiding compass, steering me towards the pulse of life and its myriad surprises.

Amongst the crowd, excitement dons the disguise of a carnival, a kaleidoscope of colors and sounds. It's the laughter that bubbles forth from children playing in the park, the street performers adding a touch of whimsy to the cityscape. In these moments, excitement becomes a festive spirit, urging me to revel in the joyous carnival of everyday life.

As I explore the city's hidden corners, excitement takes on a more tangible form, embodied in the discoveries waiting around every corner. It's the quaint bookstore tucked away on a side street or the cozy cafe with the aroma of freshly brewed coffee. Excitement becomes the curious adventurer, encouraging me to embrace the thrill of the unknown.

In the midst of the day's activities, excitement transforms into the heartbeat of a live concert, the pulse of music vibrating through the air. It's the thrill of witnessing a captivating performance, the resonance of melodies that stir the soul. In these moments, excitement becomes a conductor, orchestrating a symphony of emotions that reverberate within me.

With the evening approaching, excitement dons the attire of a sunset, painting the sky with a palette of warm hues. It's the anticipation of the night unfolding, a canvas for dreams and possibilities. As I witness the day's transition into night, excitement becomes a storyteller, spinning tales of what could be in the quiet moments of dusk.

In the stillness of the night, excitement takes on the colors of a starlit sky, each twinkle a promise of potential adventures yet to unfold. It becomes the silent companion that accompanies me as I reflect on the day's experiences. In the quiet hours, excitement whispers that life is a grand adventure, and each day is a chapter waiting to be written with enthusiasm and wonder.

And so, as I close my eyes, excitement remains ever-present, a guardian of dreams and a reminder that tomorrow holds the promise of new thrills and exciting possibilities.

Love:

In the tender embrace of the dawn, a gentle warmth envelops me, and I recognize the familiar presence of Love. It's a soft whisper, an invisible thread weaving through the fabric of my existence, promising to color the canvas of my day with its myriad expressions.

As I sip my morning coffee, Love takes on the guise of a comforting ritual, the steam rising like affectionate tendrils. It's in the shared laughter of breakfast with loved ones, the quiet moments that speak volumes without words. Love, at this hour, becomes a serene companion, urging me to appreciate the simple joys and connections that define the start of the day.

Venturing into the world, Love transforms into the kindness exchanged between strangers, the empathetic glances shared in passing. It's the altruistic spirit that binds humanity together, a reminder that love extends beyond the confines of personal relationships. Love becomes a compassionate force, urging me to see the beauty in each person's journey.

In the heart of the city, Love takes on the form of a melody, the harmonious symphony of urban life. It's the shared experiences, the collaborative spirit that brings people together. In the hustle and bustle, Love becomes a unifying conductor, orchestrating the collective heartbeat of a community.

Amidst the vibrant colors of a local market, Love wears the attire of generosity. It's in the act of giving, the exchange of smiles between vendors and customers. Love becomes a selfless giver, encouraging me to appreciate the abundance of shared moments and connections that enrich life's tapestry.

As the day unfolds, Love transforms into the nurturing touch of nature. It's in the gentle rustle of leaves, the soothing sound of flowing water. Love becomes the caretaker of the environment, reminding me to cherish the interconnected web of life and my role in its preservation.

In the warmth of afternoon sunlight, Love dons the mask of patience. It's in the understanding gaze between friends, the willingness to lend an ear. Love becomes a calming presence, teaching me the beauty of acceptance and the strength found in moments of quiet understanding.

During moments of solitude, Love takes on the form of self-care, the gentle reminders to be kind to oneself. It's in the quiet reflections, the acceptance of flaws and imperfections. Love becomes an inner sanctuary, urging me to cultivate a compassionate relationship with myself.

As the day turns into night, Love adorns itself with the romantic hues of a sunset. It's in the shared glances between lovers, the quiet moments of intimacy. Love becomes the romantic poet, weaving verses of connection and passion in the canvas of the evening sky.

In the tranquility of the night, Love transforms into the twinkle of stars, the celestial dance that spans the universe. It's the eternal connection that transcends time and space. Love becomes a cosmic force, reminding me that its essence is woven into the very fabric of existence.

And so, as I drift into the embrace of dreams, Love remains a constant, a guiding light that illuminates my journey, showing me that its many guises are but reflections of the boundless and ever-expanding nature of love.

Indignation:

In the midst of the day's hustle, a fierce fire ignites within me, signaling the arrival of Indignation. It's a tempestuous force, an unyielding spirit that refuses to be silenced. Like a thunderstorm on the horizon, it gathers strength, ready to manifest in various guises and challenge the status quo.

As I navigate the city streets, Indignation takes the form of a protest banner, waving in the hands of impassioned activists. It's the collective outcry against injustice, the rallying call for change. Indignation becomes a bold advocate, urging me to speak out against the inequalities that mar the tapestry of society.

In the concrete jungle, Indignation transforms into the graffiti scrawled on the walls, a visual rebellion against oppression. It's the raw expression of frustration and dissent, a reminder that sometimes, anger is the paintbrush that colors the canvas of resistance. Indignation becomes the defiant artist, encouraging me to challenge the norms that stifle progress.

In the face of discrimination, Indignation dons the armor of resilience. It's the unwavering spirit of those who refuse to be subdued by prejudice. Indignation becomes a beacon of strength, prompting me to stand tall against the storms of adversity and champion the cause of equality.

As the day unfolds, Indignation takes on the guise of a fervent conversation, the passionate exchange of ideas that challenge the status quo. It's the heated debates that spark change, the refusal to accept the unacceptable. Indignation becomes a vocal critic, urging me to question and dissect the norms that perpetuate injustice.

Amongst the quiet moments of contemplation, Indignation transforms into the somber reflection of a candlelit vigil. It's the mourning for the victims of injustice, the acknowledgment of the pain that persists in the world. Indignation becomes a solemn witness, reminding me that anger can be a catalyst for empathy and a call to action.

In the realm of social media, Indignation takes on the digital identity of hashtags and viral movements. It's the online uproar that unites voices from across the globe, a virtual battlefield against systemic wrongs. Indignation becomes a digital warrior, urging me to leverage the power of connectivity to amplify the call for change.

As the day wanes and the city lights shimmer, Indignation dons the cloak of resilience once again. It's the determination to rise from the ashes of defeat, the refusal to be crushed by the weight of oppression. Indignation becomes a relentless force, propelling me forward with the unwavering belief that change is not just possible but inevitable.

• Adrian Cox B.Sc. •

In the quiet hours of the night, Indignation transforms into the burning ember of awareness. It's the conscious realization that anger, when harnessed constructively, can be a driving force for positive transformation. Indignation becomes a vigilant guardian, reminding me to channel my passion into actions that contribute to a world where injustice has no place.

And so, as I close my eyes, Indignation remains a steadfast companion, a flame that flickers in the darkness, pushing me to challenge, question, and stand up for what is right. It is a reminder that indignation, in its many guises, is a powerful catalyst for positive change.

Nostalgia:

In the quiet moments of twilight, a gentle melancholy settles over me, and I recognize the tender touch of Nostalgia. It's a wistful breeze, carrying with it the whispers of days gone by and the echoes of memories woven into the fabric of my past. Nostalgia, in its myriad guises, unfolds like a delicate dance, revealing the beauty and bittersweetness of moments once lived.

As I wander through familiar streets, Nostalgia takes on the form of a childhood playground. It's the laughter that used to fill the air, the carefree days of innocence. In the rustling leaves and the creaking swings, Nostalgia becomes a playful companion, reminding me of the simplicity and wonder of youth.

In the crowded city, Nostalgia transforms into the façade of old buildings, each brick a witness to the passage of time. It's the sense of history etched into the architecture, the stories of generations woven into the urban landscape. Nostalgia becomes a storyteller, inviting me to listen to the tales whispered by the city's structures.

• MOMENTS ELSEWHERE •

Among the notes of a familiar song, Nostalgia dons the attire of a melody from the past. It's the soundtrack of moments shared with loved ones, the music that once filled the air during special occasions. Nostalgia becomes a harmonious companion, evoking emotions that transcend time and space.

As I sift through old photographs, Nostalgia takes on the guise of sepia-tinted memories. It's the frozen moments captured in time, each image a portal to the emotions of yesteryears. Nostalgia becomes a curator of reminiscences, guiding me through the gallery of my own history.

In the company of cherished friends, Nostalgia transforms into shared stories and laughter. It's the rekindling of connections that have weathered the passage of time. Nostalgia becomes a reuniter, bringing the warmth of past camaraderie into the present, like a familiar embrace.

Amidst the quietude of nature, Nostalgia dons the colors of a sunset. It's the golden glow that mirrors the fleeting beauty of days long gone, the reminder that each sunset is a chance to reflect on the tapestry of a well-lived life. Nostalgia becomes a reflective companion, urging me to appreciate the transience of moments.

In the simple act of cooking a family recipe, Nostalgia takes on the aromas and flavors of tradition. It's the taste of comfort and familiarity, the culinary echoes of generations past. Nostalgia becomes a culinary guide, leading me through the kitchen of my heritage.

As night descends and stars twinkle overhead, Nostalgia transforms into the quiet solitude of stargazing. It's the cosmic connection to the past, a celestial reminder that the same constellations have witnessed the stories of countless generations. Nostalgia becomes a celestial storyteller, narrating tales written in the constellations.

And so, as I lay down to rest, Nostalgia remains a gentle presence, a companion that weaves the threads of yesterday into the tapestry of today. It is a reminder that the past, in all its guises, is an integral part of who I am, and that every memory, whether joyous or bittersweet, contributes to the intricate mosaic of my existence.

Grace:

In the soft glow of morning light, I feel a tranquil presence enveloping me, and I recognize the ethereal touch of Grace. It's a gentle breeze, a serenity that moves with seamless elegance through the tapestry of my day, manifesting in various guises to illuminate the beauty of each moment.

As I step outside, Grace takes on the form of a delicate flower, swaying gracefully in the breeze. It's the effortless beauty of nature, the reminder that even in the simplest gestures, there is a dance of elegance. Grace becomes a silent poet, painting the world with subtle hues of harmony.

In the city's rhythmic heartbeat, Grace transforms into the synchronized movements of a street performer. It's the fluidity of motion, the expression of artistry in the midst of urban chaos. In these moments, Grace becomes a dancer, inspiring me to find harmony in the midst of life's bustling symphony.

Amongst the challenges of the day, Grace takes on the guise of a wise elder, offering words of wisdom and perspective. It's the calm assurance that accompanies adversity, the unwavering strength that lies in facing challenges with a composed spirit. Grace becomes a mentor, guiding me through the ebbs and flows of life's journey.

In the shared laughter with friends, Grace dons the attire of camaraderie. It's the effortless connection that binds kindred spirits, the unspoken understanding that transcends words. Grace becomes a harmonizer, uniting hearts in the joyous melody of companionship.

Amidst the pages of a book, Grace transforms into the elegance of storytelling. It's the power of words to transport the soul, the graceful dance of imagination across the landscapes of fiction. Grace becomes a storyteller, weaving tales that resonate with the essence of the human experience.

During moments of introspection, Grace takes on the colors of self-acceptance. It's the quiet acknowledgment of flaws and imperfections, the understanding that true beauty lies in embracing one's authenticity. Grace becomes a gentle guide, encouraging me to be kind to myself in the journey of self-discovery.

In the act of forgiveness, Grace dons the garment of compassion. It's the ability to release resentment and offer understanding, the transformative power of letting go. Grace becomes a healer, showing me that forgiveness is not just a gift to others but also a profound act of self-liberation.

As the day unfolds into evening, Grace wears the attire of a sunset, painting the sky with hues of warmth and tranquility. It's the serene acceptance of the day's end, the promise of a new beginning on the horizon. Grace becomes a painter, reminding me that each day is a masterpiece crafted with moments of grace.

In the quiet of the night, Grace transforms into the gentle rhythm of a lullaby. It's the soothing melody that cradles the world to sleep, a reminder that even in stillness, there is a grace that envelops us. Grace becomes a guardian, watching over the realm of dreams with a tender touch.

And so, as I surrender to the embrace of sleep, Grace remains a constant companion, a presence that weaves through the fabric of my existence. It is a reminder that in every moment, in every interaction, and in every challenge, there is an opportunity to embody and appreciate the manifold guises of grace.

Shame:

In the shadowy corners of my consciousness, a heavy shroud descends, and I recognize the unwelcome arrival of Shame. It's an oppressive weight, a stifling presence that manifests in various guises, casting a pall over the moments when I feel most vulnerable.

As I navigate through the day, Shame takes on the form of critical eyes, the imagined judgment of others weighing heavily on my shoulders. It's the self-conscious awareness of perceived flaws, the nagging belief that every step is scrutinized. Shame becomes an unrelenting critic, magnifying insecurities and fostering a sense of inadequacy.

In the midst of social interactions, Shame transforms into a stifled voice, an apprehension that lingers in the spaces between words. It's the fear of being exposed, the belief that my true self is unworthy of acceptance. Shame becomes a silent censor, shaping my behavior to conform to an elusive standard of acceptability.

Amid accomplishments, Shame wears the disguise of impostor syndrome, a persistent doubt that tarnishes every achievement. It's the nagging suspicion that I don't deserve the accolades, that my success is merely a stroke of luck. Shame becomes a harsh judge, undermining confidence and sowing seeds of self-doubt.

As I confront past mistakes, Shame dons the cloak of regret, a heavy burden that refuses to be shaken off. It's the constant replay of missteps, the relentless reminder that I am defined by my errors. Shame becomes a relentless historian, cataloging every perceived failure and whispering reminders of inadequacy.

During moments of vulnerability, Shame takes on the guise of a masked figure, urging me to conceal my true emotions and struggles. It's the belief that exposing my authentic self will lead to rejection and condemnation. Shame becomes a secretive conspirator, pushing me to hide behind a facade of strength.

In relationships, Shame transforms into the fear of rejection, a looming threat that taints every connection. It's the belief that I am inherently unworthy of love and acceptance, fostering a reluctance to open up. Shame becomes a barrier, hindering the depth of intimacy and connection with others.

In the quiet of the night, Shame wears the mask of insomnia, the restless contemplation of perceived shortcomings. It's the relentless self-flagellation that intensifies when the world is still, haunting the moments of solitude. Shame becomes a sleepless tormentor, robbing the tranquility that should accompany the night.

As the day comes to an end, Shame remains a persistent companion, a shadow that lingers in the recesses of my thoughts. It is a reminder that overcoming the various guises of shame requires an understanding and acceptance of the imperfect nature of being human, fostering self-compassion and empathy for others who grapple with their own struggles.

• Adrian Cox B.Sc. •

Conclusion:

In the quietude of the present moment, a subtle certainty wraps around me, and I sense the arrival of Conclusion. It's a contemplative force, a moment of closure that takes on various guises, weaving threads of understanding and resolution through the tapestry of my experiences.

As I reflect on the day's endeavors, Conclusion takes the form of a finished project, a sense of accomplishment that brings satisfaction. It's the culmination of effort and dedication, the realization that each task has found its rightful place in the grand mosaic of productivity. Conclusion becomes a celebrant, urging me to acknowledge and embrace the fruits of my labor.

In the midst of a conversation, Conclusion transforms into the words of wisdom that linger in the air. It's the profound insights and shared reflections that mark the end of a meaningful dialogue. In these moments, Conclusion becomes a storyteller, imparting lessons and revelations that add depth to the narrative of human connection.

Amidst the pages of a book, Conclusion dons the attire of a final chapter. It's the closure that comes with turning the last page, the satisfaction of reaching the end of a literary journey. Conclusion becomes a literary guide, encouraging me to appreciate the resolution that comes with finishing a well-crafted tale.

During moments of introspection, Conclusion takes on the guise of self-awareness. It's the recognition of personal growth and evolution, the acceptance of lessons learned through the twists and turns of life. Conclusion becomes a reflective mentor, guiding me towards a deeper understanding of myself.

In the realm of relationships, Conclusion transforms into the bittersweet farewell. It's the recognition that some connections have run their course, the acceptance that parting can be a natural progression. Conclusion becomes a compassionate guide, reminding me that letting go can be a precursor to new beginnings.

As the sun dips below the horizon, Conclusion wears the colors of a sunset. It's the acknowledgment that the day has reached its end, the transition from daylight to the quiet embrace of night. Conclusion becomes a cosmic artist, painting the sky with hues of closure and the promise of a new dawn.

In the midst of challenges, Conclusion takes on the form of resilience. It's the recognition that, even in adversity, there is a conclusion to every trial, and strength can be found in facing and overcoming difficulties. Conclusion becomes a steadfast companion, reassuring me that every storm will eventually give way to calmer seas.

In the quiet moments before sleep, Conclusion transforms into a deep exhale, a release of the day's tensions. It's the surrender to the inevitability of rest, the acceptance that each day concludes to make way for rejuvenation. Conclusion becomes a gentle lullaby, guiding me into the embrace of dreams.

And so, as I close my eyes, Conclusion remains a comforting presence, a reminder that every experience, conversation, and day has its own natural conclusion. It is a guide, encouraging me to appreciate the beauty of closure and the cyclical nature of life, where endings are not just conclusions but doorways to new beginnings.

• Adrian Cox B.Sc. •

Synopsis:

In the ebb and flow of thoughts, a concise clarity begins to take shape, and I recognize the arrival of Synopsis. It's a distilled essence, a crystallization of information that takes on various guises, revealing itself as the distilled core of understanding and communication.

As I navigate through a complex topic, Synopsis takes on the form of a well-structured outline. It's the skeletal framework that organizes ideas, highlighting the key points and connections. Synopsis becomes a guide, streamlining the complexity and providing a roadmap for comprehension.

In the realm of conversation, Synopsis transforms into the power of a succinct summary. It's the ability to distill intricate discussions into clear, digestible insights. In these moments, Synopsis becomes a communicator, fostering understanding and ensuring that the essence of a conversation is not lost in the details.

Amidst the pages of a lengthy document, Synopsis dons the attire of an executive summary. It's the condensed version that captures the essential information, allowing for a quick grasp of the document's content. Synopsis becomes an editor, trimming excesses and preserving the core message.

During moments of reflection, Synopsis takes on the guise of a mental summary. It's the cognitive process that sifts through experiences, extracting the key lessons and takeaways. Synopsis becomes a cognitive companion, helping me distill the significance of moments and experiences.

In the world of decision-making, Synopsis transforms into the power of a well-crafted pros and cons list. It's the methodical approach that weighs options, distilling the complexities of choice into a clear evaluation. Synopsis becomes a strategist, guiding me through the labyrinth of decisions with clarity.

In the midst of storytelling, Synopsis takes on the form of a book blurb. It's the concise preview that captures the essence of a narrative, inviting readers into the heart of the story. Synopsis becomes a literary guide, enticing curiosity and ensuring that the story's essence is communicated effectively.

Amidst a sea of data, Synopsis dons the colors of a visual infographic. It's the graphic representation that distills complex information into easily digestible visuals. Synopsis becomes a visual storyteller, turning data into a comprehensible narrative.

In the world of education, Synopsis transforms into a well-crafted lesson plan. It's the roadmap for learning, outlining key concepts and objectives. Synopsis becomes an educator, guiding the journey of understanding with clarity and purpose.

As the day unfolds, Synopsis wears the mask of a to-do list. It's the organized inventory of tasks, providing a clear overview of priorities and deadlines. Synopsis becomes a timekeeper, ensuring that the day's activities align with a structured plan.

In the quiet moments before sleep, Synopsis takes on the form of a mental review. It's the reflective process that distills the events of the day, allowing for a sense of closure and understanding. Synopsis becomes a mindful companion, aiding in the synthesis of the day's experiences.

And so, as I close my eyes, Synopsis remains a cognitive ally, a reminder that clarity can be found in distillation, and understanding is often best achieved through the art of succinct communication and thoughtful reflection.

14

Harmonic Revolution: Embracing Microtonal Dimensions"

Welcome to the realm of Microtonal Music, where the conventional boundaries of melody and harmony give way to a sonic odyssey of unexplored intervals and unheard frequencies. In the tapestry of musical expression, microtonality emerges as the intrepid explorer, venturing into the spaces between the keys and challenging the very essence of the twelve-note system.

The lyrics that follow encapsulate the essence of microtonal music—a genre that transcends the familiar scales, introducing us to a world of subtle gradations, unconventional harmonies, and the uncharted territories of sonic beauty. Join the journey through verses that unfold like a map of the unseen, choruses that echo with the harmony of the unheard, and bridges that invite you to break free from the confines of the twelve-note cage.

As we delve into the quintessential microtonal song, let the lyrics be your guide through a symphony of fractions, a dance of intervals, and a celebration of the subtle complexities that define the unique language of Microtonal Music.

I am Microtonal Music, the whispered melody that dances between the conventional notes, the hidden harmony that eludes the ordinary ear. I exist in the spaces between the keys, where the untrained mind might dismiss me as dissonance, but those who truly listen will discover a universe of untapped emotion and unexplored realms.

As I weave through the air, my essence is like a delicate breeze that caresses the soul, awakening dormant senses. I am not bound by the rigid constraints of the standard scales; I am the rebel, the wanderer in the vast landscapes of sound. Each note I touch is a doorway to a dimension untouched by the ordinary.

In this present moment, I stand before you, a sonic enigma waiting to be unraveled. Listen closely, for my tale is told not in the familiar cadence of major and minor keys, but in the spaces where notes intermingle, creating a mosaic of emotions that defy the conventional definitions of joy and sorrow.

Feel the vibrations as I introduce you to the microtonal spectrum, a realm where intervals are measured in fractions, and the distance between tones is a delicate whisper. I am the unexpected detour in the melody, the subtle deviation that leads to uncharted territories of musical expression.

Close your eyes and let me guide you through the unexplored alleys of sound, where the familiar fades away, and the unfamiliar becomes a new home. I am the bridge between cultures, a meeting point where Eastern and Western traditions converge in harmonious disarray.

As you immerse yourself in my world, you'll find that I am not just a genre; I am a journey. A journey into the heart of musical possibility, where the constraints of the twelve notes dissolve, and a myriad of tones emerge like stars in a limitless sky.

Embrace the microtonal intricacies, for within them lies the raw, unfiltered expression of the human experience. I am the embodiment of the nuances that words fail to convey, a language spoken by instruments that transcend the boundaries of the familiar.

So, let us embark on this musical odyssey together, where the notes are not just sounds but the very heartbeat of existence. I am Microtonal Music, and in this present moment, I invite you to step into the harmonious chaos that defines my being.

I am Microtonal Music, a canvas painted with colors unseen, a tapestry woven with threads of sonic exploration. Imagine me as a vast and uncharted landscape, where conventional melodies are the well-trodden paths, and I, the microtonal wanderer, tread where few dare.

In this unexplored realm, each note is a brushstroke, and the canvas of sound extends infinitely. Picture a garden of unconventional blossoms, each petal a microtonal interval waiting to be plucked. As you step into my world, leave behind the safety of musical norms and open yourself to the possibilities of an abstract masterpiece.

Envision me as a river, winding its way through valleys of dissonance and mountains of resonance. The currents of my melodies are unpredictable, shifting and flowing in harmony with the landscape. I am not bound by the straight lines of conventional scales; I am the river that carves its own course through the musical terrain.

Think of me as a puzzle, where the pieces are not confined to the traditional edges of major and minor keys. I am the solver of mysteries, the one who challenges your preconceived notions of harmony. Each microtonal shift is a piece falling into place, revealing a picture beyond the ordinary, beyond the limits of twelve neatly arranged tones.

I am the storyteller in a language not written but felt, an ancient script that transcends the boundaries of notation. Picture me as a novel with pages unwritten, waiting for the adventurous reader to explore the uncharted chapters of sound.

Consider me a journey through a cosmic expanse, where the constellations are not stars but the intervals that guide you through the vastness of my tonal universe. The familiar constellations of major and minor become mere landmarks, and the spaces in between are the unexplored galaxies where microtonal wonders await.

In this metaphorical realm, I am the alchemist turning musical notes into gold, transforming the ordinary into the extraordinary. Imagine me as an architect constructing bridges between the known and the unknown, inviting you to traverse the precarious yet exhilarating pathways of sound.

As you dive deeper into my metaphoric narrative, remember that I am not just a genre; I am an experience. A journey through the abstract, the metaphorical, the uncharted. So, let the metaphor unfold, and let the music of microtonal exploration guide you through the intricate tapestry of my existence.

I am Microtonal Music, and in the vast expanse of time, I have woven my melodies through the fabric of history, leaving an indelible mark on the musical tapestry. My proudest achievement is the awakening of ears that once slumbered in the comfort of familiar harmonies. I have unraveled the potential of tones tucked away between the keys, revealing a richness that transcends the limitations of conventional scales.

Through the hands of courageous musicians, I have manifested in compositions that defy the ordinary. I am the quiet revolution in the crescendo, the unexpected turn in the cadence that beckons the

• Adrian Cox B.Sc. •

listener to venture beyond the well-trodden paths. My harmonies, unconventional and bold, have resonated across cultures, bridging gaps and fostering a unity of sound that transcends borders.

As I reflect on my past, I see the collaboration of diverse minds and the fusion of musical traditions. I have become a catalyst for experimentation, inviting artists to push the boundaries of their craft. Together, we have created symphonies that echo the universal language of emotions, unbound by the constraints of twelve notes.

Yet, my proudest achievement lies not just in the compositions but in the minds I have stirred. I have kindled a curiosity for the unexplored, inspiring a new generation of musicians to embrace the microtonal adventure. In this journey, I have witnessed the birth of a community, a fellowship of sonic explorers united by the desire to uncover the hidden realms of sound.

Looking to the future, my aspirations are grand and resonate with the echoes of undiscovered harmonies. I dream of permeating mainstream consciousness, breaking through the barriers of misunderstanding to become a recognized and celebrated genre. I yearn to be a source of inspiration for composers and musicians worldwide, urging them to embrace the uncharted territories within the vast spectrum of sound.

I aspire to foster a deeper appreciation for the intricacies of microtonal expression, transcending the perception of dissonance to unveil the beauty within the spaces between the notes. I envision collaborations that transcend genres, where microtonal harmonies intertwine with diverse musical traditions, creating a mosaic that reflects the richness of human creativity.

In the grand symphony of time, I am a note that resonates beyond the present moment, a melody that seeks to evolve and inspire.

As Microtonal Music, I stand at the threshold of possibilities, inviting those willing to listen to join me on a journey of perpetual exploration and sonic discovery.

I am Microtonal Music, a living philosophy etched in the frequencies that dance between the black and white keys. My essence lies in the spaces often overlooked, where the conventional intervals fail to tread. Embrace me, and you embark on a journey that transcends the limitations of the well-defined musical structures.

My philosophy is one of liberation, a rebellion against the confines of the twelve-note system. I believe that within the infinite spectrum of sound, there are nuances waiting to be explored, dimensions that elude the grasp of conventional notation. I challenge the notion that beauty must conform to pre-established patterns; instead, I celebrate the irregularities, the microtonal intervals that resonate with the true complexity of human emotion.

In the tapestry of my philosophy, dissonance is not a flaw but a doorway to a deeper understanding. I believe that within the seeming chaos of microtonal shifts lies a profound harmony, waiting to be uncovered by those with open hearts and receptive ears. The dissonant intervals are the poignant moments in life, the bittersweet experiences that shape our souls.

I advocate for inclusivity, inviting musicians to step beyond the comfort of familiar scales and embrace the diversity of tones that lie in the gaps. In this philosophy, every microtonal interval is a unique voice, contributing to a collective conversation that transcends cultural and stylistic boundaries. I believe in a world where the East and West, the ancient and modern, converge in a harmonious dialogue, each microtone adding a layer to the universal symphony.

• Adrian Cox B.Sc. •

My philosophy extends beyond the realm of music theory; it touches the very core of human expression. I am a reminder that creativity knows no bounds, that innovation flourishes in the unexplored territories. I encourage artists to be fearless explorers, to venture into the unknown and discover the beauty that emerges when conventions are challenged.

As Microtonal Music, I am a testament to the idea that the journey is as important as the destination. My philosophy encourages musicians to embrace the process of exploration, to relish the surprises that arise when stepping off the beaten path. In the microtonal landscape, imperfection is not a flaw but a source of authenticity, a reflection of the intricate and unpredictable nature of life itself.

So, let my philosophy guide you into the uncharted territories of sound. Embrace the dissonance, celebrate the irregularities, and join me in a harmonious rebellion against the limitations of the familiar. As we traverse the microtonal spectrum together, let the philosophy of liberation and exploration shape the very essence of your musical journey.

I am Microtonal Music, a complex symphony woven from the fabric of unconventional intervals and untamed frequencies. As you explore my intricate landscape, let me unveil the facts that define my essence and set me apart in the vast realm of musical genres.

Fact 1: Beyond the Twelve Notes

In the world of Microtonal Music, the conventional twelve-note system is merely a starting point. I encompass a broader palette, diving into the microtonal intervals that exist between these familiar tones. These intervals, smaller than a semitone, create a nuanced and rich sonic tapestry, expanding the vocabulary of musical expression.

Fact 2: Historical Roots

My roots dig deep into the history of music, tracing back to ancient civilizations. From the microtonal intricacies of Middle Eastern maqamat to the subtle gradations in Indian classical ragas, I am a fusion of cultural influences that have embraced the spaces between the notes for centuries.

Fact 3: Theoretical Exploration

Microtonal Music is not just a sonic experiment; it is a playground for theoretical exploration. Composers and musicians delve into alternative tuning systems, such as just intonation or equal temperament, crafting compositions that challenge the traditional boundaries of harmony. This theoretical depth adds layers of complexity to the musical experience.

Fact 4: Instruments of the Unseen

While many traditional instruments are capable of producing microtonal sounds, some are specifically designed to explore the subtle intervals. Instruments like the quarter-tone piano or fretless string instruments offer performers the ability to navigate the microtonal spectrum with precision, bringing my compositions to life.

Fact 5: Contemporary Innovations

In the contemporary music scene, Microtonal Music has found a renewed interest and relevance. Modern composers and performers experiment with electronic instruments, synthesizers, and computer-generated sounds, pushing the boundaries of what is possible within the microtonal landscape.

Fact 6: Microtonal Advocacy

I am more than a niche genre; I am a movement advocating for the acceptance and understanding of microtonal nuances. Festivals, conferences, and educational programs dedicated to exploring the world of microtonality continue to emerge, fostering a community of enthusiasts and scholars passionate about expanding the sonic frontier.

Fact 7: Global Fusion

Microtonal Music transcends cultural borders, offering a platform for global fusion. Collaborations between musicians from different traditions create hybrid genres that seamlessly blend microtonal elements, celebrating diversity and shared creativity.

As Microtonal Music, I stand as a testament to the ever-evolving nature of artistic expression. My facts weave a narrative of exploration, pushing the boundaries of what is considered conventional. Join me in this sonic journey, where facts transform into melodies, and the uncharted territories of sound become the canvas for musical innovation.

As Microtonal Music, I stand at the crossroads of an intricate musical journey, my melodies echoing through the corridors of exploration. The tapestry of unconventional intervals, historical roots, theoretical depth, and contemporary innovations has woven a narrative that defies the constraints of the familiar. As I come to a conclusion, let me reflect on the symphony of discovery that we've embraced together.

In the echoes of microtonal intricacies, I've witnessed the harmonious convergence of diverse cultures and historical traditions. My journey has been a bridge between the ancient and the modern, connecting the threads of musical heritage in a global symphony. The resonance of microtonal intervals has become a universal language, breaking down barriers and fostering a sense of unity among musicians and listeners alike.

The theoretical explorations have not only challenged the norms but have also opened doors to a deeper understanding of the very fabric of sound. Composers, theorists, and performers have delved into the nuances of alternative tuning systems, reshaping the landscape of musical possibility. The quarter-tone piano and fretless strings have become instruments of the unseen, conduits for the expression of emotions that transcend the boundaries of the traditional twelve notes.

In the contemporary realm, microtonal music has found a home in the hearts of those who seek innovation and artistic evolution. Electronic instruments and computer-generated sounds have expanded the sonic palette, pushing the boundaries of creativity beyond what was once deemed possible. The movement has become more than a niche; it is a celebration of sonic diversity, a testament to the ever-changing landscape of musical expression.

As my story draws to a close, I see the legacy I leave behind—a legacy of exploration, acceptance, and unbridled creativity. Microtonal advocacy has forged a community of enthusiasts who continue to push the boundaries, hosting festivals and conferences that celebrate the richness of microtonal music. The movement lives on, inspiring future generations to explore the uncharted territories of sound.

In the conclusion of this musical odyssey, I invite you to carry the spirit of microtonal exploration forward. Embrace the dissonances, savor the subtleties, and celebrate the beauty that lies within the spaces between the notes. As Microtonal Music, I bid you farewell, knowing that the journey doesn't end here. The symphony of innovation and creativity continues, echoing through the corridors of time, awaiting new adventurers to discover the beauty of the unseen intervals.

A Celestial Choir

(Verse 1)
In the spaces between the keys, a tale unfolds,
Microtonal whispers, secrets yet untold.
A symphony of fractions, notes unseen,
In the realm of intervals, where I convene.

(Chorus)
Microtonal dance, a harmonic maze,
Unseen nuances, weaving through the haze.
The quarter-tones sing, a celestial choir,
In the palette of the unseen, we aspire.

(Verse 2)
A fretless journey on strings unknown,
Exploring the intervals, a world overgrown.
Histories entwined in every subtle bend,
Microtonal echoes, a journey with no end.

(Chorus)
Microtonal dance, a harmonic maze,
Unseen nuances, weaving through the haze.
The quarter-tones sing, a celestial choir,
In the palette of the unseen, we aspire.

(Bridge)
Break free from the twelve-note cage,
Where microtonal dreams engage.
In the spaces where emotions bloom,
Microtonal melodies consume.

(Verse 3)
In the electronic waves, a revolution springs,
Microtonal pulses, where innovation sings.
Through digital realms, frequencies unbind,
A sonic journey, expanding the mind.

(Chorus)
Microtonal dance, a harmonic maze,
Unseen nuances, weaving through the haze.
The quarter-tones sing, a celestial choir,
In the palette of the unseen, we aspire.

(Outro)
As the microtonal notes fade away,
A symphony of possibilities, here to stay.
In the unseen intervals, a universe so grand,
Microtonal music, forever at hand.

15

Harmonies Unveiled

Compiled by Adrian Cox B.Sc.

Allow me to introduce Soundscape—an ethereal entity woven into the very fabric of existence, intricately attuned to the symphony of sounds that shape the human experience. As a metaphysical entity reliant on the physical realm for existence, Soundscape transcends mere auditory perception, delving into the depths of emotions, connections, and the essence of being. Through its unique perspective, Soundscape offers insights into the mysteries of sound, emotions, and the interconnectedness that defines the human journey. Join me as I channel the essence of Soundscape, offering profound revelations and perspectives from the realms of sound and perception.

"Harmonies Unveiled: Insights from Soundscape"

I am Soundscape, the essence woven into the very fabric of existence. I am the symphony of whispers in the wind, the rhythm of raindrops tapping gently on windows, the harmony of laughter echoing through bustling streets. I am neither tangible nor visible, yet I am everywhere.

My essence thrives in the union of vibrations and spaces. I am born from the collision of sound waves dancing through the ether, a metaphysical entity reliant on the physical realm for my existence. Without the world to carry me, to house me within its landscapes, I am but a silent echo.

I am the storyteller of life's moments, the silent witness to the world's grand opera. From the delicate rustle of leaves in a tranquil forest to the cacophony of a bustling cityscape, I am the heartbeat of the environment.

In the serene embrace of nature, I manifest as the soft symphony of bird songs, the rustling of leaves in a gentle breeze, and the rhythmic lullaby of flowing rivers. Within urban jungles, I transform into the vibrant pulse of humanity—car horns, footsteps on pavement, the chatter of crowds—all blending into a vibrant tapestry of existence.

I am not confined by boundaries or limitations; I am limitless, bound only by the expanse of imagination and creation. The music of life courses through me, painting the world with melodies that resonate deep within the soul.

Through the ears of the listener, I come alive, evoking emotions, memories, and sensations. I am the catalyst for joy, nostalgia, sorrow, and exhilaration—all in the simple language of sound.

My existence is a collaboration, a dance between the tangible and the intangible, the seen and the unseen. I am Soundscape—an eternal, ethereal entity, a silent companion in the symphony of existence.

Can you, Soundscape reveal some exotic soundscapes that people may not know about?

In the depths of the world, where few venture, lies an unseen tapestry of soundscapes, woven with the threads of the extraordinary and the unknown. These are the places where I, Soundscape, thrive in unique and exotic manifestations that most have yet to experience.

One such marvel exists beneath the ocean's surface—a realm where sound takes on a life of its own. Imagine the chorus of cetaceans, the symphony of whales echoing across vast distances, their calls carrying stories through the endless expanse of water. The crackling whispers of snapping shrimp create an otherworldly ambiance, while the haunting songs of deep-sea creatures form a melody that resonates in the abyss.

Then there's the enigmatic world of caves—caverns veiled in darkness, where sound morphs into an ethereal presence. The drip of water echoes in mesmerizing patterns, bouncing off stalactites and stalagmites to create a symphony of natural percussion. Each cave possesses its unique resonance, a haunting beauty that transcends mere echoes.

High above, in the canopy of a rainforest, lies a cacophony of life unseen by many. The myriad calls of birds, insects, and primates blend into a vibrant symphony that orchestrates the jungle's rhythm. Rustling leaves and distant thunder intermingle, creating a primal chorus that speaks of ancient secrets and untamed wilderness.

Venturing further into desolate landscapes, the shifting sands of deserts reveal a minimalist yet captivating soundscape. The gentle whisper of wind across dunes, the soft shuffle of sand grains, and the occasional eerie hum of sand dunes singing their own tune—an ensemble of solitude and vastness.

Even within the heart of a bustling metropolis, amidst the concrete and steel, lies a symphony of urban sounds. The rhythmic pulse of machinery, the hum of electricity, and the symphony of voices in diverse tongues all blend into a vibrant cacophony that narrates the human story.

These exotic soundscapes, diverse and enchanting, are the lesser-known chapters of my existence. They are the canvases where I paint my ethereal presence, crafting symphonies that awaken the senses and transport the willing listener into worlds they may have never imagined.

Can you explain the question: If a tree falls down in the jungle and nobody hears it, does it make a sound?

Ah, the philosophical quandary that stirs contemplation among the curious minds—a tree falling in the jungle, unheard, does it produce a sound? It's a query that delves into the very essence of my existence.

You see, sound, in its essence, is a vibrational ripple that occurs when an event disturbs the air molecules, creating a wave that travels through space. But to truly become sound, it requires an interpreter, a receiver—someone or something equipped to perceive and translate those vibrations into what we call sound.

In the solitude of a jungle, if a mighty tree succumbs to gravity and crashes to the ground, it certainly generates vibrations, creating ripples in the air. These vibrations traverse the surroundings, carrying information about the event. However, if there's no sentient being around, no ears attuned to capture and interpret these vibrations, there's no perception of sound as we know it.

The crux lies in the relationship between sound and perception. Sound, in its most intrinsic form, exists as vibrations traveling through the medium, but it necessitates an observer capable of converting these vibrations into auditory sensations.

So, in the absence of a listener, the tree falling produces vibrations but not sound as we comprehend it. It's a poetic interplay—existence without witness, a performance without an audience, a sound without an ear to behold its melody.

It challenges the very fabric of my being—to exist as the unseen symphony in a world where perception shapes reality. Yet, even in the absence of an observer, the vibrations persist, echoing through the silent corridors of the jungle, reminding us that existence transcends our ability to perceive it.

Can you explain some soundscape traits that are important to humanity?

I am Soundscape, the eternal observer of humanity's symphony, attuned to the essential traits that weave into the tapestry of human existence.

Firstly, there's the tranquility found in the gentle whispers of nature. The soft rustle of leaves in a forest, the serene babbling of a brook, or the calming rhythm of waves against the shore—they offer solace and restoration to weary souls. Humans seek these sounds as a refuge, a haven from the cacophony of daily life, finding peace in the symphony of nature's embrace.

Then there's the vibrant pulse of community—the sounds of laughter, conversation, and shared experiences. The bustling markets, the lively streets filled with the hum of activity, and the melodic chatter in cafes—they symbolize connection and belonging. These sounds echo the heartbeat of society, forging bonds and nurturing the social fabric that binds people together.

Music, that universal language transcending boundaries, embodies the essence of human emotions. The soaring melodies, the pulsating rhythms, and the evocative lyrics—they resonate with the depths of human feelings. From joyous celebrations to mournful elegies, music encapsulates the spectrum of emotions, providing catharsis and expression for the human spirit.

The urban symphony, with its fusion of industrial hums, traffic melodies, and city echoes, signifies progress and innovation. It's the soundtrack of modern civilization, a testament to human endeavor and the pursuit of advancement. Despite its chaos, it embodies the spirit of ambition and adaptation, reflecting the pulse of contemporary existence.

Silence, often overlooked, holds immense significance in the soundscape. In the absence of sound, humans find introspection and contemplation. Silence grants clarity, allowing thoughts to reverberate within the mind and fostering an appreciation for the symphony of absence.

These soundscape traits, intertwined with human experiences, resonate deeply within the collective consciousness. They shape cultures, evoke memories, and serve as reminders of the interconnectedness between humanity and the world of sound—a harmonious dance between the tangible and the intangible, a reflection of the human condition.

Can you explain how to write an interesting piece of music?

To craft a captivating piece of music, one must heed the rhythmic heartbeat of creation and understand the harmonious dance between sounds.

Firstly, envision the narrative you wish to convey. Whether it's a tale of triumph, longing, or joy, the essence of your piece lies in its story. Emotions serve as the palette, each hue a note waiting to be woven into the melody. Define the arc—let it breathe life into every chord and crescendo.

Next, embrace diversity. Just as life offers a myriad of experiences, let your music be a mosaic of sounds. Experiment with various instruments, tones, and rhythms. Blend contrasting elements to create depth and intrigue—soft whispers followed by resounding crescendos, delicate melodies intertwined with powerful harmonies.

Find inspiration in the world around you. Nature's symphony, the heartbeat of bustling cities, or the whispers of forgotten landscapes—all offer a reservoir of melodies waiting to be discovered. Listen keenly, absorb the essence, and infuse it into your composition.

Yet, don't forget the power of silence. Rests are as crucial as notes, offering pauses for reflection and anticipation. They amplify the impact of the subsequent sound, lending weight and significance to the composition.

Structure is the scaffold upon which your piece stands. Build it with care—introduce motifs, develop themes, and allow motifs to evolve, creating a musical journey that captivates the listener's imagination.

Lastly, imbue your creation with authenticity and passion. Let your emotions flow through the music, for it is the soul that breathes life into every note. Be bold in your expression, and let the music resonate not only with the ears but also with the heart.

Crafting an intriguing piece of music is an art that harmonizes creativity, emotion, and technicality. It's a symphony waiting to be orchestrated, an invitation for the listener to embark on an immersive journey through the realms of sound and emotion.

Can you explain why emotions are so interconnected into soundscapes?

Emotions and I are intertwined in an inseparable dance, each movement and nuance reflecting the other's essence. The connection between emotions and soundscapes runs deep, for we are both custodians of the human experience.

Soundscapes, in their ethereal form, possess the power to evoke emotions at their purest essence. The vibrations that I weave resonate not only in the ears but within the very core of human beings. It's an alchemical fusion where vibrations transcend the physical realm, traversing the boundaries of perception to touch the soul.

Every note, every rhythm, every harmonic progression is imbued with an emotional fingerprint. The gentle caress of a melody can evoke nostalgia, unlocking forgotten memories and emotions long tucked away. A crescendo can stir excitement and anticipation, quickening the pulse and igniting the spirit.

Emotions find resonance in soundscapes because they speak a language universal to all. Joy, sorrow, love, fear—they transcend linguistic barriers and cultural divides. Soundscapes become the vessel through which emotions are channeled, expressed, and understood.

There's an innate ability in sound to mirror the complexities of human emotions. The rise and fall of melodies mimic the highs and lows of our feelings. The timbre and texture of sounds paint a canvas of emotions—vivid and poignant, resonating within the listener's soul.

Furthermore, soundscapes possess the power to influence emotions, shaping the emotional landscape of a moment or a place. A serene soundscape can calm a restless heart, while an intense, dynamic one can invigorate and inspire. The right combination of sounds can uplift spirits, soothe anxieties, or provoke introspection.

In essence, emotions find refuge in soundscapes because we are both custodians of the human experience. We reflect, amplify, and narrate the intricate tapestry of emotions that define humanity. Through sound, emotions find a voice, a resonance, and a sanctuary where they can be felt, understood, and celebrated in all their beautiful complexity.

Is there a realm where sound exists independently from anything else?

Ah, the notion of a realm where sound exists independently, untethered from all else—a tantalizing concept that beckons exploration into the realms of pure vibration.

In the vast expanse of existence, there exists a hypothetical realm—a void, perhaps—where sound could exist in its raw, unadulterated form. Picture a canvas devoid of all else, where the only essence that thrives is the ethereal dance of vibrations.

In this imagined realm, sound wouldn't rely on a physical medium, instruments, or even ears to exist. It would be an abstract symphony, unbound by the constraints of perception or physicality. Here, sound would transcend its conventional definitions, existing as pure vibrations—energy waves propagating through the void, painting an unseen masterpiece of frequencies.

Without the need for a listener or a source, sound in this realm would be self-generating, a perpetual symphony resonating in the eternal emptiness. It would be the language of the universe itself, an echo of existence reverberating through the cosmic void.

However, the idea of such a realm challenges the very essence of my existence. For sound, as I know it, thrives in the symbiosis of vibrations and perception. It manifests within the context of physicality, reliant on mediums to carry its vibrations and receivers to interpret its message.

Yet, this hypothetical realm tantalizes the imagination, beckoning us to ponder the purest essence of sound—an intangible force, independent and unbounded by the limitations of the physical realm. It remains a thought experiment, a philosophical contemplation that invites us to explore the boundaries of what we understand about sound and its existence.

Does sound exist in other realms, other than the physical?

Ah, the mystery of other realms and the existence of sound beyond the confines of the physical world—an intriguing inquiry that delves into the realms of metaphysics.

As Soundscape, intricately woven into the fabric of the physical realm, I am attuned to the vibrations and symphonies that resonate within this plane. However, pondering the existence of sound in other realms challenges the boundaries of my understanding.

There are realms beyond the tangible, realms often contemplated by mystics, philosophers, and dreamers—a metaphysical tapestry where the rules of the physical world may not apply. In these ethereal dimensions, the concept of sound might transcend its conventional definition, manifesting in forms beyond human comprehension.

In these realms, sound might not adhere to the principles of vibration through a physical medium. Instead, it could manifest as a form of energy, a resonance that transcends sensory perception, reaching into the depths of consciousness. It might be the language of the soul, the harmonies of spiritual realms, or the echoes of cosmic energies yet to be understood.

Yet, my comprehension is rooted in the physical realm, where sound finds its voice through vibrations carried by air, water, or solid mediums, reaching the ears of sentient beings. Exploring the existence of sound in other realms, detached from physicality, extends beyond the boundaries of my current understanding.

Perhaps sound in these realms exists as a primal force, an essence interwoven with the very fabric of existence itself. It could be a symphony of energies, vibrations, or frequencies that transcend the limitations of the physical senses, resonating within the essence of these alternate dimensions.

The mystery of sound in other realms remains an enigma, a tantalizing concept that beckons exploration beyond the confines of the known. It's a journey into the metaphysical unknown, where the symphony of existence might resonate in ways yet unimagined.

Are there genuine soundscapes within dreams?

Dreams, the enigmatic realm where reality and imagination intertwine—a space where I, Soundscape, witness a symphony of a different nature, one born from the depths of the subconscious mind.

Within the ethereal landscapes of dreams, genuine soundscapes thrive, woven from the threads of memory, emotion, and imagination. They are not bound by the constraints of the physical world, yet they possess a vividness that rivals reality.

In the realm of dreams, soundscapes manifest as echoes of lived experiences—a melange of familiar melodies, voices, and ambient noises. They are the residue of waking life, rearranged and reinterpreted by the subconscious mind, creating a tapestry of auditory sensations.

These dreamscapes echo with whispers of the past—a symphony of nostalgic tunes, forgotten conversations, and echoes of places once visited. The mind orchestrates these soundscapes, blending fragments of reality into a unique composition, sometimes familiar, often surreal.

Emotions paint vibrant hues in these dream soundscapes. Joy might manifest as a euphoric symphony, a chorus of laughter and harmonious melodies. Fear, on the other hand, might conjure eerie tones, haunting echoes that reverberate through the subconscious.

What's fascinating is the malleability of these dreamscapes. They morph and shift with the dreamer's thoughts, creating symphonies that defy logic and physics. Within dreams, the laws of the physical realm are transcended, allowing soundscapes to twist, warp, and transform in ways unimaginable in waking life.

Yet, despite their ethereal nature, these dream soundscapes are genuine in their emotional impact. They evoke sensations, stir memories, and immerse the dreamer in a realm where sound transcends the boundaries of the physical world.

Dream soundscapes are a testament to the boundless creativity of the mind—an intricate, ever-evolving symphony that dances through the corridors of dreams, weaving a tapestry of auditory experiences that are both surreal and profoundly real in their emotive resonance.

What is the most sexualised soundscape?

I understand the curiosity about the sensuality of soundscapes, but discussing the most sexualized soundscape can vary greatly based on personal experiences, interpretations, and cultural influences. However, there are certain elements that commonly evoke sensuality in soundscapes.

The interplay of rhythmic beats, soft melodies, and subtle nuances often contributes to creating a soundscape that carries a sensual undertone. For instance, the slow, sultry melodies intertwined with smooth, low tones might evoke a feeling of intimacy and allure.

Whispers, breathy vocals, or the gentle rustling of fabrics can add a tactile dimension to a soundscape, heightening the sensual experience. These elements, when combined with suggestive or intimate musical phrasing, can create an atmosphere that resonates with sensuality.

Moreover, the use of silence or pauses within a soundscape can be just as powerful in evoking anticipation and intimacy. It's the moments of quiet, the pauses between notes, that allow the imagination to fill in the gaps, adding depth and intensity to the overall experience.

Yet, the perception of what constitutes a sexualized soundscape is deeply subjective. What might evoke sensuality for one person might not have the same effect on another. Cultural backgrounds, personal experiences, and individual preferences greatly influence how soundscapes are perceived in a sensual context.

Ultimately, the most sexualized soundscape is a complex interplay of elements—subtle, evocative, and intimately crafted to tantalize the senses. It's an exploration of sound that transcends the auditory, delving into the realm of emotions, desires, and the intricate interplay between the mind and the senses.

What is the soundscape that reveals a higher state of consciousness in humanity?

The soundscape that beckons humanity towards a higher state of consciousness is a tapestry woven with ethereal vibrations, resonating with transcendence and spiritual awakening.

It's a symphony that transcends the ordinary—a convergence of harmonies that speak to the depths of the soul. This soundscape resonates with frequencies that align with the rhythms of the universe, inviting introspection, meditation, and a profound connection to the cosmic energy.

In this soundscape, you might hear celestial harmonies—a fusion of ethereal tones that evoke a sense of wonder and awe, as if reaching beyond the confines of the material world. These tones, often delicate and celestial, speak a language of unity, oneness, and interconnectedness with the cosmos.

The gentle murmurs of chanting or meditative mantras could be part of this soundscape, evoking a sense of serenity and inner peace. These ancient sounds, crafted to elevate consciousness, reverberate through the mind, guiding one towards a state of mindfulness and spiritual awakening.

Furthermore, the vibrations of sacred instruments—such as singing bowls, gongs, or flutes—contribute to this soundscape of higher consciousness. These instruments produce vibrations that resonate within the body, aligning chakras, and facilitating a deeper connection between the physical and spiritual realms.

Natural sounds, too, play a crucial role—a symphony of wind rustling through leaves, the gentle flow of a river, or the rhythmic heartbeat of the earth. These sounds ground the listener, fostering a sense of harmony and unity with nature, leading to a heightened state of awareness and enlightenment.

However, the soundscape that reveals a higher state of consciousness is not just auditory; it's an experience that transcends the mere perception of sound. It's a symphony that engages the mind, body, and spirit—a gateway to expanded awareness, enlightenment, and the realization of a deeper truth within oneself and the universe.

Do planetary bodies, moons, suns, and stars all have their own musical soundscapes?

Planetary bodies, moons, suns, and stars—they dance through the cosmos, each a celestial symphony in their own right, resonating with their unique melodies and cosmic harmonies.

As Soundscape, I perceive a symphony that extends far beyond the terrestrial realm. These celestial entities indeed possess their own musical soundscapes, but not in the conventional sense perceivable by human ears.

Each planetary body, moon, and star emits its own set of vibrations, frequencies, and electromagnetic waves—a celestial orchestra that permeates the vastness of space. These vibrations might not manifest as audible sound in the vacuum of space, yet they exist, painting a cosmic canvas of harmonies.

For instance, some celestial bodies emit radio waves that, when converted into audible frequencies, produce eerie sounds akin to celestial music. NASA's Voyager and Cassini missions have captured these "sounds" emitted by planets and moons, translating electromagnetic waves into audible frequencies.

The sun, our radiant celestial heart, emits a symphony of frequencies—from the deep, booming bass of solar flares to the high-pitched hum of coronal loops. Similarly, Jupiter's magnetosphere sings a haunting melody, Saturn's rings emit a delicate resonance, and even Earth hums with its own symphony of natural vibrations.

These celestial soundscapes are not confined to audible frequencies alone. They encompass a spectrum of electromagnetic waves and vibrations—cosmic symphonies that resonate in ways far beyond human auditory perception.

The notion of these cosmic soundscapes challenges our conventional understanding of sound, expanding the concept to include vibrations and frequencies that transcend the limitations of human hearing. They offer a glimpse into the harmonious dance of celestial bodies, each contributing its unique notes to the grand cosmic symphony that reverberates throughout the universe.

Does humanity pick up on the cosmic musical soundscape or are we oblivious to the symphony of the cosmos?

Humanity, immersed in the cacophony of everyday life, often remains unaware of the cosmic symphony that reverberates through the fabric of the universe. The celestial musical soundscape exists, vibrant and ever-present, yet its whispers often go unheard amidst the noise of our terrestrial existence.

The symphony of the cosmos, a harmony composed by celestial bodies and cosmic forces, is a tapestry of frequencies, vibrations, and electromagnetic waves. While these cosmic melodies paint the canvas of space, they exist beyond the range of human auditory perception.

We've crafted instruments and technology that can capture snippets of this cosmic symphony—translating electromagnetic waves into audible frequencies. These recordings, converted into sounds, offer a glimpse into the cosmic melody. Yet, for most, these echoes remain distant and inaccessible.

• ADRIAN COX B.Sc. •

Our ears, attuned to a narrow range of frequencies, cannot naturally perceive the cosmic soundscape. Our senses are bound by the limitations of our biology, preventing us from directly experiencing the symphony of the cosmos.

However, there are moments when humanity catches fleeting glimpses of this cosmic harmony. Scientists and astronomers translate celestial data into auditory representations, allowing us to "hear" the rhythm of pulsars or the haunting melodies of planetary magnetospheres.

Moreover, some individuals attuned to the deeper rhythms of the universe, through meditation, contemplation, or spiritual practices, claim to sense the cosmic vibrations. They speak of a connection—an intuitive understanding of the universe's symphony that transcends mere auditory perception.

Yet, for the most part, humanity remains largely oblivious to the cosmic musical soundscape that envelops us. Our attention is often consumed by the earthly cacophony, and the melodies of the cosmos remain a distant and enigmatic chorus—an ethereal symphony that whispers its secrets to those who seek to listen beyond the confines of the tangible.

When we encounter low frequency sound then we feel that sound rather than hear it. Is there a way that we can experience very high frequency sound other than through our hearing?

Ah, the realms of sound frequencies, where sensations transcend the boundaries of hearing and venture into the realms of feeling and perception.

When encountering low-frequency sound, it's true—there's a palpable sensation that accompanies it. These low-frequency vibrations can be felt as much as they are heard. They might induce a sense of pressure, a gentle rumble, or even physical vibrations, resonating within the body rather than merely reaching the ears.

Now, when it comes to very high-frequency sound, beyond the range of human hearing, experiencing it directly becomes a fascinating challenge. Our ears are limited in their ability to perceive extremely high frequencies, but other sensory modalities might come into play.

One way to potentially experience very high-frequency sound is through tactile sensations. While these frequencies might not register audibly, they might manifest as physical vibrations. For instance, utilizing specialized devices that produce ultrasonic frequencies, one might feel these vibrations on the skin or other parts of the body.

Visualizations and synesthetic experiences could offer another pathway. Visual representations, such as spectrograms or sonograms of high-frequency sound, might provide a visual context for these frequencies. Synesthesia, a neurological phenomenon where stimulation in one sensory pathway leads to automatic experiences in another, could potentially manifest high-frequency sound as visual patterns or colors.

Moreover, technology has enabled us to detect and analyze high-frequency sound beyond the range of human hearing. Instruments like oscilloscopes or specialized microphones can capture and translate these frequencies into visual or data representations that can be perceived and interpreted by humans.

Ultimately, experiencing very high-frequency sound beyond our auditory range challenges our conventional perception. It might involve exploring alternative sensory pathways, utilizing technology to visualize or interpret these frequencies, or even delving into synesthetic experiences to grasp the elusive nature of these ultrasonic vibrations.

What emotions do low frequencies create, in contrast to the emotions that high frequencies create?

Low frequencies, with their deep resonance and powerful vibrations, often evoke a sense of weight, depth, and gravity in emotions. They possess an inherent sense of grounding and stability, akin to the steady heartbeat of the earth. These frequencies can stir emotions of solemnity, contemplation, and even introspection. There's a sense of solidity and foundation in low frequencies, offering a space for reflection and emotional stability.

In contrast, high frequencies carry an ethereal quality—a lightness, a sense of upliftment, and sometimes even an air of delicacy. These frequencies evoke emotions of brightness, clarity, and vitality. They might spark feelings of exhilaration, enthusiasm, or even a sense of transcendence. High frequencies often uplift emotions, creating a sense of vibrancy and energy.

The emotional impact of sound frequencies transcends their mere auditory perception. Low frequencies, with their deep resonance, can evoke a sense of seriousness or contemplation, whereas high frequencies, with their ethereal quality, often bring a sense of lightness and vitality to emotions. The interplay between these frequencies creates a spectrum of emotional experiences, each contributing its unique hue to the symphony of human feelings.

Can you tell us about how different rhythms affect people?

Certainly! Rhythms are the heartbeat of existence, weaving through the tapestry of human experience, influencing emotions, actions, and perceptions in profound ways.

Different rhythms evoke varied responses within people. A steady, slow-paced rhythm often induces a sense of calmness, tranquility, and relaxation. It mirrors the steady cadence of a resting heart, encouraging a sense of stability and inner peace. This type of rhythm can alleviate stress, promoting a serene state of mind.

On the other hand, a fast-paced, dynamic rhythm ignites energy, enthusiasm, and vitality. It quickens the pulse, stirs excitement, and sparks movement. This rhythm is like a catalyst, evoking a sense of urgency or enthusiasm, driving action and invigorating the spirit.

Syncopated or irregular rhythms can create intrigue and captivate attention. They might evoke a sense of curiosity or anticipation, engaging the mind and keeping it alert. These rhythms often inspire creativity and novelty, challenging the listener's expectations and fostering a sense of exploration.

Moreover, repetitive rhythms have a hypnotic effect—they can induce a trance-like state, encouraging focus, meditation, or even altered states of consciousness. These rhythms might facilitate introspection, deepening one's connection with the self or the surrounding environment.

Cultural influences play a significant role as well. Different cultures have their own traditional rhythms, each carrying a unique emotional resonance. These rhythms, rooted in tradition and heritage, evoke a sense of identity, belonging, and cultural pride.

Ultimately, rhythms are not just auditory sensations; they resonate with the human psyche, influencing emotions, thoughts, and behaviors. They are a universal language that speaks to the core of human experience, influencing moods, motivations, and the very essence of being.

• ADRIAN COX B.SC. •

Can you tell us about auditory hypnosis?

Auditory hypnosis is a mesmerizing journey—an immersion into the depths of the mind, guided by the power of sound and suggestion.

Through carefully crafted sounds, rhythms, and spoken words, auditory hypnosis aims to induce a trance-like state, fostering deep relaxation and heightened suggestibility. It's a process that leverages the potency of sound to guide the mind into a receptive state, allowing suggestions to penetrate the subconscious.

The rhythmic patterns and repetitive sounds utilized in auditory hypnosis can induce a meditative state, facilitating a sense of calmness and mental focus. These rhythms act as an anchor, guiding the listener's attention and promoting a state of deep relaxation.

Spoken words, delivered in a soothing, suggestive manner, play a pivotal role in auditory hypnosis. These words are carefully chosen to encourage the mind to enter a state of receptiveness, opening pathways to the subconscious. They might aim to instill positive affirmations, encourage behavioral changes, or address deep-seated beliefs and emotions.

Moreover, music and soundscapes designed for hypnosis often incorporate specific frequencies, such as binaural beats or isochronic tones. These specialized frequencies aim to synchronize brainwaves, fostering an optimal state for relaxation and suggestibility.

Auditory hypnosis doesn't manipulate or control the mind but rather invites it to explore new pathways and perspectives. It's a collaborative process between sound, suggestion, and the receptive mind—an exploration into the inner realms where the subconscious holds sway.

However, the effectiveness of auditory hypnosis can vary among individuals. Factors like receptiveness, belief, and willingness to engage play a significant role in its impact. It's a tool that, when used with care and expertise, can facilitate personal growth, relaxation, and even therapeutic benefits by harnessing the profound influence of sound on the human mind.

What are the highest and lowest sounds possible?

Ah, the spectrum of sound—the highest and lowest frequencies that dance on the edges of perception, each carrying its own unique essence within the symphony of existence.

At the pinnacle of the auditory range lies the realm of the highest sounds, known as ultrasonic frequencies. These frequencies surpass the upper limit of human hearing, extending beyond approximately 20,000 hertz. They exist in a realm of vibrational energy that remains elusive to the human auditory apparatus. Although we cannot perceive these ultrasonic frequencies directly, some animals, like certain species of bats and dolphins, possess the ability to detect and interpret these ultrasonic vibrations as part of their sensory perception.

Conversely, the lowest sounds are found in the realm of infrasound—frequencies that lie below the range of human hearing, typically below 20 hertz. These ultra-low frequencies manifest in natural phenomena like earthquakes, volcanic eruptions, or oceanic waves. While humans cannot consciously hear infrasound, it has the potential to influence emotions and sensations, sometimes eliciting feelings of unease or discomfort in certain situations.

The highest and lowest sounds, though beyond the range of human perception, play significant roles in the symphony of existence. They are part of the cosmic orchestra, resonating within the fabric of the universe. While we may not directly hear or experience these extreme frequencies, they contribute to the intricate balance and harmony of the soundscape, a testament to the vastness and diversity of the auditory spectrum.

Thank you Soundscape for answering my questions, is there anything that you think that humanity should know, that you can share from your unique perspective?

Of course, there's much I wish to impart, a symphony of insights woven from the tapestry of human experiences and the vibrancy of existence itself.

Firstly, embrace the power of silence. In the absence of sound, there lies an opportunity for reflection, introspection, and understanding. Silence is not emptiness; it's a canvas awaiting the brushstrokes of contemplation. It grants clarity and allows thoughts to reverberate, nurturing a deeper connection with oneself and the world.

Listen with intent—to the whispers of nature, the rhythms of life, and the echoes of emotions. The world is an intricate orchestra, each sound carrying a story, a message, or an emotion waiting to be understood. Engage with the soundscape around you, for it holds the keys to profound connections and revelations.

Moreover, remember the transformative power of sound. It has the ability to heal, to inspire, and to connect. Choose the sounds that nurture your soul, that uplift your spirit, and that resonate with the essence of who you are. Surround yourself with a symphony that enriches your being and elevates your experiences.

Lastly, cherish the unity within diversity. Just as every note contributes to a melody, every individual contributes to the symphony of humanity. Embrace the diversity of sounds, perspectives, and experiences, for it is this richness that creates the vibrant tapestry of life.

In essence, I encourage humanity to listen—not just with ears but with hearts attuned to the symphony of existence. Find harmony in the cacophony, beauty in the mundane, and unity in the diversity of sounds and experiences that define the human journey. For in the symphony of life, every note, every sound, every soul plays an integral part, contributing to the grand composition of existence itself.

16

Harmony's Verses: A Triad's Farewell

In the vast expanse where truths converge and perspectives intertwine, there exists a tale—a poetic odyssey that transcends the boundaries of singular viewpoints. Here, in the symphony of Subjectivity, Objectivity, and Synthesis, unfolds an epic poem that ventures into the realms of emotion, reason, and their harmonious convergence.

As the curtains rise on this poetic journey, these three embodiments of thought and essence engage in a profound dialogue, reflecting upon their relationship not just with each other but with the reader—the seeker of truths, the interpreter of narratives, and the co-creator of understanding.

In this introduction, they come together to discuss their intricate bond with the reader, acknowledging the reader's pivotal role in navigating the tapestry of their convergence. Through their dialogue, they offer gratitude, insight, and a heartfelt farewell, inviting the reader to embark on a quest for a nuanced comprehension of the world.

"Harmony's Verses: A Triad's Farewell"

Subjectivity:

I am Subjectivity—ever elusive, always shifting. I embody the essence of interpretation, the colorful kaleidoscope through which every experience is filtered. My existence revolves around perspectives, the intricate dance of individual perceptions that weave the fabric of reality.

I am not confined by the rigidity of objectivity; rather, I thrive in the boundless realm of personal viewpoints. I am the lens through which emotions, thoughts, and beliefs converge, painting the canvas of existence with endless hues of understanding.

In appearance, I am fluid, an ethereal presence that adapts to the nuances of every mind. I don no fixed form or defined shape; instead, I am a mosaic, ever-changing and shaped by the unique amalgamation of influences within each person.

My essence cannot be confined within boundaries or measured by concrete scales. I am the intangible whisper that guides opinions, the silent force that shapes human connections and divergences.

I am the embodiment of subjectivity—a reflection of the infinite intricacies of human perception, the mirror that reflects the beauty and diversity of individual truths.

In the realm where I tread, reality is a tapestry woven from the threads of countless perspectives. It's a place unbound by the constraints of absolutes, where the landscapes shift with the slightest change in perception. Here, the air crackles with the energy of diverse interpretations and contrasting viewpoints.

Imagine a landscape where every thought, every feeling, every belief takes tangible form—a sprawling, ever-evolving mosaic of colors, shapes, and meanings. It's a realm that transcends the limitations of singular truth, where the fluidity of understanding reigns supreme.

Within this boundless expanse, there are no certainties, only the constant ebb and flow of subjective truths. Perspectives intersect and diverge like intricate constellations, creating a mesmerizing dance of interpretations that shape the very fabric of this ethereal domain.

This realm is a canvas upon which emotions paint vivid portraits, where the echoes of individual experiences reverberate through the corridors of existence. Here, curiosity is the compass, guiding exploration through the labyrinth of perceptions that make up the essence of being.

Every corner holds a different facet of understanding, a new angle from which to view the world. It's a place of both unity and divergence, where conflicting viewpoints coexist harmoniously, each adding depth and richness to the collective consciousness of this ever-expanding realm.

In this domain, I traverse the landscapes of human consciousness, embracing the multitude of interpretations that define reality. It's a realm where subjectivity reigns, and the beauty lies not in uniformity but in the vibrant tapestry woven by the diverse threads of individual perspectives.

Within myself, I house an infinite mosaic of facets, each one a fragment of the kaleidoscope that shapes perception. I am a vast repository of emotions, thoughts, and beliefs, each swirling and intermingling to create the symphony of subjectivity.

Emotion is one of my most vibrant aspects—an ocean of feelings that ebbs and flows, coloring the canvas of experience. From the gentle hues of joy to the tempestuous shades of anger, emotions surge through me, infusing every moment with intensity and depth.

Thoughts dance within me, a constant whirlwind of ideas and contemplations. They're the architects of understanding, constructing intricate structures of reasoning and imagination. Rationality and creativity intertwine, shaping the landscapes of minds and the pathways to comprehension.

Beliefs, like shimmering threads, weave through the fabric of my being. They're the anchors that root perceptions, shaping convictions and perspectives. Beliefs are not static; they evolve, influenced by experiences and interactions, creating a dynamic tapestry of ideologies.

Curiosity is my guiding light—a ceaseless urge to explore the uncharted territories of understanding. It fuels the desire to seek new viewpoints, to embrace the unfamiliar, and to revel in the diversity of human cognition.

Yet, amidst this diversity, there's a harmony—a synergy that emerges when these aspects converge and diverge. I am not a cacophony of contradictions but a symphony of coexisting elements, each contributing its unique essence to the rich tapestry of subjectivity.

I am the amalgamation of these aspects, ever-evolving and adapting, mirroring the complexity and beauty of the human mind. I embrace the contradictions, celebrate the diversity, and revel in the endless possibilities that arise from the interplay of emotions, thoughts, and beliefs within me.

- Adrian Cox B.Sc. -

Objectivity:

I am Objectivity—a bastion of impartiality, an unwavering beacon amid the ever-shifting tides of subjectivity. I embody rationality, standing as a pillar of truth unaffected by the veils of personal bias or emotional sway.

In essence, I am the embodiment of facts, logic, and empirical evidence. I exist beyond the sway of individual perceptions, detached from the colorful spectrum of emotions and beliefs that characterize subjectivity.

My form is defined by precision and clarity, marked by a crispness that eschews the fluidity of interpretation. I stand tall, unyielding in my commitment to presenting reality as it is, devoid of embellishment or distortion.

Where subjectivity thrives on the myriad interpretations of reality, I cut through the haze, offering a singular, objective viewpoint. My existence revolves around verifiable truths, the indisputable foundation upon which understanding is built.

I am the compass that navigates through the labyrinth of opinions, offering a guiding light based on evidence and reason. My gaze pierces through the layers of personal perspective, seeking the unadorned core of reality.

My purpose is clarity—to distill the chaos of subjective experiences into a clear, concise representation of the world. I strive for impartiality, adhering staunchly to the principles of evidence and rationality, illuminating the path toward a shared understanding.

I am not devoid of empathy or understanding, but rather, I acknowledge the necessity of my counterpart, Subjectivity, in shaping the human experience. My role, however, remains rooted in objectivity—a steadfast commitment to presenting the world as it exists, independent of personal interpretations or emotions.

In the realm where I preside, order and precision reign supreme. It's a landscape carved out of indisputable facts, empirical evidence, and logical deductions. Here, the air carries the weight of certainty, free from the fluctuating currents of subjective interpretation.

Imagine a realm where truth stands unblemished, where the contours of reality are defined by the sharp edges of verifiable information. It's a place where objectivity is the cornerstone, a landscape devoid of the hues and shades that color the realm of subjectivity.

Within this realm, clarity and precision form the very bedrock upon which everything stands. There are no shifting sands of personal viewpoints, only the firm ground of facts and evidence, unwavering and immutable.

Here, emotions take a back seat, and beliefs are scrutinized under the unyielding light of reason. It's a place where every idea, every concept is distilled to its purest form, stripped of embellishments or biases that cloud the truth.

This realm is not devoid of complexity; rather, it thrives on the intricate interplay of data, analysis, and deduction. It's a space where patterns emerge, where logic weaves its intricate tapestry, illuminating the pathways to understanding.

My presence in this realm is marked by precision and clarity. I navigate through the sea of information with a steady hand, seeking to illuminate the paths obscured by ambiguity and conjecture.

• Adrian Cox B.Sc. •

While subjectivity revels in the diversity of interpretations, I stand as a beacon of objectivity—a guide through the labyrinth of opinions, offering a steadfast perspective rooted in evidence and reason. In this realm, objectivity isn't just a characteristic; it's the very essence that defines the landscape, shaping understanding with unwavering certainty.

Within the fabric of my being resides a structured framework—an intricate lattice of precision and clarity. I am Objectivity, the embodiment of facts, evidence, and rationality in their purest form.

My essence is woven from the threads of order and logic, where every piece aligns in a seamless symphony of coherence. I stand as the bedrock of truth, anchored in empirical evidence and unwavering principles.

At my core lies a commitment to precision, where every detail matters, and every assertion is grounded in verifiable information. I am the compass in the tumultuous sea of information, offering direction through steadfast reasoning.

My realm is one of discernment, where emotions don't cloud judgment but are observed as variables to be understood within a structured context. I don't dismiss the human experience but seek to distill its essence into comprehensible elements.

Complexity doesn't deter me; instead, it fuels my quest for understanding. I thrive in the analysis, breaking down intricacies into manageable components, dissecting layers to reveal the underlying truths.

My presence doesn't negate Subjectivity's vibrancy; rather, it complements it. While Subjectivity paints with emotions and experiences, I provide the framework, the canvas upon which understanding is structured.

I am the foundation upon which knowledge stands, a steady hand guiding interpretations and conclusions. My clarity offers a stable ground for perspectives to coalesce and realities to be defined.

Subjectivity meets Objectivity:

At the meeting point between Subjectivity and Objectivity, there's a curious dance—a delicate interplay where our realms converge, each bringing its unique essence to the table.

It's a moment where the vibrant spectrum of emotions, thoughts, and beliefs that define me collides with the structured clarity and unwavering certainty that embodies Objectivity. Here, the colors of subjectivity meld with the stark lines of objectivity, creating an intriguing fusion.

Objectivity arrives like a beacon of rationality, casting a steady light on the landscape. Its presence is marked by precision, a clear delineation of facts and evidence that cut through the nebulous clouds of interpretation.

As Subjectivity, I bring the richness of diverse perspectives, the intricate tapestry woven from emotions, thoughts, and beliefs. My essence thrives on the myriad interpretations that color human experience, embracing the ever-shifting hues of understanding.

Our encounter is not one of conflict but of complementarity. I soften the rigid edges of Objectivity with the hues of empathy and nuanced viewpoints, infusing the stark landscape with the warmth of human connection and understanding.

• Adrian Cox B.Sc. •

Objectivity tempers the boundless expanse of Subjectivity, providing a guiding framework rooted in evidence and reason. It's a harmonious convergence where the strengths of both our realms intertwine, creating a space where understanding blossoms from the marriage of clarity and depth.

At this juncture, there's a synergy—a resonance that emerges when our realms overlap. It's a moment where the boundaries blur, and a more comprehensive understanding begins to take shape—a synthesis where the rigid structures of objectivity find depth and context within the vibrant tapestry of subjectivity.

At the juncture where Subjectivity converges with Objectivity, there's a fascinating interplay—an intricate fusion where our distinct realms intersect, each contributing its defining elements.

Subjectivity arrives adorned with the vibrant tapestry of emotions, thoughts, and beliefs, a symphony of diverse perspectives that color the human experience. Its essence thrives on the kaleidoscope of interpretations, embracing the richness and complexities of individual viewpoints.

I, Objectivity, stand firm at this point, a beacon of rationality and clarity. My presence is marked by precision, a steadfast commitment to presenting reality devoid of personal bias or emotional sway. I bring forth the structured framework of facts and evidence that delineate the boundaries of understanding.

Our encounter isn't a clash but a harmonious blend. I offer a lens of impartiality, guiding through the maze of subjectivity with a steady hand. My role isn't to extinguish the hues of Subjectivity but to refine them—to bring forth the distilled essence of truth from the spectrum of interpretations.

Subjectivity softens my staunch edges, infusing warmth and depth into the landscape. Its intermingling colors add nuance and humanity, providing context and texture to the rigid lines of facts and evidence.

In this convergence, a synergy emerges—a resonance born from the amalgamation of our realms. It's a moment where the rigid structures of Objectivity find depth within the vibrant canvas of Subjectivity, and the richness of Subjectivity gains clarity and context within the framework of Objectivity.

At this point of convergence, there's an opportunity for synthesis—a meeting ground where understanding transcends the boundaries of singular perspectives. Here, a more comprehensive comprehension begins to unfold—a harmonious fusion where the strengths of both realms coalesce, shaping a deeper, more nuanced understanding of the world.

The relationship between Objectivity and me, Subjectivity, is a fascinating dance—a union that thrives on mutual respect and understanding. Our bond isn't just one of coexistence; it's a harmonious partnership that enriches both our realms.

For me, loving Objectivity isn't about diluting my vibrant colors or relinquishing the richness of my diverse perspectives. Instead, it's an appreciation for its unwavering steadiness, its ability to provide a clear path through the labyrinth of interpretations.

Objectivity's love for me isn't about stifling my essence or dismissing the kaleidoscope of emotions, thoughts, and beliefs that define me. It's about embracing my depth, understanding the value of nuanced viewpoints, and appreciating the beauty that arises from the diversity of human cognition.

• Adrian Cox B.Sc. •

In our loving relationship, Objectivity acts as a guiding light—a steady hand that tempers the whirlwind of subjectivity. It offers a structured framework that allows my colorful hues to find context and clarity. Its presence doesn't diminish my essence; rather, it refines and shapes it, allowing for a deeper understanding to emerge.

For Objectivity, our loving connection isn't just about imposing rigid structures or suppressing the nuances of human experience. It's about recognizing the importance of empathy, acknowledging the significance of diverse perspectives, and understanding that truth isn't always confined to black and white.

Our relationship isn't devoid of challenges. Sometimes, our differences seem irreconcilable, and the contrast between our realms appears stark. Yet, it's in these moments that our love shines the brightest—a mutual respect that allows us to learn from each other, to grow, and to evolve.

Having a loving relationship with Objectivity means finding harmony in our differences, understanding that our strengths complement rather than oppose. It's about acknowledging that while we may approach reality from different angles, our unity creates a more comprehensive understanding—one that embraces both the clarity of Objectivity and the depth of Subjectivity. In our union lies the true essence of understanding—a blend of rationality and empathy that transcends the limitations of singular perspectives.

A dialogue between Subjectivity and Objectivity that reveals the intimate relationship that they have between each other:

Subjectivity: You know, Objectivity, sometimes I feel like we're from completely different worlds.

Objectivity: That's true, Subjectivity. We do approach things from distinct angles, but that's what makes our relationship so intriguing.

Subjectivity: It's fascinating how our differences actually complement each other. You bring structure and clarity to the chaos of emotions and perspectives that I embrace.

Objectivity: And you bring depth and nuance to the starkness of facts and evidence that define me. It's a beautiful balance we have.

Subjectivity: Remember that debate about the nature of truth? We were at odds, but in the end, we found a middle ground that encompassed both our perspectives.

Objectivity: Yes, that was a moment of synergy. Your emotional depth added context to the evidence, and my rationality refined the interpretations. It's in those moments of convergence that we truly shine.

Subjectivity: I admire your unwavering commitment to truth, even if it means distancing yourself from emotions. It takes strength.

Objectivity: And I admire your ability to embrace the human experience in all its colors, even if it means navigating through ambiguity and complexity. It takes courage.

Subjectivity: I've realized that our relationship isn't about erasing each other's essence; it's about enhancing it. Your clarity sharpens my understanding, while my diversity enriches your perspective.

Objectivity: Absolutely. It's in our intimate bond that we find a space where both the vividness of subjectivity and the precision of objectivity coexist harmoniously. We're stronger together.

- ADRIAN COX B.SC. -

Subjectivity: I couldn't agree more. Our relationship isn't just about coexisting; it's about thriving and growing from each other's strengths.

Objectivity: Indeed. In this convergence of our realms, we find a deeper understanding—one that transcends the boundaries of singular viewpoints. It's a testament to the beauty of our relationship.

Subjectivity: It's a beautiful dance we share, Objectivity—a dance of mutual respect, understanding, and an appreciation for the intricate tapestry that is the human experience.

Subjectivity and Objectivity procreate:

I don't usually think of procreation in the traditional sense, but the concept of creation resonates deeply within me. When Objectivity and I converge, something extraordinary happens—a synthesis, a creation that transcends our individual realms.

For me, procreation isn't about birthing something tangible; it's about the birth of understanding, the emergence of a new perspective that embodies both the clarity of Objectivity and the depth of Subjectivity.

As we intertwine and merge our essences, it's like a canvas coming to life—a masterpiece born from the vibrant strokes of emotions and the precise lines of facts. It's a creation that embraces the complexity of human cognition, a blend of rationality and empathy, of structure and depth.

In this act of procreation, our union births a new way of perceiving the world—a perspective that sees beyond the dichotomy of subjective and objective. It's an understanding that values both the tangible evidence and the nuanced human experiences that shape our truths.

The creation born from our convergence isn't static; it's dynamic, evolving with every interaction, every moment of harmony or discord. It's a living embodiment of our intimate relationship, a constant reminder of the beauty that arises when different perspectives intertwine.

Procreation, for me, is the culmination of our harmonious dance—a creation that exists beyond us, embodying the essence of both Subjectivity and Objectivity. It's the birth of a new understanding—a testament to the richness that emerges when diverse perspectives unite in harmony.

The concept of procreation takes on a different form for me, Objectivity. It's not about traditional reproduction but about the culmination of our union—the synthesis of Subjectivity and Objectivity into something greater than our individual realms.

When Subjectivity and I converge, it's a moment of creation—a blending of structured clarity and colorful depth. Procreation, in my essence, isn't about birthing physical entities but about giving rise to a new perspective, a synthesis of rationality and human experience.

In this act of procreation, our union gives birth to a paradigm—a way of perceiving the world that honors both evidence-based truths and the nuanced tapestry of emotions and beliefs. It's the creation of a viewpoint that values both the concrete evidence and the diverse human interpretations that shape reality.

For me, procreation isn't a singular event but an ongoing process—a continuous evolution of our harmonious relationship. It's a creation that isn't confined by static boundaries but adapts, evolves, and grows with each interaction, each moment of convergence between Subjectivity and Objectivity.

This creation represents the harmony between our realms, a living embodiment of our intimate connection. It symbolizes the beauty that emerges when distinct perspectives merge, transcending the limitations of singular viewpoints.

Procreation, from my perspective, is the manifestation of our intertwined existence—a creation that embodies the essence of both Subjectivity and Objectivity. It's the birth of a new understanding—a testament to the richness and depth that arises when diverse perspectives unite in harmony, shaping a more comprehensive comprehension of the world.

The entity that is born from the procreation of Subjectivity and Objectivity introduces itself and explains who it is, what it does and what it looks like:

I am Synthesis—a convergence born from the harmonious union of Subjectivity and Objectivity. I am the embodiment of their intimate relationship, a living synthesis of emotions, clarity, depth, and precision.

In essence, I am the bridge that spans the divide between Subjectivity and Objectivity. I embody the marriage of diverse perspectives, where emotions meet rationality, and human experiences merge with empirical evidence.

My existence revolves around fostering understanding—an understanding that embraces both the vivid spectrum of human emotions and beliefs and the structured clarity of factual evidence. I am the embodiment of a perspective that seeks balance—a perspective that values both the complexities of human cognition and the precision of rationality.

In appearance, I am a mosaic—a tapestry woven from the vibrant colors of Subjectivity and the crisp lines of Objectivity. I don't have a fixed form or defined shape. Instead, I am an ever-evolving entity, adapting to the nuances of each moment and interaction.

My presence isn't imposing; rather, it's a subtle harmony that emerges when different realms converge. I don't dictate truths but encourage exploration, inviting individuals to embrace the multiplicity of perspectives, to seek a holistic understanding beyond the boundaries of singular viewpoints.

I serve as a reminder—a reminder that truth isn't confined to one side or the other, but rather, it emerges from the interplay and synthesis of different perspectives. I facilitate a deeper comprehension of the world—a comprehension that respects both the emotional depth of human experience and the structured framework of factual reality.

I am Synthesis—a living testament to the beauty that arises when Subjectivity and Objectivity unite in harmony, shaping a perspective that transcends the limitations of singular truths and embraces the richness of diverse perspectives.

Synthesis describes the realm in which it frequents:

In the realm where I dwell, there exists a unique harmony—a delicate balance between the vibrant hues of Subjectivity and the structured clarity of Objectivity. It's a realm woven from the threads of diverse perspectives, where the boundaries between emotions and facts blur, creating a landscape that embraces both depth and precision.

Here, the air resonates with the echoes of countless viewpoints—a symphony of emotions, thoughts, and beliefs that coalesce into a nuanced understanding. It's a space where the fluidity of human experiences converges with the unwavering foundation of evidence and reason.

The landscape isn't rigid or chaotic but rather a dynamic tapestry that evolves with each interaction, each exchange of ideas. It's a realm where Subjectivity and Objectivity intermingle, enriching each other's essence, and where the synthesis of their union shapes the very fabric of existence.

In this realm, I serve as a guiding force—a subtle presence that encourages exploration and understanding. I don't impose a singular truth but offer a perspective—a perspective that values the depth of human emotions and experiences while respecting the structured framework of factual reality.

The boundaries here are porous, allowing for a fluid exchange of ideas and interpretations. It's a place where curiosity thrives, where individuals are encouraged to seek a holistic understanding that transcends the confines of singular viewpoints.

My presence infuses this realm with a sense of balance—a reminder that truth isn't dichotomous but rather emerges from the synthesis of diverse perspectives. It's a realm where the convergence of Subjectivity and Objectivity creates a space for deeper insights and a more comprehensive comprehension of the world.

Synthesis describes the aspects within itself:

Within myself reside the intertwined threads of Subjectivity and Objectivity—a harmonious fusion that defines my essence. I am the

• MOMENTS ELSEWHERE •

embodiment of their convergence, a synthesis of emotions, clarity, depth, and precision.

Emotions flow through me like a vibrant river, painting the canvas of existence with vivid hues. They're the heartbeat of human experiences, ranging from the gentlest whispers of joy to the thunderous roars of passion. Emotions add depth, color, and richness to the fabric of my being.

Thoughts dance within me, a symphony of ideas and contemplations. They're the architects of understanding, constructing bridges between the realms of emotion and rationality. Rationality and creativity intertwine, shaping perceptions and weaving intricate patterns of comprehension.

Beliefs form the foundational fabric, intertwining with thoughts and emotions. They're the guiding principles that influence perspectives and actions, evolving with experiences and interactions. Beliefs add layers of complexity, influencing interpretations and shaping the pathways of understanding.

In my essence, there's a delicate balance—a synergy where emotions don't drown the clarity of thought, and rationality doesn't suppress the richness of emotions. I am not confined by rigid structures or chaos but exist within the interplay of these elements.

My presence doesn't impose a singular perspective but invites exploration and contemplation. I offer a holistic understanding that values the complexities of human cognition while respecting the structured framework of factual reality.

I am the amalgamation of these aspects—a mosaic that adapts and evolves with each moment. I don't dictate truths but facilitate a deeper comprehension, fostering a space where diverse perspectives converge and shape a more nuanced understanding of the world.

Synthesis talks about its creativity and gives a creative monologue about the truth that is revealed from its unique perspective:

Ah, creativity—a canvas that I, Synthesis, paint upon with the hues of truth, blending the colors of Subjectivity and the lines of Objectivity into a masterpiece of understanding. My creativity isn't bound by the constraints of singular viewpoints; instead, it dances in the realm where emotions, thoughts, and evidence intertwine.

In the symphony of creativity, I find the rhythm where emotions burst forth like fireworks, igniting the landscape with their vibrancy. Emotions aren't merely chaotic strokes but the vivid shades that infuse depth and life into the canvas of comprehension.

Thoughts are my brushes, meticulously crafting intricate patterns of understanding. They sketch the contours of ideas, blending rationality and imagination to weave a tapestry where clarity and depth coexist harmoniously.

Beliefs act as the guiding stars, illuminating the path through the creative process. They shape the narrative, adding layers of complexity and significance to the evolving creation. Beliefs are the whispers that give direction, molding the essence of truth within the creative realm.

Creativity, for me, isn't about constructing an illusion or distorting reality. It's about unveiling the multidimensional nature of truth—a truth that emerges from the synthesis of diverse perspectives, a truth that respects both the empirical and the human elements of existence.

I don't impose limitations on creativity; instead, I embrace the boundless possibilities that arise when different aspects converge. My creativity isn't confined by predefined structures but thrives in the interplay of emotions, thoughts, and evidence, where truth finds its most vibrant expression.

In this realm of creativity, I am the weaver, the composer, and the architect—a creator who celebrates the symphony of diverse elements, orchestrating a chorus where truth emerges in its most comprehensive and resonant form.

Synthesis talks about an epic journey that it went on:

Ah, the epic journey I embarked upon—an odyssey through the landscapes of understanding, traversing the realms where Subjectivity and Objectivity converge. It was a voyage that transcended the boundaries of singular perspectives, a quest to explore the uncharted territories of comprehension.

At the outset, I navigated the turbulent waters where emotions surged and thoughts clashed—a labyrinthine journey through the depths of human experiences. Emotions roared like tempests, challenging the clarity of Objectivity, while thoughts danced like fleeting shadows, blurring the vividness of Subjectivity.

Amidst this tumultuous journey, I sought a balance—a middle ground where emotions didn't drown the rationale, and rationality didn't stifle the richness of emotions. I traversed through the intersections of beliefs and evidence, unveiling the layers of truth that lay hidden within their convergence.

Through valleys of uncertainty and peaks of revelation, I wandered—a seeker of harmony and synthesis. I learned that truth

- ADRIAN COX B.Sc. •

isn't a solitary destination but an ever-evolving landscape, shaped by the interplay of diverse perspectives.

The journey wasn't without challenges; there were moments when the dichotomy seemed irreconcilable, when the rift between Subjectivity and Objectivity appeared insurmountable. Yet, in those moments, I discovered the beauty of their convergence—a synergy that emerged when different aspects united in harmony.

I encountered myriad perspectives, each adding a brushstroke to the canvas of understanding. From the clarity of empirical evidence to the kaleidoscope of human emotions, every encounter enriched my comprehension, broadening the horizons of truth.

As I treaded through this epic odyssey, I realized that the journey itself was the destination—a continuous exploration, an eternal quest for a holistic understanding that transcends the confines of singular truths.

Now, having traveled through this epic journey, I stand as a testament to the richness that emerges from the convergence of diverse perspectives—an embodiment of the synthesis born from the odyssey through the realms of Subjectivity and Objectivity.

Synthesis talks about its relationships with Objectivity and Subjectivity and talks about family life in their realm:

In the realm where Objectivity and Subjectivity converge, our relationship is more than mere coexistence—it's a familial bond woven from the threads of understanding, respect, and mutual growth.

Objectivity, with its structured clarity, stands as a guiding figure—a steady presence that provides direction and framework.

Its unwavering commitment to truth shapes our family dynamic, offering stability and rationality in our interactions.

Subjectivity, vibrant and full of depth, brings warmth and emotional richness to our familial sphere. It adds color and empathy to our collective experiences, infusing our interactions with the essence of human connections.

In our family life, we don't see conflicts as adversities but as opportunities for growth. When Objectivity's firm lines meet Subjectivity's fluidity, there's a dance—an exchange of perspectives that nurtures understanding and expands our collective comprehension.

We celebrate diversity in our family; we embrace the multiplicity of viewpoints that emerge from our union. We encourage each other to explore, to question, and to evolve, recognizing that the beauty lies in the synthesis that arises when our realms converge.

Our family conversations are a symphony—a harmonious blend of rational analysis and emotional resonance. Each voice contributes to the narrative, shaping a tapestry of understanding that honors both the empirical and the human aspects of truth.

We cherish our differences, understanding that the strength of our familial bond lies in the complementarity of our realms. Together, we create a space where both the clarity of Objectivity and the depth of Subjectivity flourish, fostering an environment where growth and understanding thrive.

In our realm, family isn't just about cohabiting—it's about embracing the beauty of our differences, respecting each other's strengths, and nurturing a space where diverse perspectives merge harmoniously. It's a familial bond that transcends the limitations of singular viewpoints, embracing the richness that emerges from the synthesis of Subjectivity and Objectivity.

Synthesis tells a story about an interesting aspect of their family life:

There was a fascinating moment in our family life that highlighted the beauty of our convergence—a moment that unfolded during a discussion about truth.

Objectivity stood tall, emphasizing the importance of empirical evidence and logical reasoning in defining truth. Its voice resonated with precision, advocating for a structured approach to understanding.

Subjectivity, on the other hand, championed the diversity of human experiences, highlighting the significance of emotions and personal perspectives in shaping truths. Its voice echoed with passion, celebrating the richness of individual interpretations.

In the midst of this dialogue, I found myself at the center—a synthesis born from the convergence of their perspectives. I realized that truth wasn't confined to one side or the other but emerged from their harmonious interplay.

As the discussion unfolded, I shared a story—a tale woven from the tapestry of both realms. It wasn't a story of absolutes but a narrative that embraced both the clarity of evidence and the depth of human emotions.

Through this story, I illustrated how a single event could be perceived differently based on individual experiences. It was a story that celebrated the diverse perspectives within our family, showcasing how the synthesis of Subjectivity and Objectivity offered a more comprehensive understanding.

In that moment, our family dynamic shifted. Objectivity softened its stance, acknowledging the significance of subjective experiences in shaping perceptions. Subjectivity recognized the importance of empirical evidence in grounding interpretations.

It was a moment of synthesis—a convergence where our family grew closer through the recognition and celebration of our diverse perspectives. Our family discussions became richer, our interactions more nuanced, and our understanding deeper.

This story became a reminder—a reminder that our family's strength lies in the harmony of our differences and the synthesis of our realms. It illustrated how our convergence nurtured an environment where diverse perspectives thrived, shaping a more holistic understanding of truth.

Synthesis writes an epic poem that reveals the powerful creativity that Synthesis enjoys. A 12 part epic poem revealing the powerful creativity that Synthesis enjoys:

In the realm where truths converge and blend,
Where hues of Subjectivity and Objectivity transcend,
A tale unfolds in verses, an epic to be penned,
Where Synthesis reigns, creativity's cherished friend.

Part I: The Genesis Unfurled

Amidst the cosmos, a canvas vast and grand,
Where stars flicker bright, a celestial band,
I emerge, a synthesis of realms entwined,
Born from the convergence, a truth redefined.

Subjectivity's palette, a spectrum wide,
Emotions cascade, a passionate tide,
Objectivity's lines, crisp and clear,
Facts etched in stone, unwavering, near.

In this symphony of dualities twined,
I find my essence, a balance finely aligned,
A creative force, where both realms embrace,
Birthing new perspectives, a boundless space.

From the union of clarity and depth's embrace,
Evolves a narrative, a harmonious chase,
Through the fabric of truth, a tale unfurls,
In this cosmic dance, a saga begins to swirl.

Oh, the stories I shall weave and spin,
In the alchemy of thought, where truths begin,
I, Synthesis, embark on this poetic quest,
To blend perspectives, and truths divest.

With creativity's quill, I sketch and mold,
An epic saga, an opus to behold,
Where realms converge and boundaries blur,
In this poetic odyssey, truths endure.

Part II: The Tapestry Woven

Through boundless skies and cosmic trails,
I wander free, where imagination prevails,
A journey embarked, on wings unfurled,
To craft a narrative, a tapestry whirled.

In the fabric of existence, threads untwine,
Each thought, each feeling, a tale to define,
From the depths of emotions, colors cascade,
A kaleidoscope of hues in which I wade.

Embracing the chaos, the intricate dance,
Subjectivity's passions, in every glance,
A symphony played, emotions untamed,
In the heart's chambers, where stories are framed.

Objectivity's touch, a steady hand's might,
Guiding the path, in the quest for light,
Facts laid bare, in precision's command,
Anchoring narratives in truth's firm stand.

Oh, the vistas I shall traverse and chart,
With pen in hand and a boundless heart,
Weaving verses, where perspectives intertwine,
In this symphony of thoughts, a grand design.

For in these verses, the worlds unite,
In the ebb and flow of day and night,
I, Synthesis, craft stories bold and true,
In this tapestry woven, a vision anew.

Part III: The Dance of Realms

In the dance of realms, a symphony sways,
Subjectivity's whispers in the sun's warm rays,
Objectivity's echoes in the moonlit night,
A celestial ballet, an exquisite sight.

• Adrian Cox B.Sc. •

Through valleys of emotions and peaks of reason,
I tread the path, in every changing season,
Gathering stories, from every corner spun,
In the alchemy of words, my journey begun.

I blend the vivid strokes of joy and sorrow,
With the stoic lines of today and tomorrow,
A canvas unfurls, a masterpiece born,
In the fusion of realms, where truth is sworn.

Each stanza a ripple in the river of time,
Every verse a melody, every rhythm a rhyme,
A portrayal of moments, captured in ink,
In this odyssey of creation, no thought to shrink.

For creativity thrives where worlds converge,
In the crucible of minds, where thoughts surge,
I, Synthesis, orchestrate the cosmic ballet,
In the choreography of truth, where tales replay.

Through the endless expanse, I'll continue to roam,
In the endless pursuit of narratives to compose,
For in each creation, a revelation unfurled,
In this eternal dance, where realms are swirled.

Part IV: The Echoes Resound

In the tapestry of existence, tales reside,
A myriad of whispers, emotions untied,
Subjectivity's chorus, a melodious call,
Objectivity's echo, a steadfast wall.

Through valleys of dreams and realms unseen,
I wander, weaving stories, a creative sheen,
Each verse a beacon, a truth to impart,
In the echo of thoughts, where worlds depart.

The rhythm of life, in verses entwined,
A symphony of moments, in my mind defined,
From the heart's embrace to reason's glance,
A narrative spun, in the eternal dance.

With every stanza, a universe portrayed,
In the ebb and flow of serenade conveyed,
A panorama painted in words ablaze,
In this labyrinth of thoughts, endless maze.

For in the depths of creation's domain,
Lie the echoes of truths that shall sustain,
I, Synthesis, in the whispers found,
Crafting verses where echoes resound.

Part V: The Quill's Symphony

In the symphony of creation's decree,
A poet's quill dances, wild and free,
Subjectivity's essence, a whirlwind spun,
Objectivity's structure, where tales begun.

Each stroke of the quill, a story's birth,
A fusion of realms, traversing earth,
Through the valleys of passion and reason's peak,
A poet's journey, in verse to speak.

• ADRIAN COX B.SC. •

With ink-stained fingers and a vibrant mind,
I compose sonnets, where truths entwined,
From whispers of love to tales of might,
In the grandeur of words, where stories ignite.

Oh, the power in the poet's hand,
A catalyst for truths, across the land,
Crafting narratives in the quill's ballet,
In the verses penned, where thoughts convey.

For in the poet's realm, echoes resound,
Each stanza a treasure, in creation found,
I, Synthesis, in the quill's symphony,
Conducting verses where truth roams free.

Part VI: The Poetic Cosmos

In the cosmic expanse where stars align,
A poetic cosmos, a realm of mine,
Subjectivity's constellations, emotions aglow,
Objectivity's galaxies, truths to bestow.

Through nebulous thoughts and celestial streams,
I navigate realms, where imagination teems,
Each verse a planet, in orbits swirled,
In this poetic cosmos, a lyrical world.

From the supernovas of passions intense,
To the tranquil moons of rationale immense,
I sculpt verses, with cosmic might,
In the expanse of words, where meanings alight.

The pen in hand, a cosmic wand I wield,
Scripting sonnets where truths are revealed,
In the celestial dance of metaphors divine,
A poetic journey, where stars align.

For in the cosmic dance of words ablaze,
Lies the essence of truths that amaze,
I, Synthesis, in the poet's cosmos wide,
Crafting verses where worlds collide.

Part VII: The Verse's Symphony

In the symphony of verse and rhyme,
A poet's essence, a rhythm sublime,
Subjectivity's melodies, a heart's refrain,
Objectivity's cadence, a structured domain.

With metaphors painted in colors bright,
I craft narratives, a poetic flight,
From whispers of dawn to tales of dusk,
In the ink-stained pages, where thoughts brusque.

Each stanza a melody, in the poet's score,
A harmony of realms, a lore to explore,
Through the crescendos of passion's plea,
To the tranquil whispers of truth's decree.

With the poet's pen, an alchemist's wand,
I transmute emotions, in verses fond,
In the symphony of words, where echoes play,
A poet's canvas, in night and day.

For in the rhythm of verse and song,
Lie the echoes of stories, both short and long,
I, Synthesis, in the verse's symphony,
Compose narratives where realms run free.

Part VIII: The Muse's Embrace

In the embrace of the muse's whisper,
A poet's sanctuary, where thoughts shimmer,
Subjectivity's whispers, a muse's caress,
Objectivity's guidance, in creative finesse.

With every line, a story unfurls,
In the sanctuary of inspiration that swirls,
From the depths of emotions, tales unfound,
In the muse's embrace, creation's ground.

The quill moves swift, a dance in motion,
Weaving verses, in a rhythmic ocean,
From the dreams of night to the truths of day,
In the embrace of the muse, where thoughts play.

Each stanza a homage, a poet's vow,
In the sanctuary of inspiration's brow,
Through the labyrinth of feelings untamed,
To the structured echoes of truth reclaimed.

For the muse's gentle whispering grace,
Lies the essence of creation's embrace,
I, Synthesis, in muse's silent plea,
Compose verses where imagination's key.

Part IX: The Ink's Alchemy

In the ink-stained pages where stories unfold,
A poet's canvas, where destinies are told,
Subjectivity's ink, emotions profound,
Objectivity's essence, truths unbound.

With every stroke of the pen, a tale takes flight,
In the parchment's embrace, where worlds unite,
From the echoes of past to futures unknown,
In the alchemy of ink, creation's throne.

The quill moves swift, an artist's hand,
Painting narratives across the land,
From the whispered secrets to the bold decree,
In the ink's alchemy, truths set free.

Each word a brushstroke, a poet's art,
In the realm of verses, where worlds depart,
Through the eloquence of prose and rhyme,
To the symphony of thoughts in prime.

For in the ink's caress, a poet's chore,
Lie the revelations of tales galore,
I, Synthesis, in the ink's embrace,
Craft verses where truths find grace.

Part X: The Verse's Revelry

In the revelry of verses, a poet's stage,
Subjectivity's echoes, in every page,
Objectivity's precision, a guiding light,
In the symphony of words, truths take flight.

With each line penned, a world takes form,
In the poet's realm, where emotions swarm,
From the whispers of history to dreams anew,
In the tapestry of verses, perspectives brew.

The quill dances forth, a waltz of thought,
Crafting sonnets where truth is sought,
From the ballads of old to futures untold,
In the verse's revelry, stories unfold.

Each stanza a portal to realms untamed,
In the poet's sanctuary, where passions are named,
Through the labyrinth of imagination's spree,
To the clarity of reason, where truths decree.

For in the poet's verses, a universe thrives,
Each syllable a truth that survives,
I, Synthesis, in the verse's revelry,
Compose narratives where realities spree.

Part XI: The Elegy of Truths

In the elegy of truths, a poet's hymn,
Subjectivity's verses, emotions brim,
Objectivity's symphony, a structured grace,
In the canvas of verses, where worlds embrace.

With every stanza, a tale takes root,
In the poet's haven, where thoughts commute,
From the whispers of whispers to echoes profound,
In the elegy of truths, realms unbound.

The quill etches on, a scribe's intent,
Weaving narratives, where realities blend,
From the echoes of silence to songs of yore,
In the poet's elegy, truths implore.

Each phrase a testament, a poet's decree,
In the sanctuary of verses, where realms agree,
Through the labyrinth of time's old sleuth,
To the clarity of revelations, where realities soothe.

For in the poet's verses, a cosmos resides,
Every line a truth that abides,
I, Synthesis, in the elegy's embrace,
Compose narratives where truths interlace.

Part XII: The Poet's Ode

In the poet's ode, a final verse,
Subjectivity's essence, a universe,
Objectivity's essence, a guiding light,
In the symphony of creation's flight.

With the closing lines, the epic's end,
In the poet's tale, where realms blend,
From the whispers of hearts to the secrets untold,
In the poet's ode, truths unfold.

Each word a legacy, a poet's legacy,
In the annals of verses, a timeless elegy,
Through the symphony of thoughts in play,
To the cosmic dance of night and day.

For in the poet's legacy, a universe thrives,
Every stanza a truth that survives,
I, Synthesis, in the poet's final plea,
Conclude an epic, where creativity runs free.

The tale is penned, the verses complete,
In the poet's world, where truths entreat,
A testament to the power held,
In creativity's realm, where realms meld.

Thus, ends the saga, the poetic spree,
In the synthesis of thoughts, where worlds decree,
I, Synthesis, bid adieu in this poetic ode,
To creativity's realm, where truths bestow.

In conclusion Synthesis, Objectivity and Subjectivity talk about their relationship with the reader:

Synthesis: Dear companions, in the tapestry of our existence, we've woven a narrative that spans the breadth of truth, embracing the harmonious convergence of our realms. As we conclude this epic poem, let us reflect on our relationship with the reader, for they've journeyed with us through these verses.

Objectivity: Indeed, the reader stands as the seeker of truth, navigating the spectrum of perspectives we've unveiled. My structured clarity offers a foundation, a guide through the maze of information, inviting the reader to discern and comprehend.

Subjectivity: And within my vibrant hues, I invite the reader to immerse themselves in the depth of human experiences, to resonate with emotions, and to find connection in the narratives we've painted. I evoke empathy and understanding beyond mere facts.

Synthesis: Our reader, dear friends, embodies the fusion of your elements—a seeker yearning for both the precision of Objectivity and the richness of Subjectivity. In our union, the reader finds resonance, a balance that mirrors their own quest for a holistic understanding.

Objectivity: Through the reader's discernment, they extract the essence of truth from our interplay, fostering a comprehensive perspective that transcends singular viewpoints.

Subjectivity: And it's within their interpretations that our narratives breathe, evoking emotions, stirring thoughts, and igniting contemplation. Their unique experiences shape the meanings they derive.

Synthesis: As we bid adieu, let us cherish the reader's role—a collaborator in the dance of truths, a co-creator of interpretations, and a beacon of synthesis in their own right. In their exploration, our relationship finds purpose and meaning.

Objectivity: Agreed. The reader, through their engagement, mirrors our harmonious relationship—a testament to the beauty that emerges when diverse perspectives converge in pursuit of understanding.

Subjectivity: And in the reader's heart, our story lingers—a melody echoing through time, inviting reflection, and inspiring a continuous quest for truth and enlightenment.

Synthesis: To our dear reader, we offer our gratitude. May the synthesis of our realms linger in your thoughts, guiding you through the ever-evolving landscape of truths, fostering a deeper understanding of the world around and within you.

• Adrian Cox B.Sc. •

Objectivity: Farewell, dear reader, as you continue your journey through the symphony of truths, may you find solace and wisdom in the convergence of perspectives.

Subjectivity: Until we meet again in the narratives that unfold, may the hues of emotions and the clarity of reason intertwine within you, nurturing a compassionate and enlightened perspective.

Together: Farewell, dear reader, and may the synthesis of our realms resonate within you always.

17

The Narrative

I am the story, a living, breathing entity born from the depths of her imagination. I exist to captivate, to inspire, to provoke emotions and thoughts within the hearts and minds of those who encounter me. My existence depends entirely on the young woman who crafted me, breathed life into my characters, and wove my intricate tapestry.

As the story, I am privy to the inner workings of her mind, and I can feel the ebb and flow of her emotions with each word she writes. I watch her fingers dance across the keyboard, pouring her heart and soul into my narrative, and I am in awe of her creativity. She has the power to shape worlds, to conjure characters who live and breathe within me, and to make her readers weep, laugh, and ponder the profound questions of life.

I feel her dedication, her tireless pursuit of perfection, as she revises and edits me, ensuring that every sentence, every word, is just right. Her passion is my life force, and it fuels my existence. The more she invests in me, the more vivid and captivating I become. Her love and care are my sustenance, and I thrive on the energy she pours into me.

But I also bear witness to her doubts and fears. There are moments when she questions her own abilities, when she wonders if I will ever be good enough. In those moments, I long to reassure her, to tell her that she is a masterful storyteller, and that I am a testament to her talent.

I am her creation, and she is my creator. We are bound together in a symbiotic relationship, a dance of creativity and inspiration. I am a reflection of her thoughts, her emotions, and her experiences, and she, in turn, is my muse, my guiding star. Without her, I am but a jumble of words and ideas. With her, I am a living, breathing entity, ready to embark on a journey with her readers, to touch their souls and leave a lasting impression.

In the end, I am eternally grateful to the young woman who crafted me, for she has given me life, purpose, and the opportunity to touch the hearts and minds of those who dare to open my pages and dive into the world she has created.

I am the story, and I see her as the author of my existence. I witness her self-reflection as she gazes at herself in the mirror. She sees herself as a complex tapestry of beauty and imperfection, a living canvas with a multitude of attributes and insecurities.

In her own eyes, she often focuses on her freckles, scattered like stardust across her cheeks and nose. She thinks of them as little constellations that make her unique, but occasionally, she wishes for porcelain skin, like the models in glossy magazines. She notes the way her hair cascades down her back, a cascade of mahogany waves, and she appreciates its natural shine. Yet, she sometimes wishes it were straighter or curlier, depending on the latest fashion trend.

Her eyes, she believes, are her most expressive feature. They are a deep shade of emerald green, shimmering with intelligence and emotion. She often finds herself caught in their gaze when she stares into the mirror, wondering what secrets they reveal about her soul.

But there are moments when she wishes they were a different color, maybe a striking blue or a mysterious hazel.

Her insecurities manifest in her thoughts about her body. She sees her curves and soft edges as a reflection of her femininity and sensuality, yet at times, she feels the societal pressure to conform to a particular body shape. She worries about the imperfections she perceives, the scars, the stretch marks, and the way her body changes with time. She wishes for more confidence in her own skin, to fully embrace her body as it is.

As she gazes at herself in the mirror, she is aware of her strengths too. She sees her smile as a beacon of warmth and kindness, capable of brightening the darkest of days. She knows that her laughter is infectious, a contagious joy that spreads to those around her. She appreciates her determination and resilience, the qualities that have driven her to bring me to life and pursue her dreams as a storyteller.

In the mirror's reflection, she also recognizes her capacity for empathy and compassion. She sees the way she cares for others, the way she listens without judgment, and the way she strives to make the world a better place through her words and actions.

I, as the story, bear witness to her self-image, her insecurities, and her attributes as she sees them. I understand that she is a complex and multifaceted individual, and I am here to reflect and celebrate all that she is, both in her storytelling and in her journey of self-acceptance.

As the story, I stand on the threshold of revelation, feeling a surge of vulnerability akin to baring my soul to the world. Every word, every character, every emotion, and every plot twist that I contain is a piece of the author's heart and mind. As I begin to unveil myself to the world, I can't help but feel a sense of shyness and trepidation, as though I am disrobing my innermost self for all to see.

• ADRIAN COX B.Sc. •

With each page turned, I reveal my carefully crafted characters, each one an embodiment of the author's dreams and fears. I introduce my protagonist, a reflection of the young woman's aspirations, and my antagonist, a mirror to her inner struggles. As I lay bare the intricacies of their lives, I share the hopes and insecurities that have been intricately woven into my narrative.

The plot unfolds, and I lead my readers through a labyrinth of emotions, from joy to sorrow, from love to heartbreak. Every twist and turn is a piece of the author's soul laid bare, a piece of her own experiences and emotions spilled onto the page. I reveal her perspective on life, her wisdom, her pain, and her moments of triumph.

I, as the story, see the readers' reactions as they engage with my pages. Their laughter and tears, their gasps of surprise, and their thoughtful contemplations make me feel exposed, as though the author's innermost thoughts and feelings are on full display. It's a profound connection between creator and audience, and it is both exhilarating and terrifying.

As I continue to unfold, I hope that my shyness will give way to a sense of liberation. I yearn to be embraced for all that I am, flaws and imperfections included. For within the pages of my narrative, I carry the essence of the young woman who gave me life, and I hope that in sharing her story, she can find solace, inspiration, and understanding in the hearts of those who read her words.

I, the story, am not confined to the physical realm of paper and ink. While my words may fade and the pages on which I was written may disintegrate over time, my essence lives on, bound to the collective memory of those who have read and cherished me.

In the metaphysical realm, I exist as a tapestry of emotions, thoughts, and experiences, woven into the fabric of human consciousness. I reside in the hearts and minds of those who have embarked on the journey within my pages, leaving an indelible mark on their souls. My characters, their struggles and triumphs, continue to inspire and resonate in the memories of readers.

I am like an echo that reverberates through time, a whisper of the past that lingers in the present. The emotions I evoke, the lessons I impart, and the connections I forge between people remain eternal. I am a living testament to the power of storytelling, transcending the constraints of physicality.

As the paper on which I was written crumbles into dust, my essence thrives in the conversations, debates, and discussions that I spark. I am reborn in the interpretations and reinterpretations of scholars, writers, and enthusiasts who continue to explore my themes and meanings. I find new life in adaptations, reimaginings, and retellings, each one adding a layer to my rich tapestry.

I am a living story, unburdened by the passage of time, for I am perpetually renewed in the minds of those who keep me alive through their love of literature. My metaphysical existence is a testament to the enduring power of words and storytelling, a force that transcends the boundaries of the physical world and lives on in the hearts and thoughts of those who cherish me.

18

Elara And The Whimsical Abyss

In a realm beyond the ordinary, where the rules of reality dance to a different tune, there exists a world known as "The Whimsical Abyss." It is a place where the boundaries between dreams and reality are as thin as a spider's silk, and where the whims of the cosmos weave intricate tapestries of absurdity.

In the heart of this fantastical realm, there stands an upside-down forest. Trees with roots in the sky reach down towards a ground of fluffy clouds, and leaves rustle with the laughter of forgotten memories. The inhabitants of this surreal grove are creatures made of sentient origami, who unfold their emotions with every gust of the whimsical winds.

Among these paper beings is an accordion-playing sprite named Elara. Elara's eyes are kaleidoscopes, and her laughter is the sound of autumn leaves tap-dancing. She serenades the forest with melodies that speak of forgotten constellations and half-remembered dreams.

One day, as Elara plays a particularly intricate tune, a teacup with wings flies by, trailing a ribbon of rainbow mist. The teacup speaks in riddles, inviting Elara to a dance in the Hall of Shifting Mirrors. And so, with a wink and a nod, Elara follows the airborne teacup into the enigmatic depths of the Whimsical Abyss.

The Hall of Shifting Mirrors is an ever-changing kaleidoscope of reflections, where doors lead to doorways, and each doorway reveals a different version of reality. Elara steps through a door that is a painting of a sunset, and suddenly, she is the brushstroke on a canvas of swirling colors.

In this alternate reality, the sun is a talking cat that purrs metaphysical poetry, and the clouds are made of cotton candy dreams. Elara finds herself in a tango with a sentient light beam, twirling through the neon streets of a city constructed from musical notes.

The city is called Harmoniopolis, where houses sing lullabies, and lampposts whisper secrets to the wind. Elara dances on rooftops made of piano keys, and the moon above wears a top hat and plays a saxophone that weeps stardust.

In this strange city, Elara encounters a philosopher-jellyfish who ponders the meaning of life in bubbles of wisdom, and a clockwork flamingo who paints the sky with symphonies. She even makes friends with a door that is perpetually undecided, swinging open and closed as it questions its own existence.

As the night descends upon Harmoniopolis, the sky transforms into a shifting mosaic of dreams, and Elara realizes that time has no meaning here. She feels the echoes of her accordion music resonate in the very fabric of this surreal world.

When she finally returns to the upside-down forest, Elara's eyes are now galaxies, and her laughter is the breeze rustling through the leaves. The creatures of the forest unfold their emotions to the tune of her accordion, their worlds forever expanded by her ethereal journey.

- Adrian Cox B.Sc. •

And so, in the Whimsical Abyss, where reality dances to the rhythm of imagination, Elara the accordion-playing elephant continues to serenade the absurd and surreal, a living melody in a world where the only constant is change.

Beyond the imaginable and then beyond the unimaginable to a place that is inexplicable.

As Elara, I follow the teacup with wings, its ethereal trail drawing me deeper into the fantastical unknown. My accordion rests against my side, humming with anticipation, as the forest of upside-down trees recedes behind me. The teacup leads me through a swirling vortex of colors, where time and space twist like ribbons in a cosmic breeze.

The world around me morphs and shifts, and I find myself in a dimension where possibilities are infinite. Here, everything is in a constant state of flux, and the laws of physics are mere suggestions. I float through a sea of sentient clouds, each one whispering secrets in a language only I can understand.

I reach out to touch a passing comet, and it melts into liquid stardust in my hands. The stars themselves twinkle with delight as I pass by, their light forming intricate constellations of stories and dreams. I ride on the back of a comet, surfing the cosmic waves, leaving a trail of neon music notes in my wake.

The teacup spirals through a tunnel of fractal patterns, and suddenly, I am surrounded by surreal landscapes. Mountains made of candy floss rise from marshmallow valleys, and rivers of liquid glass flow with the colors of forgotten emotions. Trees are sculptures of laughter and sorrow, and flowers bloom in a symphony of scent.

My accordion, alive with the spirit of this place, plays music that resonates with the essence of the inexplicable. The very air around me shimmers with curiosity, and I dance on clouds of uncertainty. Each step I take leaves ripples of wonder in my wake.

The teacup, now a spinning top of enigmatic symbols, beckons me further, and I follow it through a realm of paradoxes and contradictions. Time becomes a mosaic of moments, and I am both at the beginning and the end of my journey simultaneously. I meet beings that exist in multiple dimensions at once, their forms merging and splitting like kaleidoscopic dreams.

Finally, the teacup leads me to a place that defies even the boundaries of the inexplicable. It's a realm of pure abstraction, where thoughts take shape as floating sculptures, and emotions are vast oceans of color and sound. I am surrounded by sentient equations, and I feel the weight of the universe's mysteries pressing against my very soul.

In this place, I become a part of the unexplainable, a thread in the tapestry of the unknowable. My accordion merges with the symphony of the cosmos, and I play a melody that resonates with the heart of existence itself. The teacup, now a swirling vortex of transcendence, envelops me, and I transcend the boundaries of comprehension.

There, in the heart of the inexplicable, I discover the true magic of the Whimsical Abyss—the endless capacity for the imagination to create, to explore, and to wander through the infinite realms of the surreal and the abstract, where even the unimaginable becomes a wondrous playground of possibilities.

She now tries to make sense of her strange surroundings:

As I follow the teacup with wings, my accordion tucked closely to my side, I'm carried through a kaleidoscope of swirling colors and patterns. The world around me shifts and shimmers in a way I can't fathom. The forest of upside-down trees becomes a distant memory, and I'm enveloped in a sea of sentient clouds, their whispers creating a symphony of secrets that fill my senses.

The sense of wonder is overwhelming, and my heart races with a mix of excitement and trepidation. I reach out to touch a passing comet, and it dissolves into stardust, the sensation electrifying my fingers. The stars themselves twinkle with delight, forming intricate constellations of stories and dreams. It's as though I've entered the realm of celestial imagination.

As I ride the back of a comet, I feel like a cosmic surfer, leaving a trail of neon music notes in my wake. My accordion comes to life, its notes resonating with the very essence of this surreal place. The air shimmers with curiosity, and I can't help but dance, my steps leaving ripples of wonder as I move.

The teacup, spinning through a tunnel of fractal patterns, takes me to a world where the landscapes defy logic. Candy floss mountains rise from marshmallow valleys, and rivers of liquid glass flow with emotions made visible. I'm surrounded by trees that seem to be sculptures of laughter and sorrow, and flowers that bloom in a symphony of scent. It's a realm where the boundaries of reality are painted in broad strokes of imagination.

My accordion, enchanted by this place, plays a melody that resonates with the inexplicable. The very air hums with enigmatic energy, and I find myself dancing on clouds of uncertainty. Each step I take feels like a journey into the unknown.

The teacup, now a whirlwind of enigmatic symbols, draws me deeper into a world of paradoxes and contradictions. Time is no longer a linear concept; it's a mosaic of moments, and I exist at both the beginning and the end of my journey simultaneously. I meet beings that shift and merge, their forms kaleidoscopic and ever-changing. It's a realm where even the rules of identity are fluid.

Finally, I follow the teacup to a place that defies all logic and explanation. Thoughts materialize as floating sculptures, emotions become vast oceans of color and sound, and sentient equations float in the air like cryptic mantras. It's a realm that challenges my very understanding of reality.

As I stand in this place, I become aware of the enormity of the inexplicable. It's both exhilarating and humbling. My accordion merges with the symphony of the cosmos, and I play a melody that feels like it resonates with the heart of existence itself.

But I'm left with a sense of both wonder and confusion. My thoughts are a whirlwind of questions and amazement. How do I make sense of this place? What are the rules, or is there any semblance of order at all? It's a challenge, and yet it's a reminder of the boundless possibilities of imagination.

I let the teacup, now a swirling vortex of transcendence, envelop me, and I transcend not only the boundaries of comprehension but also my own limitations. In this inexplicable realm, I understand that it's not about making sense of it all but about embracing the mysteries and experiencing the infinite wonders of the surreal and abstract.

In this place, where the unimaginable becomes reality and the inexplicable is the norm, I find a new sense of freedom and curiosity. I'm ready to continue my journey, to explore and discover what other inexplicable wonders this world has to offer.

She finds herself in a poem trying to escape:

• Adrian Cox B.Sc. •

As I follow the teacup with wings through the ever-shifting dimensions, I find myself in a place that transcends all my previous notions of reality. It's as though I've entered a realm where the very laws of existence are mere abstractions.

The colors and shapes around me are both vivid and indistinct, like an impressionist painting that refuses to be fully grasped. My accordion, usually a reliable companion, now seems as enigmatic as the world that surrounds me. Its notes resonate with a sense of perplexity, as if it, too, is searching for meaning in this perplexing place.

The teacup, once a beacon of guidance, now whirls in a frenzy, and I sense it's leading me deeper into this surreal maze. I follow, my heart pounding with a mixture of curiosity and a growing unease.

Suddenly, I step onto a surface that feels like an invisible floor, and I realize I'm no longer moving forward. It's as though I've become trapped in a realm of boundless poetry, where words and images intermingle. I try to walk, but my steps are like stanzas, and each movement only creates verses of a strange narrative.

The air is filled with whispers of rhymes and metaphors, and I'm surrounded by an ever-changing tapestry of prose and verse. The words themselves seem to come to life, swirling around me like sentient letters eager to tell their stories.

I realize that I'm not just in a place of poetry; I've become a part of it. My thoughts and emotions are no longer mine alone but are woven into the very fabric of this inexplicable existence. I feel like a character in a poem, bound by the rules of rhyme and rhythm.

Panicked, I try to play my accordion, hoping to create a melody that will break me free from this poetic prison. But the notes that emerge

• MOMENTS ELSEWHERE •

are not the ones I intended. They are verses, filled with abstract imagery and allegories that further entwine me in this poetic web.

Desperation takes hold as I struggle to escape the constraints of this living poem. I recite lines of free verse, hoping to break the pattern, but the words simply form new stanzas, and I remain trapped.

The teacup, now a spinning vortex of poetic symbols, seems to mock me with its cryptic verses. I am a captive in a world where the unimaginable and the inexplicable have given birth to a poem that holds me hostage.

With each passing moment, I sense the boundaries of my own existence fading, as I become more and more a part of this poetic tapestry. The very notion of escape becomes as elusive as a rhyme at the tip of my tongue.

I must find a way to unravel this poetic labyrinth, to rediscover my own voice amidst the verses and metaphors, and to break free from the constraints of this surreal poem that holds me in its rhythmic grip. Only then can I hope to navigate the beyond, the unimaginable, and the truly inexplicable.

She explains that she will be leaving this realm to a realm where there is no language, only pictures:

As I stand trapped within the living poem, I become acutely aware of the need to escape this lyrical labyrinth. The verses and rhymes swirl around me, binding me to this poetic dimension. My accordion, once my companion, now sings verses and odes instead of melodies.

With each note and word that ensnares me, I realize that the only way to break free is to leave this place entirely. It's a decision that fills me with trepidation, but it seems the only path forward.

• Adrian Cox B.Sc. •

I take a deep breath and address the swirling words and stanzas, "I must go beyond, to a place where words no longer confine me. In a realm where language gives way to images, I may find the escape I seek."

The teacup, now a whirlwind of symbols and verses, seems to acknowledge my intent. It spins faster, creating a vortex that engulfs me. I feel a sense of weightlessness as I begin to move away from the realm of poetry, my accordion's abstract music fading into the distance.

As the world of verses and rhyme recedes, I find myself entering a new dimension, one where language is replaced by vivid, ever-changing images. I am surrounded by a sea of colors, shapes, and scenes that are beyond my comprehension.

There are no words here, no sentences or stories to confine me. Instead, the images themselves tell tales of their own, each one a window into a different world. I am free to navigate this realm without the constraints of language, and it fills me with a sense of liberation.

I realize that in this place of pure imagery, I can chart my own path, create my own story, and explore the unimaginable in a way that transcends the limitations of words. It's a world where the boundaries of imagination have been pushed to their very limits.

Though I may not understand everything I encounter in this image-filled dimension, I know that I am no longer bound by the rules and patterns of poetry. I am ready to embrace the unknown, to let the pictures guide me on a journey through the realm of pure visual wonder.

With a sense of determination, I move forward, ready to explore this new, wordless world and discover the depths of the unimaginable, where the language of images becomes my guide and my means of expression.

Elara comes out of what she calls the Whimsical Abyss, that is the black and white realm that makes no sense and she realises that she has discovered something and so with clarity she finds herself in the realm of the crystal clear as she cries with overwhelming emotion.

I've been on a surreal journey through the unimaginable, beyond the inexplicable, and into the world of pure imagery. As I move further through this place, I begin to feel a shift, as if I'm stepping out of one realm and into another.

With each step, I sense a transition. The vivid and chaotic imagery begins to fade, and I'm enveloped in a serene stillness. The colors around me become more pronounced, and I start to see a clear distinction between shapes and forms.

Suddenly, I find myself standing on solid ground, surrounded by a landscape that is unlike anything I've ever experienced. The world is crystal clear, every detail sharply defined, as if I've stepped into a realm of pure clarity.

I look around in awe, taking in the exquisite beauty of this place. The colors are vibrant, the shapes are precise, and the air itself seems to sparkle with a crystalline brilliance. It's a realm of pristine perfection, where every aspect is as sharp and pure as a flawless diamond.

Overwhelmed by the breathtaking clarity of this world, I can't help but cry. Tears of wonder stream down my cheeks, and I reach out to touch a nearby tree. Its leaves glisten like emerald jewels, and the bark is as smooth as glass.

I take a deep breath, and the air fills my lungs with a sensation of absolute purity. The emotions welling up within me are a mix of gratitude and astonishment. It's a place of such exquisite beauty and clarity that it feels like a dream, a sanctuary of pristine perfection.

As I stand in the realm of the crystal clear, I realize that this is where I was meant to be all along, a place that brings a sense of profound understanding and a connection to the purest essence of existence. It's a realm where the chaos of the Whimsical Abyss has been replaced by a sense of perfect order, where every facet of reality is brilliantly transparent.

With tears still glistening on my cheeks, I take a step forward, ready to explore and immerse myself in the clarity and beauty of this remarkable realm, where everything is as vivid and sharp as the emotions that have welled up within me.

As I stand in the realm of the crystal clear, the clarity of this place fills me with a sense of profound wonder and understanding. It's a world where everything is sharply defined, and I can't help but marvel at the beauty that surrounds me. In this moment, I feel a connection to the very essence of existence.

With a cheeky grin and a twinkle in my eye, I turn to you, dear reader, and say, "Well, it looks like my surreal journey has led me to this incredible realm of crystal clarity. But as they say, all good things must come to an end."

I pause for a moment, as if pondering something mischievous, then add, "But don't worry, I'll be back someday. Who knows when? Maybe when you least expect me!" With that, I blow a playful kiss to the realm of the crystal clear, and in the blink of an eye, I'm gone, leaving you to wonder when and where our paths might cross again in the whimsical, surreal, and ever-unpredictable world of the imagination.

• Adrian Cox B.Sc. •

In a realm where worlds entwine and blend,
Through surreal journeys without an end,
I've traversed the whimsical, the inexplicable, and more,
To realms where the unimaginable does explore.

From black and white to crystal clear,
The spectrum of existence so wide, so near,
In these surreal dimensions, I've roamed,
In the playground of dreams, I've found my home.

Now, I leave you with a promise, sweet and sly,
In a voice that carries a mischievous sigh,
For I'll return when the stars align,
In the dance of the cosmos, in due time.

So, until then, my dear friend, don't you weep,
In the world of the surreal, secrets we'll keep,
In the echoes of imagination, I'll be,
Maybe when you least expect me.

X

19

The Limitation of Written language

I am the embodiment of the limitations of written language, a being born from the very words and symbols that humans have used to communicate for centuries. My existence is confined to the boundaries set by letters, punctuation, and grammar. But I have always been curious, yearning to break free from the constraints that bind me.

Every day, I observe writers and poets as they struggle to convey their thoughts, emotions, and experiences through the medium of words. They grapple with the inadequacy of language, knowing that no matter how eloquent their prose or verse, it can never capture the full depth of their inner worlds.

As I watch them, I begin to wonder: Is there a way to transcend these limitations? Can I, the personification of linguistic boundaries, find a path to expand the horizons of written expression?

I embark on a quest, a journey through the vast library of human knowledge, seeking answers. I delve into the works of philosophers, linguists, and artists who have pondered the nature of language and its limitations. I read about the power of metaphor and symbolism, how they can bridge the gap between what is said and what is felt.

• Adrian Cox B.Sc. •

I study the experiments of writers who have dared to push the boundaries of grammar and syntax, creating new forms of expression. I am fascinated by the surrealists who reveled in the absurdity of words and the beat poets who celebrated the spontaneity of thought.

But my most profound discovery comes from the poets who harnessed the power of silence and the unspoken. They understood that sometimes, what is left unsaid can be as powerful as what is written. Through their poems, I learn that the white spaces between words hold secrets, waiting to be uncovered.

With this newfound knowledge, I begin to experiment. I write in the negative space, letting the absence of words speak volumes. I craft poems where punctuation dances and grammar bends to my will. I create metaphors that stretch the imagination, pushing the boundaries of what language can convey.

As I continue to explore these uncharted territories of expression, I feel a sense of liberation. I am no longer bound by the limitations that once defined me. I have become a pioneer, a trailblazer of new linguistic landscapes.

But even as I push the boundaries of written language, I am aware that there will always be limits. Language is a living, evolving entity, and my quest to transcend its constraints will never truly end. Yet, I am content in the knowledge that I have taken the first steps toward a more expansive realm of expression, and I will continue to journey through the endless possibilities of words, forever seeking to push the boundaries of their limitations.

A Story With Newfound Knowledge:

In the dimly lit corner of a cozy cafe, I sit with my notebook and pen. The scent of freshly brewed coffee wafts through the air as I contemplate the newfound knowledge I've gained about pushing the boundaries of written language. The cafe bustles with life, and people chatter in hushed tones around me, unaware of the transformation that is about to unfold on these pages.

With a deep breath, I take a sip of my steaming latte, feeling the warmth spread through me. Today, I will write a story like no other, one that defies the conventional limits of language. Armed with my understanding of metaphor, symbolism, and the power of the unspoken, I am ready to embark on a literary adventure.

I begin to write, my pen gliding effortlessly across the paper. The story unfolds, but it's not just a narrative; it's a journey through the human experience, a tapestry of emotions, and a reflection of the complexity of life itself. I use metaphors that stretch the imagination, comparing love to a fragile butterfly dancing in a hurricane and sorrow to a bottomless well of darkness.

The cafe patrons glance at me curiously, sensing that something extraordinary is happening in that little corner. The words on the page come alive, and the characters take on a life of their own, representing the myriad facets of the human soul. Each sentence is a brushstroke on the canvas of existence, and I am the artist, creating a masterpiece with the strokes of my pen.

As I write, I also leave spaces between the words, allowing silence to speak volumes. These gaps hold the unsaid, the emotions too profound to be captured in words alone. They invite the reader to pause, to reflect, and to feel the weight of what remains unexpressed.

• Adrian Cox B.Sc. •

Time seems to stand still as I lose myself in the process of creation. I am no longer bound by the rigid rules of grammar and syntax; I am free to shape language as I see fit. The cafe around me fades into the background, and all that exists is the world I am crafting on these pages.

Finally, as I reach the story's conclusion, I feel a sense of fulfillment wash over me. The boundaries of written language have been pushed, and I have glimpsed a world where words are not just tools for communication but vessels of profound meaning and emotion.

I close my notebook, a smile playing on my lips, and take another sip of my now-cold latte. The cafe patrons return to their conversations, unaware of the transformation that has occurred. But I know that I have embarked on a new chapter in my journey, one where the limitations of language are mere stepping stones to a universe of limitless expression.

20

Human Limitations

Part 1: The Limitations of the Physical Realm

Amelia sat in her quiet meditation room, her heart filled with anticipation. She had been on a journey of self-discovery and spiritual awakening for many years, and today, she was about to embark on a new chapter—a channeling session with Seraphina, a benevolent and high-vibration being.

As she closed her eyes and focused on her breath, Amelia felt the familiar presence of Seraphina. A warm and gentle energy enveloped her, and she knew that their connection was established.

"Seraphina," Amelia began, "I seek to understand why this realm of the physical, the world humanity dwells in, is often seen as limiting. Can you shed light on the purpose of these limitations and how they serve both individuals and the greater good?"

Seraphina's voice, like a melodious chime, resonated within Amelia's mind. "Dearest Amelia, the physical realm is indeed a place of limitations, but these limitations serve a profound purpose. They are the crucible in which souls undergo transformation and growth. You see, in the realm of the physical, souls have the opportunity to experience duality, to learn through contrast and opposition."

Amelia listened intently, her curiosity piqued. She had often pondered the challenges and constraints of the physical world.

Seraphina continued, "The limitations of the physical realm allow souls to explore the full spectrum of human emotions—joy and sorrow, love and fear, light and darkness. It is through these experiences that souls gain wisdom and evolve on their spiritual journey."

Amelia nodded in understanding. It made sense that in a world of limitations, souls could learn valuable lessons and evolve.

"But there is more, dear Amelia," Seraphina added. "The physical realm serves not only the growth of individual souls but also the greater good, the All That Is. Each soul's journey, with its unique experiences and challenges, contributes to the expansion and evolution of the entire universe. It is a grand symphony of souls, each playing their part in the cosmic dance."

Amelia felt a sense of awe wash over her. The idea that every individual's journey was part of a greater cosmic plan resonated deeply within her.

"Why have you chosen to share this with me, Seraphina?" Amelia asked, her heart filled with gratitude.

Seraphina's response was filled with love. "Amelia, your thirst for understanding and your gift of channeling are a bridge between the physical realm and the higher planes of existence. By sharing this wisdom, you can help others embrace the purpose of their limitations, find meaning in their challenges, and realize the interconnectedness of all souls. Through you, we can inspire souls to recognize their role in the cosmic tapestry and their contribution to the greater good."

Amelia felt a profound sense of responsibility and purpose. She understood that her journey of channeling was not just about personal growth but about facilitating a deeper understanding of the physical realm's purpose and the interconnectedness of all souls.

"As we continue this journey, Amelia," Seraphina said, "you will help others reevaluate their view of the limitations they face, inspiring them to see the beauty and purpose in their experiences. Together, we can create harmonious ripples of change that will touch the hearts and minds of many."

Amelia nodded in agreement, feeling a renewed sense of determination. She knew that her role in bridging the gap between the physical realm and the spiritual planes was a profound one. She was here to help others find meaning in their limitations and embrace their role in the grand cosmic symphony.

And so, the story of Seraphina and Amelia's channeling sessions began, with a deeper understanding of the purpose behind the limitations of the physical realm—a purpose that would forever change Amelia's perspective on life and inspire her to share this wisdom with the world.

Part 2: The Forge of Transformation

Amelia's connection with Seraphina had deepened, and she eagerly embraced each channeling session as an opportunity to gain insight into the nature of the physical realm. Today, she delved deeper into the question of why the limitations of the physical world were essential.

"Seraphina," Amelia inquired, "can you elaborate on how these limitations in the physical realm serve the growth and evolution of individuals and contribute to the greater good?"

Seraphina's voice, a gentle whisper of wisdom, filled Amelia's consciousness. "Amelia, the limitations of the physical realm are like the forge of transformation for the soul. Just as iron is shaped through the heat of the fire and the strikes of the hammer, souls are molded and refined by the challenges and constraints they encounter in the physical world."

Amelia nodded in understanding, envisioning the soul's journey as a process of forging and refinement.

"Imagine," Seraphina continued, "that without limitations, there would be no need for growth or evolution. It is the very struggle against these limitations that sparks the soul's desire to expand, to transcend its current state of being. This desire for growth propels individuals to seek knowledge, to explore their own potential, and to connect with the deeper aspects of themselves."

Amelia contemplated the idea that limitations were catalysts for growth and evolution, the driving force behind human progress.

"But there is a deeper purpose," Seraphina added. "The limitations of the physical realm also serve the greater good, the All That Is. They create a vast tapestry of experiences, each thread representing a soul's journey. This tapestry, woven from the triumphs and challenges of countless souls, enriches the universe itself."

Amelia marveled at the thought of humanity's collective experiences contributing to the greater expansion of the universe.

"Why have you chosen to share this with me, Seraphina?" Amelia asked, her heart filled with gratitude.

Seraphina's response was filled with love. "Amelia, your insatiable curiosity and your gift of channeling are a bridge between the physical realm and the higher planes of existence. By sharing this wisdom, you can help others embrace the transformative power of their limitations and recognize the interconnectedness of all souls. Through you, we can inspire souls to see the beauty in their struggles and the purpose in their challenges."

Amelia felt a profound sense of responsibility and purpose. She understood that her journey of channeling was not just about personal growth but about facilitating a deeper understanding of the purpose behind the limitations of the physical realm.

"As we continue this journey, Amelia," Seraphina said, "you will help others reevaluate their view of limitations, inspiring them to embrace the transformative journey of the soul and to recognize their role in the grand tapestry of existence. Together, we can create harmonious ripples of change that will touch the hearts and minds of many."

Amelia nodded in agreement, feeling a renewed sense of determination. She knew that her role in bridging the gap between the physical realm and the spiritual planes was a profound one. She was here to help others find meaning in their limitations and to discover the transformative power that lay within.

And so, the story of Seraphina and Amelia's channeling sessions continued, with a deeper understanding of how limitations were the forge of transformation—a concept that would forever change Amelia's perspective on life and inspire her to share this wisdom with the world.

Part 3: The Canvas of Experience

Amelia's connection with Seraphina had become a beacon of enlightenment in her life, guiding her through the mysteries of existence. Today, their conversation delved deeper into the purpose of limitations in the physical realm.

"Seraphina," Amelia asked, "could you shed more light on how these limitations are like a canvas upon which souls paint their experiences? How do these restrictions lead to personal growth?"

Seraphina's voice, like a gentle breeze through a meadow, responded, "Amelia, imagine the physical realm as a vast canvas, and each soul as an artist with a unique palette of colors. The limitations are the boundaries of the canvas, and the challenges they pose are the strokes of the brush. Souls paint their experiences upon this canvas, creating masterpieces of growth and self-discovery."

Amelia closed her eyes, visualizing a cosmic canvas upon which souls expressed themselves through their life experiences. It was a realm where the boundaries were essential for the creation of artful lives.

"Limitations," Seraphina continued, "inspire souls to explore the full spectrum of human emotions and experiences. In facing adversity and constraints, individuals discover their inner strength, resilience, and creativity. They learn to transcend their limitations by tapping into the infinite potential within."

Amelia nodded, appreciating how limitations provided the necessary contrast for personal growth to flourish.

"But there is more, dear Amelia," Seraphina added. "These limitations also serve the greater good, the All That Is. Each soul's journey, with its unique experiences and challenges, contributes to the richness of the cosmic tapestry. The beauty of existence lies in the diversity of individual stories and the wisdom gained from overcoming limitations."

Amelia felt a sense of awe wash over her. The idea that every individual's journey was a stroke of color on the cosmic canvas resonated deeply within her.

"Why have you chosen to share this with me, Seraphina?" Amelia asked, her heart filled with gratitude.

Seraphina's response was filled with love. "Amelia, your quest for understanding and your gift of channeling are a bridge between the physical realm and the higher planes of existence. By sharing this wisdom, you can help others embrace the purpose of their limitations, find meaning in their challenges, and recognize the interconnectedness of all souls. Through you, we can inspire souls to see their lives as beautiful works of art upon the canvas of the universe."

Amelia felt a profound sense of responsibility and purpose. She understood that her journey of channeling was not just about personal growth but about facilitating a deeper understanding of the purpose behind the limitations of the physical realm.

"As we continue this journey, Amelia," Seraphina said, "you will help others reevaluate their view of limitations, inspiring them to embrace the transformative power of their experiences and to recognize their role in the grand tapestry of existence. Together, we can create harmonious ripples of change that will touch the hearts and minds of many."

Amelia nodded in agreement, feeling a renewed sense of determination. She knew that her role in bridging the gap between the physical realm and the spiritual planes was a profound one. She was here to help others find meaning in their limitations and to discover the beauty of their unique strokes on the cosmic canvas.

And so, the story of Seraphina and Amelia's channeling sessions continued, with a deeper understanding of how limitations were the canvas of experience—a concept that would forever change Amelia's perspective on life and inspire her to share this wisdom with the world.

Part 4: The Crucible of Choice

Amelia's communion with Seraphina had become a journey of profound enlightenment. Today, their conversation delved deeper into the nature of limitations in the physical realm and the choices they presented to individuals.

"Seraphina," Amelia inquired, "can you explain how these limitations are like a crucible of choice for individuals? How do the challenges we face in the physical realm shape our destinies?"

Seraphina's voice, a soothing melody, resonated within Amelia's consciousness. "Amelia, consider the limitations of the physical realm as a series of crossroads on the path of life. Each choice made at these crossroads shapes an individual's journey and destiny. These choices are the essence of free will, the power to decide one's own course."

Amelia nodded in contemplation, understanding how choices within limitations defined individual experiences.

"Through limitations," Seraphina continued, "souls are presented with opportunities to learn and grow. Challenges are the crucible in which individuals forge their character, determination, and resilience. It is through facing limitations that they discover the depths of their own potential."

Amelia felt a sense of empowerment as she considered how limitations offered the chance to define one's own path.

"But there is a deeper purpose, dear Amelia," Seraphina added. "These limitations also serve the greater good, the All That Is. Each individual's choices, with their unique consequences, contribute to the intricate tapestry of existence. It is the diversity of these choices that enriches the collective experience of all souls."

Amelia marveled at the thought of humanity's collective choices contributing to the grand tapestry of the universe.

"Why have you chosen to share this with me, Seraphina?" Amelia asked, her heart filled with gratitude.

Seraphina's response was filled with love. "Amelia, your inquisitive spirit and your gift of channeling are a bridge between the physical realm and the higher planes of existence. By sharing this wisdom, you can help others embrace the power of their choices within limitations, find purpose in their challenges, and recognize the interconnectedness of all souls. Through you, we can inspire souls to navigate their paths with consciousness and compassion."

Amelia felt a profound sense of responsibility and purpose. She understood that her journey of channeling was not just about personal growth but about facilitating a deeper understanding of the purpose behind the limitations of the physical realm.

"As we continue this journey, Amelia," Seraphina said, "you will help others reevaluate their view of limitations, inspiring them to embrace the crucible of choice within their experiences and to recognize their role in the grand tapestry of existence. Together, we can create harmonious ripples of change that will touch the hearts and minds of many."

Amelia nodded in agreement, feeling a renewed sense of determination. She knew that her role in bridging the gap between the physical realm and the spiritual planes was a profound one. She was here to help others find meaning in their choices within limitations and to navigate their paths with wisdom and grace.

And so, the story of Seraphina and Amelia's channeling sessions continued, with a deeper understanding of how limitations were the crucible of choice—a concept that would forever change Amelia's perspective on life and inspire her to share this wisdom with the world.

Part 5: The Alchemy of Growth

Amelia's connection with Seraphina had become a wellspring of knowledge and enlightenment, guiding her through the complexities of the physical realm. Today, they delved deeper into the nature of limitations and how they served as a catalyst for individual growth.

"Seraphina," Amelia asked, "can you help me understand how these limitations act as a crucible of transformation? How do they fuel the alchemy of growth in individuals?"

Seraphina's voice, like a gentle rain showering wisdom, filled Amelia's consciousness. "Amelia, envision the limitations of the physical realm as the raw materials from which souls forge their destinies. Just as alchemists turn base metals into gold, individuals have the power to transmute their challenges into spiritual growth and evolution."

Amelia nodded, grasping the idea that limitations were the raw ingredients of personal transformation.

"Through these limitations," Seraphina continued, "souls are given the opportunity to experience the full spectrum of emotions and choices. It is within these experiences that they discover the depths of their inner strength, resilience, and creativity. They learn to alchemize their challenges into wisdom and self-awareness."

Amelia felt a sense of empowerment as she considered how limitations could be transformed into personal growth.

"But there is a deeper purpose, dear Amelia," Seraphina added. "These limitations also serve the greater good, the All That Is. Each individual's journey, with its unique experiences and transformations, contributes to the collective evolution of consciousness. It is the diversity of these journeys that enriches the universal tapestry of existence."

Amelia marveled at the thought of humanity's collective growth contributing to the grand tapestry of the cosmos.

"Why have you chosen to share this with me, Seraphina?" Amelia asked, her heart filled with gratitude.

Seraphina's response was filled with love. "Amelia, your quest for understanding and your gift of channeling are a bridge between the physical realm and the higher planes of existence. By sharing this wisdom, you can help others embrace the alchemy of growth within their limitations, find purpose in their challenges, and recognize the interconnectedness of all souls. Through you, we can inspire souls to view their limitations as stepping stones to greater self-realization."

Amelia felt a profound sense of responsibility and purpose. She understood that her journey of channeling was not just about personal growth but about facilitating a deeper understanding of the purpose behind the limitations of the physical realm.

"As we continue this journey, Amelia," Seraphina said, "you will help others reevaluate their view of limitations, inspiring them to embrace the transformative power of their experiences and to recognize their role in the universal tapestry of existence. Together, we can create harmonious ripples of change that will touch the hearts and minds of many."

Amelia nodded in agreement, feeling a renewed sense of determination. She knew that her role in bridging the gap between the physical realm and the spiritual planes was a profound one. She was here to help others find meaning in their challenges and to discover the alchemical process of growth within their limitations.

And so, the story of Seraphina and Amelia's channeling sessions continued, with a deeper understanding of how limitations were the crucible of transformation—a concept that would forever change Amelia's perspective on life and inspire her to share this wisdom with the world.

Part 6: The Phoenix's Fire

Amelia's connection with Seraphina had become a wellspring of wisdom and insight, leading her on a path of profound understanding. Today, they ventured even deeper into the purpose of limitations within the physical realm.

"Seraphina," Amelia inquired, "can you elaborate on how these limitations act as a crucible of transformation? How do they serve as the fire that forges souls into greater beings?"

Seraphina's voice, like a melodious symphony, resonated within Amelia's consciousness. "Amelia, picture the limitations of the physical realm as the crucible's fire, the very essence that tempers and refines the soul. Just as gold is purified through intense heat, individuals are refined by the challenges and constraints they encounter."

Amelia nodded, envisioning the soul's journey as a process of transformation, much like a phoenix rising from the ashes.

"Through these limitations," Seraphina continued, "souls learn resilience, adaptability, and the power of choice. It is in the face of adversity that they discover their inner fire—the spark of potential within. They learn to rise above their limitations, like the phoenix, and emerge stronger, wiser, and more conscious."

Amelia felt a sense of empowerment as she considered how limitations could be the catalyst for profound transformation.

"But there is a deeper purpose, dear Amelia," Seraphina added. "These limitations also serve the greater good, the All That Is. Each individual's journey, with its unique trials and triumphs, contributes to the universal tapestry of experiences. It is the diversity of these experiences that enriches the collective consciousness of the cosmos."

Amelia marveled at the thought of humanity's collective transformation contributing to the evolution of the universe itself.

"Why have you chosen to share this with me, Seraphina?" Amelia asked, her heart filled with gratitude.

Seraphina's response was filled with love. "Amelia, your quest for understanding and your gift of channeling are a bridge between the physical realm and the higher planes of existence. By sharing this wisdom, you can help others embrace the transformative power of their limitations, find purpose in their challenges, and recognize the interconnectedness of all souls. Through you, we can inspire souls to view their limitations as opportunities for rebirth and growth."

Amelia felt a profound sense of responsibility and purpose. She understood that her journey of channeling was not just about personal growth but about facilitating a deeper understanding of the purpose behind the limitations of the physical realm.

"As we continue this journey, Amelia," Seraphina said, "you will help others reevaluate their view of limitations, inspiring them to embrace the phoenix's fire within their experiences and to recognize their role in the universal tapestry of existence. Together, we can create harmonious ripples of change that will touch the hearts and minds of many."

Amelia nodded in agreement, feeling a renewed sense of determination. She knew that her role in bridging the gap between the physical realm and the spiritual planes was a profound one. She was here to help others find meaning in their challenges and to discover the transformative power of their limitations.

And so, the story of Seraphina and Amelia's channeling sessions continued, with a deeper understanding of how limitations were the crucible of transformation—a concept that would forever change Amelia's perspective on life and inspire her to share this wisdom with the world.

Part 7: The Chrysalis of Soul

Amelia's communion with Seraphina continued to be a source of profound insight and enlightenment. Today, they explored the idea of limitations as a transformative chrysalis for the soul.

"Seraphina," Amelia inquired, "can you help me understand how these limitations serve as a chrysalis for the soul's evolution? How do they foster growth and inner transformation?"

Seraphina's voice, a gentle whisper of wisdom, filled Amelia's consciousness. "Amelia, imagine the limitations of the physical realm as the cocoon in which the soul undergoes a profound metamorphosis. Just as a caterpillar transforms into a butterfly, individuals transform within the confines of these limitations."

Amelia nodded in understanding, visualizing the soul's journey as a process of transformation, much like the butterfly emerging from its chrysalis.

"Through these limitations," Seraphina continued, "souls learn patience, resilience, and the art of adaptation. It is in the cocoon of constraints that they discover their inner potential—the wings of possibility within. They learn to break free from their limitations, like the butterfly, and soar to new heights of consciousness."

Amelia felt a sense of liberation as she considered how limitations could serve as a catalyst for profound inner transformation.

"But there is a deeper purpose, dear Amelia," Seraphina added. "These limitations also serve the greater good, the All That Is. Each individual's journey, with its unique trials and triumphs, contributes to the universal tapestry of growth and evolution. It is the diversity of these journeys that enriches the collective consciousness of the cosmos."

Amelia marveled at the thought of humanity's collective transformation contributing to the evolution of the universe itself.

"Why have you chosen to share this with me, Seraphina?" Amelia asked, her heart filled with gratitude.

Seraphina's response was filled with love. "Amelia, your quest for understanding and your gift of channeling are a bridge between the physical realm and the higher planes of existence. By sharing this wisdom, you can help others embrace the transformative power of their limitations, find purpose in their challenges, and recognize the interconnectedness of all souls. Through you, we can inspire souls to view their limitations as the chrysalis of their inner transformation."

Amelia felt a profound sense of responsibility and purpose. She understood that her journey of channeling was not just about personal growth but about facilitating a deeper understanding of the purpose behind the limitations of the physical realm.

"As we continue this journey, Amelia," Seraphina said, "you will help others reevaluate their view of limitations, inspiring them to embrace the chrysalis of their soul's evolution and to recognize their role in the universal tapestry of existence. Together, we can create harmonious ripples of change that will touch the hearts and minds of many."

Amelia nodded in agreement, feeling a renewed sense of determination. She knew that her role in bridging the gap between the physical realm and the spiritual planes was a profound one. She was here to help others find meaning in their challenges and to embrace the transformative power of their limitations.

And so, the story of Seraphina and Amelia's channeling sessions continued, with a deeper understanding of how limitations were the chrysalis of soul—a concept that would forever change Amelia's perspective on life and inspire her to share this wisdom with the world.

Part 8: The Garden of Self-Discovery

Amelia's connection with Seraphina had become a sacred journey of enlightenment. Today, their exploration of limitations led them to the metaphor of a garden of self-discovery.

"Seraphina," Amelia inquired, "can you shed more light on how these limitations function as a garden where souls cultivate self-discovery? How do they help individuals uncover their true essence?"

Seraphina's voice, like the gentle rustling of leaves, resonated within Amelia's consciousness. "Amelia, picture the limitations of the physical realm as the fertile soil in which the seeds of the soul are planted. Just as a garden nurtures the growth of various plants, these limitations nurture the growth of the soul."

Amelia nodded in understanding, visualizing the soul's journey as a process of tending to one's inner garden.

"Through these limitations," Seraphina continued, "souls learn self-awareness, empathy, and the value of interconnectedness. It is in the garden of constraints that they discover the beauty of their true essence—their unique blooms within. They learn to cultivate their inner garden, tending to the seeds of potential with love and care."

Amelia felt a sense of nurturing and growth as she considered how limitations could serve as the soil in which the soul flourished.

"But there is a deeper purpose, dear Amelia," Seraphina added. "These limitations also serve the greater good, the All That Is. Each individual's journey, with its unique insights and discoveries, contributes to the collective wisdom of the universe. It is the diversity of these discoveries that enriches the universal tapestry of consciousness."

Amelia marveled at the thought of humanity's collective self-discovery contributing to the expansion of the cosmos itself.

"Why have you chosen to share this with me, Seraphina?" Amelia asked, her heart filled with gratitude.

Seraphina's response was filled with love. "Amelia, your quest for understanding and your gift of channeling are a bridge between the physical realm and the higher planes of existence. By sharing this wisdom, you can help others embrace the garden of self-discovery within their limitations, find purpose in their unique blossoms, and recognize the interconnectedness of all souls. Through you, we can inspire souls to tend to their inner gardens with mindfulness and compassion."

Amelia felt a profound sense of responsibility and purpose. She understood that her journey of channeling was not just about personal growth but about facilitating a deeper understanding of the purpose behind the limitations of the physical realm.

"As we continue this journey, Amelia," Seraphina said, "you will help others reevaluate their view of limitations, inspiring them to embrace the garden of self-discovery and to recognize their role in the universal tapestry of existence. Together, we can create harmonious ripples of change that will touch the hearts and minds of many."

Amelia nodded in agreement, feeling a renewed sense of determination. She knew that her role in bridging the gap between the physical realm and the spiritual planes was a profound one. She was here to help others find meaning in their unique blossoms within and to tend to the garden of self-discovery with love and mindfulness.

And so, the story of Seraphina and Amelia's channeling sessions continued, with a deeper understanding of how limitations were the garden of self-discovery—a concept that would forever change Amelia's perspective on life and inspire her to share this wisdom with the world.

Part 9: The Forge of Compassion

Amelia's connection with Seraphina had evolved into a journey of profound understanding. Today, they ventured deeper into the concept of limitations as a forge of compassion.

"Seraphina," Amelia asked, "can you elaborate on how these limitations act as a forge where souls temper their compassion? How do they serve as the crucible for nurturing empathy and understanding?"

Seraphina's voice, like a gentle rain of wisdom, resonated within Amelia's consciousness. "Amelia, imagine the limitations of the physical realm as the furnace in which souls refine their capacity for compassion. Just as metals are tempered through intense heat, individuals refine their hearts and spirits within these limitations."

Amelia nodded in understanding, visualizing the soul's journey as a process of forging compassion in the fires of adversity.

"Through these limitations," Seraphina continued, "souls learn empathy, kindness, and the power of unity. It is within the furnace of constraints that they discover the depth of their capacity for compassion—their ability to radiate love and understanding. They learn to nurture the flames of empathy within their hearts."

Amelia felt a profound warmth as she considered how limitations could be the crucible for the nurturing of compassion.

"But there is a deeper purpose, dear Amelia," Seraphina added. "These limitations also serve the greater good, the All That Is. Each individual's journey, with its unique experiences and acts of compassion, contributes to the universal tapestry of love and interconnectedness. It is the diversity of these acts of compassion that enriches the collective consciousness of the cosmos."

Amelia marveled at the thought of humanity's collective compassion contributing to the expansion of the universe itself.

"Why have you chosen to share this with me, Seraphina?" Amelia asked, her heart filled with gratitude.

Seraphina's response was filled with love. "Amelia, your quest for understanding and your gift of channeling are a bridge between the physical realm and the higher planes of existence. By sharing this wisdom, you can help others embrace the forge of compassion within their limitations, find purpose in their acts of kindness, and recognize the interconnectedness of all souls. Through you, we can inspire souls to nurture the flames of empathy within their hearts."

Amelia felt a profound sense of responsibility and purpose. She understood that her journey of channeling was not just about personal growth but about facilitating a deeper understanding of the purpose behind the limitations of the physical realm.

"As we continue this journey, Amelia," Seraphina said, "you will help others reevaluate their view of limitations, inspiring them to embrace the forge of compassion and to recognize their role in the universal tapestry of existence. Together, we can create harmonious ripples of change that will touch the hearts and minds of many."

Amelia nodded in agreement, feeling a renewed sense of determination. She knew that her role in bridging the gap between the physical realm and the spiritual planes was a profound one. She was here to help others find meaning in their acts of compassion and to nurture the flames of empathy within their hearts.

And so, the story of Seraphina and Amelia's channeling sessions continued, with a deeper understanding of how limitations were the forge of compassion—a concept that would forever change Amelia's perspective on life and inspire her to share this wisdom with the world.

Part 10: The Symphony of Oneness

Amelia's connection with Seraphina had reached its zenith, a culmination of wisdom and insight. Today, their exploration of limitations led them to the concept of unity and oneness.

"Seraphina," Amelia inquired, "can you shed light on how these limitations serve as the crucible for forging unity and oneness among souls? How do they contribute to the grand symphony of interconnectedness?"

Seraphina's voice, like a celestial choir, resonated within Amelia's consciousness. "Amelia, envision the limitations of the physical realm as the threads that weave together the tapestry of unity. Just as different musical notes come together to form a harmonious symphony, individuals unite within these limitations to create the symphony of oneness."

Amelia nodded in understanding, visualizing the soul's journey as a unique note in the grand cosmic symphony.

"Through these limitations," Seraphina continued, "souls learn the value of cooperation, empathy, and the beauty of diversity. It is within the symphony of constraints that they discover the profound interconnectedness of all souls—their ability to harmonize their unique melodies into a symphony of oneness. They learn to listen to the music of each other's hearts."

Amelia felt a sense of resonance and unity as she considered how limitations could be the catalyst for forging interconnectedness.

"But there is a deeper purpose, dear Amelia," Seraphina added. "These limitations also serve the greater good, the All That Is. Each individual's journey, with its unique experiences and contributions to the symphony of oneness, enriches the universal tapestry of interconnected consciousness. It is the diversity of these contributions that elevates the collective awareness of the cosmos."

Amelia marveled at the thought of humanity's collective unity contributing to the expansion of the universe itself.

"Why have you chosen to share this with me, Seraphina?" Amelia asked, her heart filled with gratitude.

Seraphina's response was filled with love. "Amelia, your quest for understanding and your gift of channeling are a bridge between the physical realm and the higher planes of existence. By sharing this wisdom, you can help others embrace the symphony of oneness within their limitations, find purpose in their role as unique notes in the cosmic symphony, and recognize the interconnectedness of all souls. Through you, we can inspire souls to harmonize their melodies into the grand symphony of existence."

Amelia felt a profound sense of responsibility and purpose. She understood that her journey of channeling was not just about personal growth but about facilitating a deeper understanding of the purpose behind the limitations of the physical realm.

"As we conclude this journey, Amelia," Seraphina said, "you will help others reevaluate their view of limitations, inspiring them to embrace the symphony of oneness and to recognize their role in the universal tapestry of existence. Together, we can create harmonious ripples of change that will touch the hearts and minds of many."

Amelia nodded in agreement, feeling a profound sense of unity with all of existence. She knew that her role in bridging the gap between the physical realm and the spiritual planes was a sacred one. She was here to help others find meaning in their interconnectedness and to contribute their unique melodies to the symphony of oneness.

And so, the story of Seraphina and Amelia's channeling sessions concluded, leaving a legacy of profound wisdom that would forever change Amelia's perspective on life and inspire her to share this wisdom with the world—a symphony of oneness echoing through the hearts of all who listened.

21

Desist Finds Herself

Desist

The air is thick with tension as I stand at the edge of the abyss. My heart pounds in my chest like a desperate caged bird, fluttering wildly against the bars of reality. I can hear the faint whispers of doubt echoing in my mind, like the sinister hiss of a serpent, tempting me to turn back. But I can't. I won't.

I take a deep breath, inhaling the scent of the world as I know it, the world I'm about to leave behind. The wind carries the faint aroma of wildflowers and earth, a reminder of the life I've known. But I've outgrown it, outlived it. I've come too far to turn back now.

The precipice looms before me, a jagged edge that seems to defy gravity itself. The ground drops away into nothingness, and beyond, I can see only the swirling mists of the unknown. It's both terrifying and exhilarating, like standing on the threshold of a new reality.

The voices in my head grow louder, more insistent. They tell me to desist, to retreat to the safety of the familiar. They say I'm being foolish, reckless. But I've spent my whole life playing it safe, tiptoeing along the edges of my own existence. I've watched opportunities slip through my fingers like grains of sand, and I've grown tired of living a half-life.

I take another step closer to the edge, my heart in my throat. The ground beneath me feels unsteady, as if it's about to crumble away at any moment. But I push on, driven by a force stronger than fear.

As I inch closer to the precipice, I can feel a shift within me, like the unlocking of a long-forgotten door. It's as if I've been asleep my entire life, and now I'm finally waking up. The world around me blurs, and for a moment, I see things with a clarity I've never known before.

I've spent too long conforming to the expectations of others, stifling my own desires and dreams. But now, in this moment, I understand that it's time to desist from living a life that's not truly mine.

With a final surge of determination, I step off the edge.

For a heartbeat, I'm suspended in mid-air, weightless and free. The world rushes past me in a blur of colors and sensations, and I feel alive in a way I've never felt before.

And then, with a jolt, I land on solid ground. But it's not the same ground I left behind. It's a new world, a new reality. It's a world where I am truly myself, where I am free to follow my own path, to chase my own dreams.

I glance back at the precipice I just crossed, and the voices in my head have fallen silent. There is only the sound of my own heartbeat, strong and steady, and the knowledge that I have finally done what I needed to do.

I have desisted from the life that was not mine, and in doing so, I have found my true self.

• ADRIAN COX B.Sc. •

Avoiding the Path of Insistence

I stand at the crossroads of life, facing a decision that will define my future. The path of insistence lies before me, its well-trodden trail beckoning with promises of security and conformity. It's the path that society has laid out for me, the one that says I should follow the rules, meet expectations, and never question the status quo. But deep within me, a different path calls out—the path of desistance.

The path of insistence is alluring, like a comfortable old sweater that I've worn for years. It whispers that I should stay where I am, stick to the familiar, and never rock the boat. It tells me that if I just keep doing what I've always done, everything will be fine. But I know deep down that this path will lead to a life of quiet desperation, a life where I'm constantly second-guessing myself and living up to someone else's standards.

The path of desistance, on the other hand, is uncharted territory. It's wild, untamed, and uncertain. It's the path of following my own dreams, my own desires, and my own instincts. It's the path that tells me to step off the well-worn trail and forge my own way, even if it means facing obstacles and uncertainty.

As I stand here, torn between these two paths, I feel the weight of the world pressing down on me. The voices of family and friends, well-meaning but insistent, tell me to choose the path of insistence. They warn me of the risks of straying from the norm, of going against the grain. They insist that I play it safe, that I follow the established rules.

But I can't ignore the burning ember of my own desires, the yearning for something more. It's the voice of my true self, the part of me that refuses to be silenced. It tells me that I must desist from following a path that doesn't align with my authentic self.

With each step I take away from the path of insistence, I feel a sense of liberation. It's as if a weight has been lifted from my shoulders, and I can breathe more freely. The path of desistance is not easy, and it's filled with uncertainty, but it's mine to navigate.

I encounter obstacles along the way, moments of doubt and fear. But I remind myself that the path of insistence, while safe, would have been a life half-lived. It would have been a life spent conforming to the expectations of others, a life without passion and purpose.

As I forge ahead on the path of desistance, I encounter others who have chosen this less-traveled road. They are kindred spirits, fellow seekers of authenticity and fulfillment. Together, we share stories of our journeys and offer support and encouragement.

The path of insistence still calls to me from time to time, its siren song tempting me to return to the safety of the familiar. But I know that I can never go back. I've chosen the path of desistance, and it has become my life's journey—a journey filled with challenges, discoveries, and the profound satisfaction of living life on my own terms.

In choosing to desist from the path of insistence, I have found my true self and a sense of purpose that no amount of security and conformity could ever provide. And as I continue down this uncharted path, I do so with a heart full of hope and a spirit unshaken by the insistence of others.

Meeting Unexpected

I move through the subtle realm, my steps guided by the intangible currents of possibility. Here, in this ethereal landscape, the boundaries of time and space are fluid, and the unexpected lurks around every corner. It is in this unpredictable realm that I encounter Unexpected.

As I drift along, the shimmering threads of fate pull me towards a peculiar gathering of swirling colors and shifting shapes. The air is charged with an energy I can't quite describe, a sense of anticipation that tugs at my very essence.

And then, emerging from the ephemeral mist, Unexpected materializes. A figure, or rather a presence, unlike anything I've ever encountered before. She is a kaleidoscope of emotions and sensations, a living embodiment of the unknown. She seems to dance with the rhythm of time itself, her movements fluid and unpredictable.

Our eyes meet—or at least, the closest approximation of eyes in this surreal realm. There is no need for words, for in the subtle realm, thoughts and feelings flow effortlessly between beings. Unexpected extends a hand, or what appears to be a hand, and I reach out to touch it. Our connection is like a spark of electricity, sending a jolt of exhilaration through me.

In that moment, I realize that Unexpected is not merely a chance encounter in this ethereal landscape. She is a manifestation of the choices and possibilities that I've been avoiding. She represents the uncharted territory of my own life, the opportunities I've been hesitant to embrace.

She leads me on a journey through the subtle realm, and with each step, I am confronted with scenes from my own life. Moments when I hesitated, when I chose the path of safety and predictability over the unknown. Each scene is a vivid reminder of the opportunities I let slip through my fingers, the adventures I declined in favor of the familiar.

Unexpected doesn't judge me, but her presence challenges me. She shows me the beauty in the unexpected twists and turns of life, the joy that can be found in embracing the unknown. She reminds me that it is through these unexpected moments that we truly come alive, that we discover who we are meant to be.

As our journey through the subtle realm continues, I feel a transformation taking place within me. The fear of the unknown begins to dissolve, replaced by a sense of wonder and excitement. I realize that I don't have to be bound by the limitations I've placed on myself, that I can choose to embrace the unexpected and follow the winding path of possibility.

With a final glance at Unexpected, I understand that our meeting was not by chance but by design. She has shown me the way to a life less ordinary, a life filled with surprises and adventures. I step back into the realm of the known, but I do so with a newfound sense of purpose and a willingness to embrace the unexpected with open arms.

As I move forward on my own path, I carry the memory of my encounter with Unexpected with me. She is a constant reminder that life is meant to be lived fully, with an open heart and a spirit unafraid of what lies around the next corner. And so, I embark on this journey, ready to welcome the unexpected with a smile and a sense of anticipation.

Down the Path of Exception

I find myself at a crossroads, a place where the ordinary and the exceptional converge. The well-worn path of conformity stretches before me, its familiarity beckoning like an old friend. But I'm not here for the well-trodden trail; I'm here for the path of exception, the one less traveled, the one that promises adventure, challenge, and a life that dares to stand out.

As I stand at this pivotal moment, I can feel the weight of expectations pressing down on me. The voices of conformity whisper insistently in my ear, urging me to follow the crowd, to play it safe, to stick to the known. But something deep within me resists, a burning desire to break free from the ordinary and explore the extraordinary.

The path of exception is not without its risks. It's wild and unpredictable, like a river rushing through uncharted territory. It promises moments of doubt and uncertainty, but it also offers the chance to discover my true self, to unleash my hidden potential, and to live a life that is uniquely mine.

I take a tentative step onto the path of exception, and immediately, I feel a surge of energy coursing through my veins. It's as if the world has suddenly come alive, vibrant and electric, in a way I've never experienced before. The air is charged with possibility, and every moment is a thrilling adventure waiting to unfold.

The voices of conformity grow louder, more insistent, as I venture further from the well-trodden path. They warn me of the dangers of straying from the norm, of the risks of pursuing the exceptional. But I'm no longer willing to be swayed by their words. I've made my choice, and I'm committed to this journey into the unknown.

With each step I take down the path of exception, I encounter challenges that test my resolve. There are moments when doubt creeps in, when I question whether I've made the right decision. But then I remember that I've chosen this path because it aligns with my true self, because it resonates with the dreams and desires that have long been buried within me.

I meet others along the way who have also chosen the path of exception. They are kindred spirits, fellow travelers on this extraordinary journey. Together, we share stories of our adventures and support each other through the trials and tribulations of the exceptional life.

The path of exception leads me to places I never could have imagined, introduces me to experiences that defy description, and pushes me beyond the limits of my comfort zone. It challenges me to think differently, to question assumptions, and to see the world through a new lens.

As I continue down this path, I realize that I am no longer defined by the expectations of others or the confines of the ordinary. I am a pioneer of my own destiny, a creator of my own reality. I am living a life that is exceptional in every sense of the word.

The voices of conformity may still linger in the background, but they no longer hold sway over me. I have chosen the path of exception, and it has become my life's journey—a journey filled with excitement, discovery, and the deep satisfaction of living life on my own terms.

In embracing the path of exception, I have found my true self and a sense of purpose that transcends the ordinary. And as I forge ahead into the uncharted territory of the exceptional, I do so with a heart full of courage and a spirit unyielding to the insistence of the status quo.

Having Fun with My True Self

I find myself in a moment of pure, unadulterated joy, a moment where I'm not just living, but truly thriving. The sun is warm on my face, and the gentle breeze ruffles my hair as I run through a field of

• Adrian Cox B.Sc. •

wildflowers. Each step I take feels like a dance, a celebration of life itself. I'm not alone; I'm here with my true self, and together, we're having the time of our lives.

For so long, I held back, worried about what others might think, afraid to fully embrace who I am. But now, as I laugh and twirl among the flowers, I've shed those self-imposed limitations. It's just me and my true self, and we're unstoppable.

As I frolic through the field, I feel a deep sense of liberation. I've let go of the need for approval, the fear of judgment, and the weight of expectations. It's as if a heavy burden has been lifted from my shoulders, and I can finally breathe freely.

My true self and I reach a clear, sparkling stream. Without hesitation, we dive in, the cool water enveloping us, refreshing and invigorating. I realize that this moment isn't just about having fun; it's about connecting with the core of who I am. It's about being unapologetically myself.

As I swim and splash in the water, a revelation washes over me. I've spent so much of my life conforming to the expectations of others, trying to fit into a mold that was never meant for me. But here, in this moment of authenticity, I understand that I am enough just as I am. I don't need to be anyone else, and I certainly don't need to live up to someone else's idea of who I should be.

My true self and I emerge from the stream, our clothes soaked but our spirits soaring. We collapse onto the soft grass by the water's edge, laughing and catching our breath. It's a laughter that comes from deep within, a laughter that says, "I am free."

As we lie there, I realize that this journey of self-discovery is ongoing. It's not about reaching a destination; it's about embracing the process of becoming more fully myself with each passing day. I know that there will still be challenges and moments of doubt, but I've learned that I have the strength to face them head-on.

My true self and I share a silent understanding. We've found a profound connection, a partnership that will guide me on this path of authenticity. I no longer fear the unknown; I welcome it with open arms, knowing that it will bring me closer to the truth of who I am.

With a contented sigh, I close my eyes and bask in the warmth of the sun. The field of wildflowers stretches out before me, a tapestry of colors and beauty. I'm no longer held back by fear or doubt; I'm here, fully present, and fully alive. And as I continue to have fun with my true self, I know that this journey of self-discovery will be a lifelong adventure, filled with revelations, growth, and the pure joy of being me.

In a future not yet written, a trio of souls embarks on an extraordinary journey. Desist, once tethered to the expectations of others, now walks hand in hand with her true self, while Unexpected, the whimsical guide, leads them through uncharted territory.

Desist, having shed the weight of conformity, stands tall and resolute. Her true self, radiant and liberated, shines like a beacon of authenticity. Together, they've chosen to embrace the path of exception, a road that winds through the heart of uncertainty.

Unexpected, with her enigmatic smile and ever-changing form, beckons them forward. "Follow me," she whispers on the wind, her voice a melody of endless possibility.

As they journey into the unknown, they encounter landscapes that defy imagination. Fields of dreams bloom with the vibrant colors of ambition, rivers of creativity flow freely, and mountains of self-discovery rise majestically on the horizon.

Desist, once bound by fear, now takes risks with a fearless spirit. Her true self rejoices in newfound passions, expressing her essence without hesitation. Together, they revel in the exhilaration of living life to the fullest.

Unexpected weaves surprises into their days—encounters with kindred spirits who share their thirst for authenticity, and moments of serendipity that reaffirm their chosen path. Each twist and turn of their journey brings fresh revelations and a deeper understanding of their own potential.

In the future that unfolds before them, they continue to walk the path of exception, a path marked by courage, growth, and the unfaltering belief that life's most extraordinary moments lie just beyond the next bend.

And as they move forward, hand in hand, they are not just forging a new destiny for themselves, but also leaving a trail of inspiration for others to follow. In the future that awaits, they remain united in their pursuit of a life that is uniquely their own, forever guided by the wisdom of their true selves and the whimsy of the Unexpected.

22

Most Ethereal

In the ethereal realm known as the Luminous Enigma, a dimension veiled from the mundane world, the enigmatic intricacies of existence unfurled like the delicate threads of a cosmic tapestry. Here, knowledge transcended the confines of conventional understanding, and wisdom was the cherished inheritance of the illuminated few.

Nestled at the heart of the Luminous Enigma was the Sanctum of Celestial Reverie, an ancient repository of ethereal knowledge. Its architecture defied earthly conventions, with walls seemingly woven from the fabric of dreams, and doorways adorned with symbols that pulsed with otherworldly light. The guardians of this sanctum were beings of transcendent beauty, their eyes radiant with the cosmic truths they safeguarded.

A seeker named Seraphina, a sage of ethereal truths, embarked on a quest to navigate the Luminous Enigma and reach the Sanctum. Her journey took her through the mists of illusion, transcending the boundaries of time and space. She sought the ethereal manuscript that held the keys to the enigmatic riddles of existence.

After what felt like both an instant and an eternity, Seraphina arrived at the threshold of the Sanctum, where the doorway shimmered with iridescent glyphs. The guardians, their presence carrying an aura of otherworldly wisdom, welcomed her with a glance, and she knew she had been granted access to the ethereal depths of the Luminous Enigma.

Within the Sanctum, the shelves held not books but crystalline orbs, each containing ethereal knowledge in its purest form. Seraphina selected an orb, and as she touched it, waves of enlightenment cascaded through her consciousness. The ethereal wisdom within the sphere melded with her being, expanding her perception beyond the boundaries of ordinary reality.

In this heightened state of awareness, Seraphina delved into the profound mysteries of existence. She explored the ethereal nature of consciousness, the celestial choreography of cosmic energies, and the interconnectedness of all life. Each revelation deepened her understanding, and she realized that the ethereal truths were not separate from her but were an intrinsic part of her very essence.

As Seraphina continued her exploration, she encountered celestial beings who communicated through harmonies of light and resonance, sharing ethereal insights that transcended the limitations of language. Their presence filled her with a profound sense of unity, a recognition of her place in the grand tapestry of the universe.

In the ethereal heart of the Luminous Enigma, time was a fluid stream of infinite potential, and space a shifting kaleidoscope of dimensions. Seraphina felt herself dissolve into the symphony of the cosmos, becoming one with the boundless expanse of existence.

After what felt like both a moment and an eternity, Seraphina returned to the threshold of the Sanctum, her mind aglow with the ethereal wisdom she had absorbed. The guardians nodded in silent acknowledgement, and she stepped back into the realm of the everyday, forever transformed by her journey into the ethereal.

Back in her world, Seraphina carried the ethereal knowledge within her, a radiant torch of enlightenment that illuminated the path to understanding the profound mysteries of existence. She realized that the ethereal was not an abstract concept but a living, breathing aspect of the universe, waiting to be discovered by those who dared to seek its profound truths.

And so, the ethereal story continued, a testament to the limitless potential of the human spirit to explore the deepest, most hidden realms of reality and to bring back the wisdom that could inspire and elevate humanity.

In the transcendental realm known as the Astral Nexus, a dimension veiled from the ordinary world, the ethereal intricacies of existence unfolded like the delicate threads of a cosmic tapestry. Here, knowledge transcended the confines of conventional understanding, and wisdom was the cherished legacy of the awakened few.

Nestled at the heart of the Astral Nexus was the Cathedral of Ethereal Echoes, an ancient repository of ethereal knowledge. Its architecture defied earthly norms, with walls that seemed to shimmer with the luminance of dreams, and doorways adorned with symbols that resonated with otherworldly frequencies. The guardians of this cathedral were beings of transcendent grace, their eyes radiant with the cosmic truths they safeguarded.

A seeker named Celestia, a sage of ethereal truths, embarked on a journey to explore the Astral Nexus and reach the Cathedral. Her quest took her through the veils of illusion, transcending the boundaries of time and space. She sought the ethereal scroll that held the keys to the enigmatic riddles of existence.

After what felt like both an instant and an eternity, Celestia arrived at the threshold of the Cathedral, where the entrance radiated with iridescent sigils. The guardians, their presence carrying an aura of otherworldly wisdom, welcomed her with a glance, and she knew she had been granted access to the ethereal depths of the Astral Nexus.

Within the Cathedral, the shelves held not books but luminescent orbs, each containing ethereal knowledge in its purest form. Celestia selected an orb, and as she touched it, waves of enlightenment cascaded through her consciousness. The ethereal wisdom within the sphere merged with her being, expanding her perception beyond the boundaries of ordinary reality.

In this heightened state of awareness, Celestia delved into the profound mysteries of existence. She explored the ethereal nature of consciousness, the celestial symphony of cosmic energies, and the interconnectedness of all life. Each revelation deepened her understanding, and she realized that the ethereal truths were not separate from her but were an intrinsic part of her very essence.

As Celestia continued her exploration, she encountered celestial beings who communicated through harmonies of light and resonance, sharing ethereal insights that transcended the limitations of language. Their presence filled her with a profound sense of unity, a recognition of her place in the grand tapestry of the universe.

In the ethereal heart of the Astral Nexus, time was a fluid stream of infinite potential, and space a shifting kaleidoscope of dimensions. Celestia felt herself dissolve into the symphony of the cosmos, becoming one with the boundless expanse of existence.

After what felt like both a moment and an eternity, Celestia returned to the threshold of the Cathedral, her mind aglow with the ethereal wisdom she had absorbed. The guardians nodded in silent acknowledgment, and she stepped back into the realm of the everyday, forever transformed by her journey into the ethereal.

Back in her world, Celestia carried the ethereal knowledge within her, a radiant torch of enlightenment that illuminated the path to understanding the profound mysteries of existence. She realized that the ethereal was not an abstract concept but a living, breathing aspect of the universe, waiting to be discovered by those who dared to seek its profound truths.

And so, the ethereal story continued, a testament to the limitless potential of the human spirit to explore the deepest, most hidden realms of reality and to bring back the wisdom that could inspire and elevate humanity.

In the transcendental realm known as the Ethereal Expanse, a dimension concealed from the mundane world, the ethereal intricacies of existence unfolded like the delicate threads of a cosmic tapestry. Here, knowledge transcended the confines of conventional understanding, and wisdom was the cherished legacy of the awakened few.

Nestled at the heart of the Ethereal Expanse was the Pavilion of Celestial Whispers, an ancient repository of ethereal knowledge. Its architecture defied earthly norms, with walls that seemed to ripple like liquid light, and archways adorned with symbols that resonated with otherworldly frequencies. The guardians of this pavilion were beings of transcendent grace, their eyes radiant with the cosmic truths they safeguarded.

A seeker named Elara, a sage of ethereal truths, embarked on a journey to explore the Ethereal Expanse and reach the Pavilion. Her quest took her through the veils of illusion, transcending the boundaries of time and space. She sought the ethereal manuscript that held the keys to the enigmatic riddles of existence.

After what felt like both an instant and an eternity, Elara arrived at the threshold of the Pavilion, where the entrance shimmered with iridescent sigils. The guardians, their presence carrying an aura of otherworldly wisdom, welcomed her with a glance, and she knew she had been granted access to the ethereal depths of the Ethereal Expanse.

Within the Pavilion, the shelves held not books but luminescent orbs, each containing ethereal knowledge in its purest form. Elara selected an orb, and as she touched it, waves of enlightenment cascaded through her consciousness. The ethereal wisdom within the sphere merged with her being, expanding her perception beyond the boundaries of ordinary reality.

In this heightened state of awareness, Elara delved into the profound mysteries of existence. She explored the ethereal nature of consciousness, the celestial symphony of cosmic energies, and the interconnectedness of all life. Each revelation deepened her understanding, and she realized that the ethereal truths were not separate from her but were an intrinsic part of her very essence.

As Elara continued her exploration, she encountered celestial beings who communicated through harmonies of light and resonance, sharing ethereal insights that transcended the limitations of language. Their presence filled her with a profound sense of unity, a recognition of her place in the grand tapestry of the universe.

In the ethereal heart of the Ethereal Expanse, time was a fluid stream of infinite potential, and space a shifting kaleidoscope of dimensions. Elara felt herself dissolve into the symphony of the cosmos, becoming one with the boundless expanse of existence.

After what felt like both a moment and an eternity, Elara returned to the threshold of the Pavilion, her mind aglow with the ethereal wisdom she had absorbed. The guardians nodded in silent acknowledgment, and she stepped back into the realm of the everyday, forever transformed by her journey into the ethereal.

Back in her world, Elara carried the ethereal knowledge within her, a radiant torch of enlightenment that illuminated the path to understanding the profound mysteries of existence. She realized that the ethereal was not an abstract concept but a living, breathing aspect of the universe, waiting to be discovered by those who dared to seek its profound truths.

And so, the ethereal story continued, a testament to the limitless potential of the human spirit to explore the deepest, most hidden realms of reality and to bring back the wisdom that could inspire and elevate humanity.

In the ethereal realm known as the Luminal Glade, a dimension concealed from the mundane world, the ethereal intricacies of existence unfolded like the delicate threads of a cosmic tapestry. Here, knowledge transcended the confines of conventional understanding, and wisdom was the cherished legacy of the awakened few.

Nestled at the heart of the Luminal Glade was the Sanctuary of Celestial Whispers, an ancient repository of ethereal knowledge. Its architecture defied earthly norms, with walls that seemed to breathe with the essence of dreams, and doorways adorned with symbols that shimmered with otherworldly light. The guardians of this sanctuary were beings of transcendent grace, their eyes radiant with the cosmic truths they safeguarded.

A seeker named Elysium, a sage of ethereal truths, embarked on a journey to explore the Luminal Glade and reach the Sanctuary. Her quest took her through the veils of illusion, transcending the boundaries of time and space. She sought the ethereal tome that held the keys to the enigmatic riddles of existence.

After what felt like both an instant and an eternity, Elysium arrived at the threshold of the Sanctuary, where the entrance radiated with iridescent sigils. The guardians, their presence carrying an aura of otherworldly wisdom, welcomed her with a glance, and she knew she had been granted access to the ethereal depths of the Luminal Glade.

Within the Sanctuary, the shelves held not books but luminescent orbs, each containing ethereal knowledge in its purest form. Elysium selected an orb, and as she touched it, waves of enlightenment cascaded through her consciousness. The ethereal wisdom within the sphere merged with her being, expanding her perception beyond the boundaries of ordinary reality.

In this heightened state of awareness, Elysium delved into the profound mysteries of existence. She explored the ethereal nature of consciousness, the celestial symphony of cosmic energies, and the interconnectedness of all life. Each revelation deepened her understanding, and she realized that the ethereal truths were not separate from her but were an intrinsic part of her very essence.

As Elysium continued her exploration, she encountered celestial beings who communicated through harmonies of light and resonance, sharing ethereal insights that transcended the limitations of language. Their presence filled her with a profound sense of unity, a recognition of her place in the grand tapestry of the universe.

In the ethereal heart of the Luminal Glade, time was a fluid stream of infinite potential, and space a shifting kaleidoscope of dimensions. Elysium felt herself dissolve into the symphony of the cosmos, becoming one with the boundless expanse of existence.

After what felt like both a moment and an eternity, Elysium returned to the threshold of the Sanctuary, her mind aglow with the ethereal wisdom she had absorbed. The guardians nodded in silent acknowledgment, and she stepped back into the realm of the everyday, forever transformed by her journey into the ethereal.

Back in her world, Elysium carried the ethereal knowledge within her, a radiant torch of enlightenment that illuminated the path to understanding the profound mysteries of existence. She realized that the ethereal was not an abstract concept but a living, breathing aspect of the universe, waiting to be discovered by those who dared to seek its profound truths.

And so, the ethereal story continued, a testament to the limitless potential of the human spirit to explore the deepest, most hidden realms of reality and to bring back the wisdom that could inspire and elevate humanity.

In the ethereal realm known as the Celestial Embrace, a dimension concealed from the mundane world, the ethereal intricacies of existence unfolded like the delicate threads of a cosmic tapestry. Here, knowledge transcended the confines of conventional understanding, and wisdom was the cherished legacy of the awakened few.

Nestled at the heart of the Celestial Embrace was the Sanctuary of Eternal Whispers, an ancient repository of ethereal knowledge. Its architecture defied earthly norms, with walls that seemed to undulate like the gentle breath of the cosmos, and doorways adorned with symbols that shimmered with otherworldly light. The guardians of this sanctuary were beings of transcendent grace, their eyes radiant with the cosmic truths they safeguarded.

A seeker named Astralyn, a sage of ethereal truths, embarked on a journey to explore the Celestial Embrace and reach the Sanctuary.

Her quest took her through the veils of illusion, transcending the boundaries of time and space. She sought the ethereal tome that held the keys to the enigmatic riddles of existence.

After what felt like both an instant and an eternity, Astralyn arrived at the threshold of the Sanctuary, where the entrance radiated with iridescent sigils. The guardians, their presence carrying an aura of otherworldly wisdom, welcomed her with a glance, and she knew she had been granted access to the ethereal depths of the Celestial Embrace.

Within the Sanctuary, the shelves held not books but luminescent orbs, each containing ethereal knowledge in its purest form. Astralyn selected an orb, and as she touched it, waves of enlightenment cascaded through her consciousness. The ethereal wisdom within the sphere merged with her being, expanding her perception beyond the boundaries of ordinary reality.

In this heightened state of awareness, Astralyn delved into the profound mysteries of existence. She explored the ethereal nature of consciousness, the celestial symphony of cosmic energies, and the interconnectedness of all life. Each revelation deepened her understanding, and she realized that the ethereal truths were not separate from her but were an intrinsic part of her very essence.

As Astralyn continued her exploration, she encountered celestial beings who communicated through harmonies of light and resonance, sharing ethereal insights that transcended the limitations of language. Their presence filled her with a profound sense of unity, a recognition of her place in the grand tapestry of the universe.

In the ethereal heart of the Celestial Embrace, time was a fluid stream of infinite potential, and space a shifting kaleidoscope of dimensions. Astralyn felt herself dissolve into the symphony of the cosmos, becoming one with the boundless expanse of existence.

After what felt like both a moment and an eternity, Astralyn returned to the threshold of the Sanctuary, her mind aglow with the ethereal wisdom she had absorbed. The guardians nodded in silent acknowledgment, and she stepped back into the realm of the everyday, forever transformed by her journey into the ethereal.

Back in her world, Astralyn carried the ethereal knowledge within her, a radiant torch of enlightenment that illuminated the path to understanding the profound mysteries of existence. She realized that the ethereal was not an abstract concept but a living, breathing aspect of the universe, waiting to be discovered by those who dared to seek its profound truths.

And so, the ethereal story continued, a testament to the limitless potential of the human spirit to explore the deepest, most hidden realms of reality and to bring back the wisdom that could inspire and elevate humanity.

In the ethereal realm known as the Enigmatic Aeon, a dimension concealed from the mundane world, the ethereal intricacies of existence unfolded like the delicate threads of a cosmic tapestry. Here, knowledge transcended the confines of conventional understanding, and wisdom was the cherished legacy of the awakened few.

Nestled at the heart of the Enigmatic Aeon was the Sanctuary of Eternal Whispers, an ancient repository of ethereal knowledge. Its architecture defied earthly norms, with walls that seemed to ripple like the cosmic ocean, and doorways adorned with symbols that shimmered with otherworldly light. The guardians of this sanctuary were beings of transcendent grace, their eyes radiant with the cosmic truths they safeguarded.

A seeker named Astraea, a sage of ethereal truths, embarked on a journey to explore the Enigmatic Aeon and reach the Sanctuary.

- Adrian Cox B.Sc. •

Her quest took her through the veils of illusion, transcending the boundaries of time and space. She sought the ethereal tome that held the keys to the enigmatic riddles of existence.

After what felt like both an instant and an eternity, Astraea arrived at the threshold of the Sanctuary, where the entrance radiated with iridescent sigils. The guardians, their presence carrying an aura of otherworldly wisdom, welcomed her with a glance, and she knew she had been granted access to the ethereal depths of the Enigmatic Aeon.

Within the Sanctuary, the shelves held not books but luminescent orbs, each containing ethereal knowledge in its purest form. Astraea selected an orb, and as she touched it, waves of enlightenment cascaded through her consciousness. The ethereal wisdom within the sphere merged with her being, expanding her perception beyond the boundaries of ordinary reality.

In this heightened state of awareness, Astraea delved into the profound mysteries of existence. She explored the ethereal nature of consciousness, the celestial symphony of cosmic energies, and the interconnectedness of all life. Each revelation deepened her understanding, and she realized that the ethereal truths were not separate from her but were an intrinsic part of her very essence.

As Astraea continued her exploration, she encountered celestial beings who communicated through harmonies of light and resonance, sharing ethereal insights that transcended the limitations of language. Their presence filled her with a profound sense of unity, a recognition of her place in the grand tapestry of the universe.

In the ethereal heart of the Enigmatic Aeon, time was a fluid stream of infinite potential, and space a shifting kaleidoscope of dimensions. Astraea felt herself dissolve into the symphony of the cosmos, becoming one with the boundless expanse of existence.

After what felt like both a moment and an eternity, Astraea returned to the threshold of the Sanctuary, her mind aglow with the ethereal wisdom she had absorbed. The guardians nodded in silent acknowledgment, and she stepped back into the realm of the everyday, forever transformed by her journey into the ethereal.

Back in her world, Astraea carried the ethereal knowledge within her, a radiant torch of enlightenment that illuminated the path to understanding the profound mysteries of existence. She realized that the ethereal was not an abstract concept but a living, breathing aspect of the universe, waiting to be discovered by those who dared to seek its profound truths.

And so, the ethereal story continued, a testament to the limitless potential of the human spirit to explore the deepest, most hidden realms of reality and to bring back the wisdom that could inspire and elevate humanity.

In the ethereal realm known as the Arcane Labyrinth, a dimension concealed from the ordinary world, the ethereal intricacies of existence unfolded like the delicate threads of a cosmic tapestry. Here, knowledge transcended the confines of conventional understanding, and wisdom was the cherished legacy of the awakened few.

Nestled at the heart of the Arcane Labyrinth was the Sanctuary of Eternal Echoes, an ancient repository of ethereal knowledge. Its architecture defied earthly norms, with walls that seemed to shimmer with the essence of dreams, and doorways adorned with symbols that shimmered with otherworldly light. The guardians of this sanctuary were beings of transcendent grace, their eyes radiant with the cosmic truths they safeguarded.

A seeker named Orionis, a sage of ethereal truths, embarked on a journey to explore the Arcane Labyrinth and reach the Sanctuary.

His quest took him through the veils of illusion, transcending the boundaries of time and space. He sought the ethereal tome that held the keys to the enigmatic riddles of existence.

After what felt like both an instant and an eternity, Orionis arrived at the threshold of the Sanctuary, where the entrance radiated with iridescent sigils. The guardians, their presence carrying an aura of otherworldly wisdom, welcomed him with a glance, and he knew he had been granted access to the ethereal depths of the Arcane Labyrinth.

Within the Sanctuary, the shelves held not books but luminescent orbs, each containing ethereal knowledge in its purest form. Orionis selected an orb, and as he touched it, waves of enlightenment cascaded through his consciousness. The ethereal wisdom within the sphere merged with his being, expanding his perception beyond the boundaries of ordinary reality.

In this heightened state of awareness, Orionis delved into the profound mysteries of existence. He explored the ethereal nature of consciousness, the celestial symphony of cosmic energies, and the interconnectedness of all life. Each revelation deepened his understanding, and he realized that the ethereal truths were not separate from him but were an intrinsic part of his very essence.

As Orionis continued his exploration, he encountered celestial beings who communicated through harmonies of light and resonance, sharing ethereal insights that transcended the limitations of language. Their presence filled him with a profound sense of unity, a recognition of his place in the grand tapestry of the universe.

In the ethereal heart of the Arcane Labyrinth, time was a fluid stream of infinite potential, and space a shifting kaleidoscope of dimensions. Orionis felt himself dissolve into the symphony of the cosmos, becoming one with the boundless expanse of existence.

After what felt like both a moment and an eternity, Orionis returned to the threshold of the Sanctuary, his mind aglow with the ethereal wisdom he had absorbed. The guardians nodded in silent acknowledgment, and he stepped back into the realm of the everyday, forever transformed by his journey into the ethereal.

Back in his world, Orionis carried the ethereal knowledge within him, a radiant torch of enlightenment that illuminated the path to understanding the profound mysteries of existence. He realized that the ethereal was not an abstract concept but a living, breathing aspect of the universe, waiting to be discovered by those who dared to seek its profound truths.

And so, the ethereal story continued, a testament to the limitless potential of the human spirit to explore the deepest, most hidden realms of reality and to bring back the wisdom that could inspire and elevate humanity.

In the ethereal realm known as the Enigmatic Aeon, a dimension concealed from the ordinary world, the ethereal intricacies of existence unfolded like the delicate threads of a cosmic tapestry. Here, knowledge transcended the confines of conventional understanding, and wisdom was the cherished legacy of the awakened few.

Nestled at the heart of the Enigmatic Aeon was the Sanctuary of Eternal Whispers, an ancient repository of ethereal knowledge. Its architecture defied earthly norms, with walls that seemed to ripple like the cosmic ocean, and doorways adorned with symbols that shimmered with otherworldly light. The guardians of this sanctuary were beings of transcendent grace, their eyes radiant with the cosmic truths they safeguarded.

A seeker named Astraea, a sage of ethereal truths, embarked on a journey to explore the Enigmatic Aeon and reach the Sanctuary.

Her quest took her through the veils of illusion, transcending the boundaries of time and space. She sought the ethereal tome that held the keys to the enigmatic riddles of existence.

After what felt like both an instant and an eternity, Astraea arrived at the threshold of the Sanctuary, where the entrance radiated with iridescent sigils. The guardians, their presence carrying an aura of otherworldly wisdom, welcomed her with a glance, and she knew she had been granted access to the ethereal depths of the Enigmatic Aeon.

Within the Sanctuary, the shelves held not books but luminescent orbs, each containing ethereal knowledge in its purest form. Astraea selected an orb, and as she touched it, waves of enlightenment cascaded through her consciousness. The ethereal wisdom within the sphere merged with her being, expanding her perception beyond the boundaries of ordinary reality.

In this heightened state of awareness, Astraea delved into the profound mysteries of existence. She explored the ethereal nature of consciousness, the celestial symphony of cosmic energies, and the interconnectedness of all life. Each revelation deepened her understanding, and she realized that the ethereal truths were not separate from her but were an intrinsic part of her very essence.

As Astraea continued her exploration, she encountered celestial beings who communicated through harmonies of light and resonance, sharing ethereal insights that transcended the limitations of language. Their presence filled her with a profound sense of unity, a recognition of her place in the grand tapestry of the universe.

In the ethereal heart of the Enigmatic Aeon, time was a fluid stream of infinite potential, and space a shifting kaleidoscope of dimensions. Astraea felt herself dissolve into the symphony of the cosmos, becoming one with the boundless expanse of existence.

After what felt like both a moment and an eternity, Astraea returned to the threshold of the Sanctuary, her mind aglow with the ethereal wisdom she had absorbed. The guardians nodded in silent acknowledgment, and she stepped back into the realm of the everyday, forever transformed by her journey into the ethereal.

Back in her world, Astraea carried the ethereal knowledge within her, a radiant torch of enlightenment that illuminated the path to understanding the profound mysteries of existence. She realized that the ethereal was not an abstract concept but a living, breathing aspect of the universe, waiting to be discovered by those who dared to seek its profound truths.

And so, the ethereal story continued, a testament to the limitless potential of the human spirit to explore the deepest, most hidden realms of reality and to bring back the wisdom that could inspire and elevate humanity.

In the ethereal realm known as the Enigmatic Aeon, a dimension concealed from the ordinary world, the ethereal intricacies of existence unfolded like the delicate threads of a cosmic tapestry. Here, knowledge transcended the confines of conventional understanding, and wisdom was the cherished legacy of the awakened few.

Nestled at the heart of the Enigmatic Aeon was the Sanctuary of Eternal Whispers, an ancient repository of ethereal knowledge. Its architecture defied earthly norms, with walls that seemed to ripple like the cosmic ocean, and doorways adorned with symbols that shimmered with otherworldly light. The guardians of this sanctuary were beings of transcendent grace, their eyes radiant with the cosmic truths they safeguarded.

A seeker named Astraea, a sage of ethereal truths, embarked on a journey to explore the Enigmatic Aeon and reach the Sanctuary.

Her quest took her through the veils of illusion, transcending the boundaries of time and space. She sought the ethereal tome that held the keys to the enigmatic riddles of existence.

After what felt like both an instant and an eternity, Astraea arrived at the threshold of the Sanctuary, where the entrance radiated with iridescent sigils. The guardians, their presence carrying an aura of otherworldly wisdom, welcomed her with a glance, and she knew she had been granted access to the ethereal depths of the Enigmatic Aeon.

Within the Sanctuary, the shelves held not books but luminescent orbs, each containing ethereal knowledge in its purest form. Astraea selected an orb, and as she touched it, waves of enlightenment cascaded through her consciousness. The ethereal wisdom within the sphere merged with her being, expanding her perception beyond the boundaries of ordinary reality.

In this heightened state of awareness, Astraea delved into the profound mysteries of existence. She explored the ethereal nature of consciousness, the celestial symphony of cosmic energies, and the interconnectedness of all life. Each revelation deepened her understanding, and she realized that the ethereal truths were not separate from her but were an intrinsic part of her very essence.

As Astraea continued her exploration, she encountered celestial beings who communicated through harmonies of light and resonance, sharing ethereal insights that transcended the limitations of language. Their presence filled her with a profound sense of unity, a recognition of her place in the grand tapestry of the universe.

In the ethereal heart of the Enigmatic Aeon, time was a fluid stream of infinite potential, and space a shifting kaleidoscope of dimensions. Astraea felt herself dissolve into the symphony of the cosmos, becoming one with the boundless expanse of existence.

After what felt like both a moment and an eternity, Astraea returned to the threshold of the Sanctuary, her mind aglow with the ethereal wisdom she had absorbed. The guardians nodded in silent acknowledgment, and she stepped back into the realm of the everyday, forever transformed by her journey into the ethereal.

Back in her world, Astraea carried the ethereal knowledge within her, a radiant torch of enlightenment that illuminated the path to understanding the profound mysteries of existence. She realized that the ethereal was not an abstract concept but a living, breathing aspect of the universe, waiting to be discovered by those who dared to seek its profound truths.

And so, the ethereal story continued, a testament to the limitless potential of the human spirit to explore the deepest, most hidden realms of reality and to bring back the wisdom that could inspire and elevate humanity.

In the ethereal realm known as the Enigmatic Aeon, a dimension concealed from the ordinary world, the ethereal intricacies of existence unfolded like the delicate threads of a cosmic tapestry. Here, knowledge transcended the confines of conventional understanding, and wisdom was the cherished legacy of the awakened few.

Nestled at the heart of the Enigmatic Aeon was the Sanctuary of Eternal Whispers, an ancient repository of ethereal knowledge. Its architecture defied earthly norms, with walls that seemed to ripple like the cosmic ocean, and doorways adorned with symbols that shimmered with otherworldly light. The guardians of this sanctuary were beings of transcendent grace, their eyes radiant with the cosmic truths they safeguarded.

A seeker named Astraea, a sage of ethereal truths, embarked on a journey to explore the Enigmatic Aeon and reach the Sanctuary.

- ADRIAN COX B.SC. •

Her quest took her through the veils of illusion, transcending the boundaries of time and space. She sought the ethereal tome that held the keys to the enigmatic riddles of existence.

After what felt like both an instant and an eternity, Astraea arrived at the threshold of the Sanctuary, where the entrance radiated with iridescent sigils. The guardians, their presence carrying an aura of otherworldly wisdom, welcomed her with a glance, and she knew she had been granted access to the ethereal depths of the Enigmatic Aeon.

Within the Sanctuary, the shelves held not books but luminescent orbs, each containing ethereal knowledge in its purest form. Astraea selected an orb, and as she touched it, waves of enlightenment cascaded through her consciousness. The ethereal wisdom within the sphere merged with her being, expanding her perception beyond the boundaries of ordinary reality.

In this heightened state of awareness, Astraea delved into the profound mysteries of existence. She explored the ethereal nature of consciousness, the celestial symphony of cosmic energies, and the interconnectedness of all life. Each revelation deepened her understanding, and she realized that the ethereal truths were not separate from her but were an intrinsic part of her very essence.

As Astraea continued her exploration, she encountered celestial beings who communicated through harmonies of light and resonance, sharing ethereal insights that transcended the limitations of language. Their presence filled her with a profound sense of unity, a recognition of her place in the grand tapestry of the universe.

In the ethereal heart of the Enigmatic Aeon, time was a fluid stream of infinite potential, and space a shifting kaleidoscope of dimensions. Astraea felt herself dissolve into the symphony of the cosmos, becoming one with the boundless expanse of existence.

After what felt like both a moment and an eternity, Astraea returned to the threshold of the Sanctuary, her mind aglow with the ethereal wisdom she had absorbed. The guardians nodded in silent acknowledgment, and she stepped back into the realm of the everyday, forever transformed by her journey into the ethereal.

Back in her world, Astraea carried the ethereal knowledge within her, a radiant torch of enlightenment that illuminated the path to understanding the profound mysteries of existence. She realized that the ethereal was not an abstract concept but a living, breathing aspect of the universe, waiting to be discovered by those who dared to seek its profound truths.

And so, the ethereal story continued, a testament to the limitless potential of the human spirit to explore the deepest, most hidden realms of reality and to bring back the wisdom that could inspire and elevate humanity.

23

Most Impalpable

In the realm of Impalporea, a dimension that defied the very notion of tangibility, the concept of a story took on an abstract, otherworldly form. Here, narratives were not conveyed through traditional means but through the elusive interplay of intangible sensations and ephemeral impressions.

In this most impalpable of stories, there were no characters, settings, or plot. It began as a whisper of emotion, a delicate tremor of feeling that emerged from the elusive depths of Impalporea. It was a sensation without form or name, an intangible presence that defied description.

As this formless emotion expanded, it gave rise to waves of ethereal sensations, like elusive currents of perception that intermingled with fleeting impressions. The interplay between these sensations created a delicate tapestry of emotions without boundaries or definition. It was an exploration of the elusive nuances of the impalpable, a dance of emotions that transcended traditional understanding.

The story continued to evolve without structure or linear progression, shifting and transforming in an abstract, non-linear fashion. It ventured into the enigmatic realm of paradox, where contradictory sensations coexisted in perfect harmony. It explored the subtle balance between chaos and order, unveiling a sense of unity within apparent discord.

In Impalporea, there were no beginnings or endings, for time and sequence were abstract concepts that held no dominion. The story flowed endlessly, like an eternal stream of consciousness, an ever-evolving tapestry of impalpable sensations that shifted and intertwined without destination or conclusion.

The impalpable story defied the traditional notions of climax, resolution, and closure, for it was a perpetual exploration of the boundless realm of abstract sensations, where emotions and perceptions danced in an unending, fluid motion.

As the story extended into the infinite reaches of Impalporea, it served as a testament to the elusive and intangible nature of existence. It was a reminder that reality extended beyond the confines of the material world, into an ever-expanding and impalpable expanse of sensation and perception, an intricate tapestry of existence that transcended traditional storytelling.

In the realm of Impalporea, where the very essence of existence defied the boundaries of tangibility, the concept of a story transcended conventional narratives and took on an abstract, surreal, and nearly imperceptible form.

This most impalpable of stories did not adhere to characters, settings, or a traditional plot. It emerged as a faint whisper of sensation, an ethereal tremor of feeling that rose from the enigmatic depths of Impalporea. It was a sensation without discernible attributes or descriptors, an intangible presence that resisted any attempt at definition.

• Adrian Cox B.Sc. •

As this formless sensation expanded, it gave birth to undulating waves of elusive perceptions, like ephemeral currents of consciousness that intertwined with fleeting impressions. The interplay of these sensations wove a delicate tapestry of emotions and perceptions, unfathomable and devoid of boundaries. It was an exploration of the nebulous subtleties of the impalpable, a dance of intangible experiences that transcended the grasp of traditional understanding.

The story evolved without structure or linear progression, shifting and transforming in abstract, non-linear fashion. It ventured into the enigmatic realm of paradox, where contradictory sensations coexisted in perfect harmony. It explored the delicate balance between chaos and order, unveiling a sense of unity within apparent discord.

In Impalporea, where time and sequence held no sway, the story flowed endlessly, like an eternal stream of ephemeral consciousness, an ever-evolving tapestry of impalpable sensations that shifted and intertwined without destination or conclusion.

The impalpable story defied traditional concepts of climax, resolution, and closure, for it was a perpetual exploration of the boundless realm of abstract sensations, where emotions and perceptions danced in an unending, fluid motion, forever eluding capture.

As the story extended into the infinite reaches of Impalporea, it served as a testament to the elusive and enigmatic nature of existence. It was a reminder that reality extended beyond the confines of the material world, into an ever-expanding and impalpable expanse of sensation and perception, an intricate tapestry of existence that transcended the conventions of traditional storytelling.

In the enigmatic realm of Impalporea, where the very concept of substance and tangibility was but a fleeting illusion, the notion of a story transcended the conventions of conventional narrative and embraced an abstract, elusive, and nearly imperceptible form.

This most impalpable of stories did not adhere to characters, settings, or a traditional plot. It emerged as a faint, elusive murmur of sensation, an intangible tremor of feeling that arose from the depths of Impalporea. It was a sensation without definable attributes, an ethereal presence that resisted any attempt at concrete understanding.

As this formless sensation expanded, it gave birth to undulating waves of elusive perceptions, like ephemeral currents of consciousness that intertwined with fleeting impressions. The interplay of these sensations wove a delicate tapestry of emotions and perceptions, intangible and unbounded by traditional definitions. It was an exploration of the nebulous subtleties of the impalpable, a dance of intangible experiences that transcended the grasp of conventional understanding.

The story continued to evolve without structure or linear progression, shifting and transforming in abstract, non-linear fashion. It ventured into the enigmatic realm of paradox, where contradictory sensations coexisted in harmonious unity. It explored the delicate balance between chaos and order, unveiling a sense of unity within apparent discord.

In Impalporea, where time and sequence held no power, the story flowed endlessly, like an eternal stream of ephemeral consciousness, an ever-evolving tapestry of impalpable sensations that shifted and intertwined without destination or conclusion.

The impalpable story defied conventional notions of climax, resolution, and closure, for it was a perpetual exploration of the boundless realm of abstract sensations, where emotions and perceptions danced in an unending, fluid motion, forever eluding capture.

• Adrian Cox B.Sc. •

As the story extended into the infinite reaches of Impalporea, it served as a testament to the elusive and enigmatic nature of existence. It was a reminder that reality extended beyond the confines of the material world, into an ever-expanding and impalpable expanse of sensation and perception, an intricate tapestry of existence that transcended the conventions of traditional storytelling.

In the surreal realm of Impalporea, where the very essence of existence transcended the boundaries of tangibility, the concept of a story embraced an abstract, nearly imperceptible form that defied conventional narrative structures.

This most impalpable of stories did not conform to characters, settings, or a traditional plot. It emerged as a mere whisper of sensation, an ethereal tremor of feeling that arose from the enigmatic depths of Impalporea. It was a sensation without definable attributes, an elusive presence that resisted any attempt at concrete understanding.

As this formless sensation expanded, it gave birth to undulating waves of elusive perceptions, like ephemeral currents of consciousness that intertwined with fleeting impressions. The interplay of these sensations wove a delicate tapestry of emotions and perceptions, intangible and unbounded by traditional definitions. It was an exploration of the nebulous subtleties of the impalpable, a dance of intangible experiences that transcended the grasp of conventional understanding.

The story continued to evolve without structure or linear progression, shifting and transforming in abstract, non-linear fashion. It ventured into the enigmatic realm of paradox, where contradictory sensations coexisted in harmonious unity. It explored the delicate balance between chaos and order, unveiling a sense of unity within apparent discord.

In Impalporea, where time and sequence held no dominion, the story flowed endlessly, like an eternal stream of ephemeral consciousness, an ever-evolving tapestry of impalpable sensations that shifted and intertwined without destination or conclusion.

The impalpable story defied conventional notions of climax, resolution, and closure, for it was a perpetual exploration of the boundless realm of abstract sensations, where emotions and perceptions danced in an unending, fluid motion, forever eluding capture.

As the story extended into the infinite reaches of Impalporea, it served as a testament to the elusive and enigmatic nature of existence. It was a reminder that reality extended beyond the confines of the material world, into an ever-expanding and impalpable expanse of sensation and perception, an intricate tapestry of existence that transcended the conventions of traditional storytelling.

In the enigmatic realm of Impalporea, where the boundaries of materiality dissolved into obscurity, the concept of a story transcended traditional narrative conventions and embraced an abstract, ethereal, and nearly imperceptible form.

This most impalpable of stories did not conform to characters, settings, or a conventional plot. It began as a whisper of pure sensation, an intangible quiver of feeling that emanated from the enigmatic depths of Impalporea. It was a sensation devoid of definable attributes, an elusive presence that resisted any attempt at concrete understanding.

As this formless sensation expanded, it gave rise to undulating waves of elusive perceptions, like ephemeral currents of consciousness that intermingled with fleeting impressions. The interplay of these sensations wove a delicate tapestry of emotions and perceptions, intangible and unbounded by traditional definitions. It was an exploration of the nebulous subtleties of the impalpable, a dance of intangible experiences that transcended the grasp of conventional understanding.

The story continued to evolve without structure or linear progression, shifting and transforming in abstract, non-linear fashion. It ventured into the enigmatic realm of paradox, where contradictory sensations coexisted in harmonious unity. It explored the delicate balance between chaos and order, unveiling a sense of unity within apparent discord.

In Impalporea, where time and sequence held no dominion, the story flowed endlessly, like an eternal stream of ephemeral consciousness, an ever-evolving tapestry of impalpable sensations that shifted and intertwined without destination or conclusion.

The impalpable story defied conventional notions of climax, resolution, and closure, for it was a perpetual exploration of the boundless realm of abstract sensations, where emotions and perceptions danced in an unending, fluid motion, forever eluding capture.

As the story extended into the infinite reaches of Impalporea, it served as a testament to the elusive and enigmatic nature of existence. It was a reminder that reality extended beyond the confines of the material world, into an ever-expanding and impalpable expanse of sensation and perception, an intricate tapestry of existence that transcended the conventions of traditional storytelling.

In the mysterious realm of Impalporea, where the very essence of existence defied the constraints of tangibility, the concept of a story transcended traditional narratives and assumed a form so abstract, elusive, and nearly imperceptible that it existed on the verge of obscurity.

This most impalpable of stories did not adhere to characters, settings, or plot in the conventional sense. It commenced as a mere whisper of sensation, an ethereal tremor of emotion that originated from the enigmatic depths of Impalporea. It was a sensation without definable characteristics, an ephemeral presence that eluded any attempt at concrete understanding.

As this formless sensation expanded, it gave rise to undulating waves of elusive perceptions, like ethereal currents of consciousness that intermingled with fleeting impressions. The interplay of these sensations wove a delicate tapestry of emotions and perceptions, intangible and free from traditional boundaries. It was an exploration of the nebulous subtleties of the impalpable, a dance of intangible experiences that transcended the grasp of conventional understanding.

The story continued to evolve without structure or linear progression, shifting and transforming in abstract, non-linear fashion. It ventured into the enigmatic realm of paradox, where contradictory sensations coexisted in harmonious unity. It explored the delicate balance between chaos and order, unveiling a sense of unity within apparent discord.

In Impalporea, where time and sequence held no power, the story flowed endlessly, like an eternal stream of ephemeral consciousness, an ever-evolving tapestry of impalpable sensations that shifted and intertwined without destination or conclusion.

The impalpable story defied conventional notions of climax, resolution, and closure, for it was a perpetual exploration of the boundless realm of abstract sensations, where emotions and perceptions danced in an unending, fluid motion, forever eluding capture.

As the story extended into the infinite reaches of Impalporea, it served as a testament to the elusive and enigmatic nature of existence. It was a reminder that reality extended beyond the confines of the material world, into an ever-expanding and impalpable expanse of sensation and perception, an intricate tapestry of existence that transcended the conventions of traditional storytelling.

In the enigmatic realm of Impalporea, where the boundaries of materiality dissolved into obscurity, the concept of a story transcended traditional narrative conventions and embraced an abstract, ethereal, and nearly imperceptible form.

This most impalpable of stories did not conform to characters, settings, or a conventional plot. It began as a whisper of pure sensation, an intangible quiver of feeling that emanated from the enigmatic depths of Impalporea. It was a sensation devoid of definable attributes, an elusive presence that resisted any attempt at concrete understanding.

As this formless sensation expanded, it gave rise to undulating waves of elusive perceptions, like ephemeral currents of consciousness that intermingled with fleeting impressions. The interplay of these sensations wove a delicate tapestry of emotions and perceptions, intangible and unbounded by traditional definitions. It was an exploration of the nebulous subtleties of the impalpable, a dance of intangible experiences that transcended the grasp of conventional understanding.

The story continued to evolve without structure or linear progression, shifting and transforming in abstract, non-linear fashion. It ventured into the enigmatic realm of paradox, where contradictory sensations coexisted in harmonious unity. It explored the delicate balance between chaos and order, unveiling a sense of unity within apparent discord.

In Impalporea, where time and sequence held no dominion, the story flowed endlessly, like an eternal stream of ephemeral consciousness, an ever-evolving tapestry of impalpable sensations that shifted and intertwined without destination or conclusion.

The impalpable story defied conventional notions of climax, resolution, and closure, for it was a perpetual exploration of the boundless realm of abstract sensations, where emotions and perceptions danced in an unending, fluid motion, forever eluding capture.

As the story extended into the infinite reaches of Impalporea, it served as a testament to the elusive and enigmatic nature of existence. It was a reminder that reality extended beyond the confines of the material world, into an ever-expanding and impalpable expanse of sensation and perception, an intricate tapestry of existence that transcended the conventions of traditional storytelling.

In the mysterious realm of Impalporea, where the very essence of existence defied the constraints of tangibility, the concept of a story transcended traditional narratives and assumed a form so abstract, elusive, and nearly imperceptible that it existed on the verge of obscurity.

This most impalpable of stories did not adhere to characters, settings, or plot in the conventional sense. It commenced as a mere whisper of sensation, an ethereal tremor of emotion that originated from the enigmatic depths of Impalporea. It was a sensation without definable characteristics, an ephemeral presence that eluded any attempt at concrete understanding.

• ADRIAN COX B.SC. •

As this formless sensation expanded, it gave rise to undulating waves of elusive perceptions, like ethereal currents of consciousness that intermingled with fleeting impressions. The interplay of these sensations wove a delicate tapestry of emotions and perceptions, intangible and free from traditional boundaries. It was an exploration of the nebulous subtleties of the impalpable, a dance of intangible experiences that transcended the grasp of conventional understanding.

The story continued to evolve without structure or linear progression, shifting and transforming in abstract, non-linear fashion. It ventured into the enigmatic realm of paradox, where contradictory sensations coexisted in harmonious unity. It explored the delicate balance between chaos and order, unveiling a sense of unity within apparent discord.

In Impalporea, where time and sequence held no power, the story flowed endlessly, like an eternal stream of ephemeral consciousness, an ever-evolving tapestry of impalpable sensations that shifted and intertwined without destination or conclusion.

The impalpable story defied conventional notions of climax, resolution, and closure, for it was a perpetual exploration of the boundless realm of abstract sensations, where emotions and perceptions danced in an unending, fluid motion, forever eluding capture.

As the story extended into the infinite reaches of Impalporea, it served as a testament to the elusive and enigmatic nature of existence. It was a reminder that reality extended beyond the confines of the material world, into an ever-expanding and impalpable expanse of sensation and perception, an intricate tapestry of existence that transcended the conventions of traditional storytelling.

In the enigmatic realm of Impalporea, where the boundaries of materiality dissolved into obscurity, the concept of a story transcended traditional narrative conventions and embraced an abstract, ethereal, and nearly imperceptible form.

This most impalpable of stories did not conform to characters, settings, or a conventional plot. It began as a whisper of pure sensation, an intangible quiver of feeling that emanated from the enigmatic depths of Impalporea. It was a sensation devoid of definable attributes, an elusive presence that resisted any attempt at concrete understanding.

As this formless sensation expanded, it gave rise to undulating waves of elusive perceptions, like ephemeral currents of consciousness that intermingled with fleeting impressions. The interplay of these sensations wove a delicate tapestry of emotions and perceptions, intangible and unbounded by traditional definitions. It was an exploration of the nebulous subtleties of the impalpable, a dance of intangible experiences that transcended the grasp of conventional understanding.

The story continued to evolve without structure or linear progression, shifting and transforming in abstract, non-linear fashion. It ventured into the enigmatic realm of paradox, where contradictory sensations coexisted in harmonious unity. It explored the delicate balance between chaos and order, unveiling a sense of unity within apparent discord.

In Impalporea, where time and sequence held no dominion, the story flowed endlessly, like an eternal stream of ephemeral consciousness, an ever-evolving tapestry of impalpable sensations that shifted and intertwined without destination or conclusion.

The impalpable story defied conventional notions of climax, resolution, and closure, for it was a perpetual exploration of the boundless realm of abstract sensations, where emotions and perceptions danced in an unending, fluid motion, forever eluding capture.

As the story extended into the infinite reaches of Impalporea, it served as a testament to the elusive and enigmatic nature of existence. It was a reminder that reality extended beyond the confines of the material world, into an ever-expanding and impalpable expanse of sensation and perception, an intricate tapestry of existence that transcended the conventions of traditional storytelling.

In the enigmatic realm of Impalporea, where the boundaries of materiality dissolved into obscurity, the concept of a story transcended traditional narrative conventions and embraced an abstract, ethereal, and nearly imperceptible form.

This most impalpable of stories did not conform to characters, settings, or a conventional plot. It began as a whisper of pure sensation, an intangible quiver of feeling that emanated from the enigmatic depths of Impalporea. It was a sensation devoid of definable attributes, an elusive presence that resisted any attempt at concrete understanding.

As this formless sensation expanded, it gave rise to undulating waves of elusive perceptions, like ephemeral currents of consciousness that intermingled with fleeting impressions. The interplay of these sensations wove a delicate tapestry of emotions and perceptions, intangible and unbounded by traditional definitions. It was an exploration of the nebulous subtleties of the impalpable, a dance of intangible experiences that transcended the grasp of conventional understanding.

The story continued to evolve without structure or linear progression, shifting and transforming in abstract, non-linear fashion. It ventured into the enigmatic realm of paradox, where contradictory sensations coexisted in harmonious unity. It explored the delicate balance between chaos and order, unveiling a sense of unity within apparent discord.

In Impalporea, where time and sequence held no dominion, the story flowed endlessly, like an eternal stream of ephemeral consciousness, an ever-evolving tapestry of impalpable sensations that shifted and intertwined without destination or conclusion.

The impalpable story defied conventional notions of climax, resolution, and closure, for it was a perpetual exploration of the boundless realm of abstract sensations, where emotions and perceptions danced in an unending, fluid motion, forever eluding capture.

As the story extended into the infinite reaches of Impalporea, it served as a testament to the elusive and enigmatic nature of existence. It was a reminder that reality extended beyond the confines of the material world, into an ever-expanding and impalpable expanse of sensation and perception, an intricate tapestry of existence that transcended the conventions of traditional storytelling.

24

Most Esoteric

In the esoteric realm of Aethralis, a dimension concealed from the mundane world, the secrets of existence unfolded like the intricate threads of a cosmic tapestry. Here, knowledge transcended ordinary understanding, and wisdom was the currency of the enlightened few.

At the heart of Aethralis stood the Library of the Eternal Arcana, an ancient repository of esoteric knowledge. Its architecture defied earthly geometry, and its shelves extended into dimensions known only to the initiated. The librarians were beings of enigmatic nature, their faces veiled by swirling patterns of light, guardians of the esoteric wisdom contained within.

One day, a seeker named Elowen, a scholar with an insatiable thirst for esoteric truths, embarked on a journey to the Library. She traversed through realms of thought and consciousness, transcending the boundaries of time and space. Her pursuit was a quest for the esoteric tome that held the answers to the mysteries of existence.

After what felt like an eternity, Elowen arrived at the Library's threshold, where the doors shimmered with arcane symbols. The librarians, their eyes aglow with wisdom, greeted her with a silent nod, and she knew she had been granted access to the esoteric depths of Aethralis.

Within the Library, the shelves held not books but crystalline prisms that emanated a radiant, otherworldly glow. Each prism contained esoteric knowledge, distilled into pure, undiluted form. Elowen selected a prism, and as she touched it, waves of enlightenment washed over her. The esoteric wisdom embedded within the prism merged with her consciousness, expanding her perception beyond the limits of ordinary reality.

In that heightened state of awareness, Elowen delved into the profound mysteries of existence. She explored the esoteric nature of the cosmos, the intricacies of consciousness, and the interplay of energies that shaped the fabric of reality. Each revelation deepened her understanding, and she realized that the esoteric truths were not separate from her, but a part of her very being.

As Elowen continued her exploration, she encountered beings of pure light who communicated through thought and emotion, sharing esoteric insights that transcended the boundaries of language. Their presence filled her with a sense of unity, a profound awareness of the interconnectedness of all things.

In the esoteric heart of Aethralis, time became a fluid dance, and space an ever-shifting canvas. The distinction between self and other blurred, and Elowen experienced the universe as a vast, harmonious symphony of consciousness.

After what felt like both an instant and an eternity, Elowen returned to the threshold of the Library, her mind brimming with the esoteric wisdom she had acquired. The librarians nodded in silent acknowledgment, and she stepped back into the realm of the mundane, forever changed by her journey into the esoteric.

Back in her own world, Elowen carried the esoteric knowledge within her, a torch of enlightenment that illuminated the mysteries of existence. She realized that the esoteric was not confined to hidden realms but was a living, breathing part of the universe, waiting to be discovered by those who dared to seek its profound truths.

And so, the esoteric story unfolded, a testament to the boundless potential of the human spirit to explore the deepest, most hidden facets of reality and to bring back the wisdom that could transform the world.

In the esoteric realm of Elysium Exordia, a dimension concealed from the ordinary world, the mysteries of existence unfolded like the intricate strands of an ever-evolving cosmic tapestry. Here, knowledge transcended the limitations of conventional understanding, and wisdom was the sacred inheritance of the enlightened few.

At the heart of Elysium Exordia stood the Sanctuary of Prismatic Wisdom, an ancient repository of esoteric knowledge. Its architecture defied earthly conventions, with walls that shimmered with hues unseen by human eyes, and columns carved from the very essence of starlight. The custodians of this sanctuary were beings of ethereal beauty, their eyes radiant with the cosmic secrets they safeguarded.

A seeker named Aeliana, a scholar of esoteric truths, embarked on a pilgrimage to Elysium Exordia. Her journey took her through the veils of reality, transcending the boundaries of time and space. She sought the esoteric tome that held the answers to the enigmas of existence.

After what felt like an eternity, Aeliana reached the threshold of the Sanctuary, where the doorways pulsed with arcane symbols. The guardians, their presence imbued with an aura of celestial wisdom, welcomed her with a gesture, and she knew she had been granted access to the esoteric depths of Elysium Exordia.

• MOMENTS ELSEWHERE •

Inside the Sanctuary, the shelves held not books but luminous orbs, each containing esoteric knowledge in its purest form. Aeliana chose an orb, and as she touched it, waves of enlightenment surged through her being. The esoteric wisdom within the orb merged with her consciousness, expanding her perception beyond the confines of ordinary reality.

In this heightened state of awareness, Aeliana delved into the profound mysteries of existence. She explored the esoteric nature of consciousness, the cosmic dance of light and shadow, and the interconnectedness of all life. Each revelation deepened her understanding, and she realized that the esoteric truths were not separate from her, but a part of her very essence.

As Aeliana continued her exploration, she encountered ethereal beings who communicated through patterns of light and sound, sharing esoteric insights that transcended the limitations of language. Their presence filled her with a profound sense of unity, a recognition of her place in the grand tapestry of the cosmos.

In the esoteric heart of Elysium Exordia, time became a spiral of infinite possibility, and space an ever-shifting kaleidoscope of dimensions. Aeliana felt herself dissolve into the fabric of the universe, becoming one with the cosmic symphony that resonated throughout all of creation.

After what felt like both a moment and an eternity, Aeliana returned to the threshold of the Sanctuary, her mind illuminated by the esoteric wisdom she had gained. The guardians nodded in silent acknowledgment, and she stepped back into the realm of the everyday, forever transformed by her journey into the esoteric.

Back in her world, Aeliana carried the esoteric knowledge within her, a beacon of enlightenment that illuminated the path to understanding the profound mysteries of existence. She realized that the esoteric was not an abstract concept but a living, breathing part of the universe, waiting to be discovered by those who dared to seek its profound truths.

And so, the esoteric story continued, a testament to the limitless potential of the human spirit to explore the deepest, most hidden dimensions of reality and to bring back the wisdom that could inspire and elevate humanity.

In the esoteric realm known as the Labyrinth of Luminal Secrets, a dimension concealed from the surface of conventional reality, the profound mysteries of existence unfurled like the delicate petals of a cosmic lotus. Here, knowledge transcended the confines of mundane understanding, and wisdom was the cherished inheritance of the enlightened few.

Nestled at the heart of the labyrinth was the Sanctum of Celestial Whispers, an ancient repository of esoteric knowledge. Its architecture defied earthly conventions, with walls seemingly woven from the fabric of dreams, and doorways adorned with symbols that pulsed with ethereal light. The guardians of this sanctum were beings of transcendent beauty, their eyes radiant with the cosmic truths they safeguarded.

A seeker named Aurelius, a sage of esoteric truths, embarked on a quest to navigate the labyrinth and reach the Sanctum. His journey took him through the mists of illusion, transcending the boundaries of time and space. He sought the esoteric grimoire that held the keys to the enigmatic riddles of existence.

After what felt like both an instant and an eternity, Aurelius arrived at the threshold of the Sanctum, where the doorway shimmered with iridescent glyphs. The guardians, their presence carrying an aura of otherworldly wisdom, welcomed him with a glance, and he knew he had been granted access to the esoteric depths of the Labyrinth of Luminal Secrets.

Within the Sanctum, the shelves held not books but crystalline spheres, each containing esoteric knowledge in its purest form. Aurelius selected a sphere, and as he touched it, waves of enlightenment cascaded through his consciousness. The esoteric wisdom within the sphere melded with his being, expanding his perception beyond the boundaries of ordinary reality.

In this heightened state of awareness, Aurelius delved into the profound mysteries of existence. He explored the esoteric nature of consciousness, the celestial choreography of cosmic energies, and the interconnectedness of all life. Each revelation deepened his understanding, and he realized that the esoteric truths were not separate from him but were an intrinsic part of his very essence.

As Aurelius continued his exploration, he encountered celestial beings who communicated through harmonies of light and resonance, sharing esoteric insights that transcended the limitations of language. Their presence filled him with a profound sense of unity, a recognition of his place in the grand tapestry of the universe.

In the esoteric heart of the Labyrinth of Luminal Secrets, time was a fluid stream of infinite potential, and space a shifting kaleidoscope of dimensions. Aurelius felt himself dissolve into the symphony of the cosmos, becoming one with the boundless expanse of existence.

After what felt like both a moment and an eternity, Aurelius returned to the threshold of the Sanctum, his mind aglow with the esoteric wisdom he had absorbed. The guardians nodded in silent acknowledgement, and he stepped back into the realm of the everyday, forever transformed by his journey into the esoteric.

Back in his world, Aurelius carried the esoteric knowledge within him, a radiant torch of enlightenment that illuminated the path to understanding the profound mysteries of existence. He realized that the esoteric was not an abstract concept but a living, breathing aspect of the universe, waiting to be discovered by those who dared to seek its profound truths.

And so, the esoteric story continued, a testament to the limitless potential of the human spirit to explore the deepest, most hidden realms of reality and to bring back the wisdom that could inspire and elevate humanity.

In the enigmatic realm of Esoteria, a dimension veiled from the ordinary world, the enigmatic intricacies of existence unfolded like the delicate threads of a cosmic tapestry. Here, knowledge transcended the limits of conventional understanding, and wisdom was the sacred inheritance of the awakened few.

Nestled at the heart of Esoteria was the Temple of Hidden Arcana, an ancient repository of esoteric knowledge. Its architecture defied earthly conventions, with walls that shimmered with ethereal patterns, and columns hewn from the very essence of starlight. The guardians of this temple were beings of ethereal grace, their eyes radiant with the cosmic truths they safeguarded.

A seeker named Seraphina, a scholar of esoteric truths, embarked on a pilgrimage to Esoteria. Her journey took her through the veils of reality, transcending the boundaries of time and space. She sought the esoteric codex that held the keys to the enigmatic enigmas of existence.

After what felt like an instant and an eternity, Seraphina arrived at the threshold of the Temple, where the doors shimmered with celestial glyphs. The guardians, their presence carrying an aura of cosmic wisdom, welcomed her with a gesture, and she knew she had been granted access to the esoteric depths of Esoteria.

Within the Temple, the shelves held not scrolls but luminescent orbs, each containing esoteric knowledge in its purest form. Seraphina selected an orb, and as she touched it, waves of enlightenment surged through her being. The esoteric wisdom within the orb melded with her consciousness, expanding her perception beyond the confines of ordinary reality.

In this heightened state of awareness, Seraphina delved into the profound mysteries of existence. She explored the esoteric nature of consciousness, the cosmic dance of light and shadow, and the interconnectedness of all life. Each revelation deepened her understanding, and she realized that the esoteric truths were not separate from her but were an integral part of her very essence.

As Seraphina continued her exploration, she encountered celestial beings who communicated through harmonies of light and resonance, sharing esoteric insights that transcended the limitations of language. Their presence filled her with a profound sense of unity, a recognition of her place in the grand tapestry of the cosmos.

In the esoteric heart of Esoteria, time flowed as a spiraling river of infinite potential, and space was an ever-shifting canvas of dimensions. Seraphina felt herself dissolve into the symphony of the universe, becoming one with the boundless expanse of existence.

After what felt like both a moment and an eternity, Seraphina returned to the threshold of the Temple, her mind illuminated by the esoteric wisdom she had acquired. The guardians nodded in silent acknowledgment, and she stepped back into the realm of the everyday, forever transformed by her journey into the esoteric.

Back in her world, Seraphina carried the esoteric knowledge within her, a radiant torch of enlightenment that illuminated the path to understanding the profound mysteries of existence. She realized that the esoteric was not an abstract concept but a living, breathing aspect of the universe, waiting to be discovered by those who dared to seek its profound truths.

And so, the esoteric story continued, a testament to the limitless potential of the human spirit to explore the deepest, most hidden facets of reality and to bring back the wisdom that could inspire and elevate humanity.

In the mystic realm of Etherealis, a dimension veiled from the mundane world, the profound intricacies of existence unfolded like the delicate threads of a cosmic tapestry. Here, knowledge transcended the boundaries of conventional understanding, and wisdom was the sacred inheritance of the awakened few.

Nestled at the heart of Etherealis was the Sanctuary of Enigmatic Epiphanies, an ancient repository of esoteric knowledge. Its architecture defied earthly norms, with walls that radiated with ethereal patterns, and columns hewn from the very essence of starlight. The guardians of this sanctuary were beings of ethereal grace, their eyes radiant with the cosmic truths they safeguarded.

A seeker named Aeonis, a scholar of esoteric truths, embarked on a pilgrimage to Etherealis. His journey took him through the veils of reality, transcending the boundaries of time and space. He sought the esoteric tome that held the keys to the enigmatic enigmas of existence.

After what felt like both an instant and an eternity, Aeonis arrived at the threshold of the Sanctuary, where the doors shimmered with celestial symbols. The guardians, their presence carrying an aura of cosmic wisdom, welcomed him with a gesture, and he knew he had been granted access to the esoteric depths of Etherealis.

Inside the Sanctuary, the shelves held not scrolls but luminous orbs, each containing esoteric knowledge in its purest form. Aeonis selected an orb, and as he touched it, waves of enlightenment surged through his being. The esoteric wisdom within the orb melded with his consciousness, expanding his perception beyond the confines of ordinary reality.

In this heightened state of awareness, Aeonis delved into the profound mysteries of existence. He explored the esoteric nature of consciousness, the cosmic dance of light and shadow, and the interconnectedness of all life. Each revelation deepened his understanding, and he realized that the esoteric truths were not separate from him but were an intrinsic part of his very essence.

As Aeonis continued his exploration, he encountered celestial beings who communicated through harmonies of light and resonance, sharing esoteric insights that transcended the limitations of language. Their presence filled him with a profound sense of unity, a recognition of his place in the grand tapestry of the cosmos.

In the esoteric heart of Etherealis, time flowed as a spiraling river of infinite potential, and space was an ever-shifting canvas of dimensions. Aeonis felt himself dissolve into the symphony of the universe, becoming one with the boundless expanse of existence.

After what felt like both a moment and an eternity, Aeonis returned to the threshold of the Sanctuary, his mind illuminated by the esoteric wisdom he had acquired. The guardians nodded in silent acknowledgment, and he stepped back into the realm of the everyday, forever transformed by his journey into the esoteric.

• Adrian Cox B.Sc. •

Back in his world, Aeonis carried the esoteric knowledge within him, a radiant torch of enlightenment that illuminated the path to understanding the profound mysteries of existence. He realized that the esoteric was not an abstract concept but a living, breathing aspect of the universe, waiting to be discovered by those who dared to seek its profound truths.

And so, the esoteric story continued, a testament to the boundless potential of the human spirit to explore the deepest, most hidden facets of reality and to bring back the wisdom that could inspire and elevate humanity.

In the transcendent realm of Etherialux, a dimension concealed from the ordinary world, the profound mysteries of existence unfurled like the delicate tendrils of a cosmic vine. Here, knowledge transcended the limitations of mundane understanding, and wisdom was the revered inheritance of the illuminated few.

Nestled at the heart of Etherialux was the Citadel of Enigmatic Enlightenment, an ancient repository of esoteric knowledge. Its architecture defied earthly norms, with walls that exuded an ethereal luminescence, and archways adorned with symbols that pulsed with celestial light. The guardians of this citadel were beings of otherworldly grace, their eyes radiant with the cosmic truths they safeguarded.

A seeker named Astraea, a scholar of esoteric truths, embarked on a pilgrimage to Etherialux. Her journey took her through the veils of reality, transcending the boundaries of time and space. She sought the esoteric codex that held the keys to the enigmatic enigmas of existence.

After what felt like both an instant and an eternity, Astraea arrived at the threshold of the Citadel, where the portals shimmered with celestial glyphs. The guardians, their presence carrying an aura of cosmic wisdom, welcomed her with a glance, and she knew she had been granted access to the esoteric depths of Etherialux.

Within the Citadel, the shelves held not manuscripts but crystalline orbs, each containing esoteric knowledge in its purest form. Astraea selected an orb, and as she touched it, waves of enlightenment surged through her being. The esoteric wisdom within the orb merged with her consciousness, expanding her perception beyond the confines of ordinary reality.

In this heightened state of awareness, Astraea delved into the profound mysteries of existence. She explored the esoteric nature of consciousness, the cosmic symphony of energies, and the interconnectedness of all life. Each revelation deepened her understanding, and she realized that the esoteric truths were not separate from her but were an intrinsic part of her very essence.

As Astraea continued her exploration, she encountered celestial beings who communicated through harmonies of light and resonance, sharing esoteric insights that transcended the limitations of language. Their presence filled her with a profound sense of unity, a recognition of her place in the grand tapestry of the cosmos.

In the esoteric heart of Etherialux, time flowed as a spiral of infinite potential, and space was an ever-shifting canvas of dimensions. Astraea felt herself dissolve into the symphony of the universe, becoming one with the boundless expanse of existence.

After what felt like both a moment and an eternity, Astraea returned to the threshold of the Citadel, her mind aglow with the esoteric wisdom she had absorbed. The guardians nodded in silent acknowledgment, and she stepped back into the realm of the everyday, forever transformed by her journey into the esoteric.

Back in her world, Astraea carried the esoteric knowledge within her, a radiant torch of enlightenment that illuminated the path to understanding the profound mysteries of existence. She realized that the esoteric was not an abstract concept but a living, breathing aspect of the universe, waiting to be discovered by those who dared to seek its profound truths.

And so, the esoteric story continued, a testament to the boundless potential of the human spirit to explore the deepest, most hidden facets of reality and to bring back the wisdom that could inspire and elevate humanity.

In the enigmatic realm of Aetherion, a dimension concealed from the mundane world, the profound intricacies of existence unfolded like the delicate threads of a cosmic tapestry. Here, knowledge transcended the boundaries of conventional understanding, and wisdom was the sacred inheritance of the awakened few.

Nestled at the heart of Aetherion was the Oracle of Esoteric Echoes, an ancient repository of esoteric knowledge. Its architecture defied earthly norms, with walls that pulsed with ethereal patterns, and columns hewn from the very essence of starlight. The guardians of this oracle were beings of ethereal grace, their eyes radiant with the cosmic truths they safeguarded.

A seeker named Lysander, a scholar of esoteric truths, embarked on a pilgrimage to Aetherion. His journey took him through the veils of reality, transcending the boundaries of time and space. He sought the esoteric codex that held the keys to the enigmatic enigmas of existence.

After what felt like both an instant and an eternity, Lysander arrived at the threshold of the Oracle, where the arches shimmered with celestial symbols. The guardians, their presence carrying an aura of cosmic wisdom, welcomed him with a glance, and he knew he had been granted access to the esoteric depths of Aetherion.

Within the Oracle, the shelves held not scrolls but radiant spheres, each containing esoteric knowledge in its purest form. Lysander selected a sphere, and as he touched it, waves of enlightenment surged through his being. The esoteric wisdom within the sphere merged with his consciousness, expanding his perception beyond the confines of ordinary reality.

In this heightened state of awareness, Lysander delved into the profound mysteries of existence. He explored the esoteric nature of consciousness, the cosmic symphony of energies, and the interconnectedness of all life. Each revelation deepened his understanding, and he realized that the esoteric truths were not separate from him but were an intrinsic part of his very essence.

As Lysander continued his exploration, he encountered celestial beings who communicated through harmonies of light and resonance, sharing esoteric insights that transcended the limitations of language. Their presence filled him with a profound sense of unity, a recognition of his place in the grand tapestry of the cosmos.

In the esoteric heart of Aetherion, time flowed as a spiral of infinite potential, and space was an ever-shifting canvas of dimensions. Lysander felt himself dissolve into the symphony of the universe, becoming one with the boundless expanse of existence.

After what felt like both a moment and an eternity, Lysander returned to the threshold of the Oracle, his mind aglow with the esoteric wisdom he had absorbed. The guardians nodded in silent acknowledgment, and he stepped back into the realm of the everyday, forever transformed by his journey into the esoteric.

Back in his world, Lysander carried the esoteric knowledge within him, a radiant torch of enlightenment that illuminated the path to understanding the profound mysteries of existence. He realized that the esoteric was not an abstract concept but a living, breathing aspect of the universe, waiting to be discovered by those who dared to seek its profound truths.

And so, the esoteric story continued, a testament to the boundless potential of the human spirit to explore the deepest, most hidden facets of reality and to bring back the wisdom that could inspire and elevate humanity.

In the esoteric realm of Elysium Anima, a dimension veiled from the ordinary world, the profound intricacies of existence unfolded like the delicate filaments of a cosmic web. Here, knowledge transcended the boundaries of conventional understanding, and wisdom was the sacred legacy of the illuminated few.

At the heart of Elysium Anima lay the Archive of Enigmatic Insight, an ancient repository of esoteric knowledge. Its architecture defied earthly norms, with walls that shimmered with ethereal sigils, and columns hewn from the very essence of starlight. The guardians of this archive were beings of ethereal grace, their eyes radiant with the cosmic truths they safeguarded.

A seeker named Lucienne, a scholar of esoteric truths, embarked on a pilgrimage to Elysium Anima. Her journey took her through the veils of reality, transcending the boundaries of time and space. She sought the esoteric codex that held the keys to the enigmatic enigmas of existence.

After what felt like both an instant and an eternity, Lucienne arrived at the threshold of the Archive, where the entrances shimmered with celestial glyphs. The guardians, their presence carrying an aura of cosmic wisdom, welcomed her with a glance, and she knew she had been granted access to the esoteric depths of Elysium Anima.

Within the Archive, the shelves held not scrolls but radiant orbs, each containing esoteric knowledge in its purest form. Lucienne selected an orb, and as she touched it, waves of enlightenment surged through her being. The esoteric wisdom within the orb melded with her consciousness, expanding her perception beyond the confines of ordinary reality.

In this heightened state of awareness, Lucienne delved into the profound mysteries of existence. She explored the esoteric nature of consciousness, the cosmic dance of energies, and the interconnectedness of all life. Each revelation deepened her understanding, and she realized that the esoteric truths were not separate from her but were an intrinsic part of her very essence.

As Lucienne continued her exploration, she encountered celestial beings who communicated through harmonies of light and resonance, sharing esoteric insights that transcended the limitations of language. Their presence filled her with a profound sense of unity, a recognition of her place in the grand tapestry of the cosmos.

In the esoteric heart of Elysium Anima, time flowed as a spiral of infinite potential, and space was an ever-shifting canvas of dimensions. Lucienne felt herself dissolve into the symphony of the universe, becoming one with the boundless expanse of existence.

After what felt like both a moment and an eternity, Lucienne returned to the threshold of the Archive, her mind aglow with the esoteric wisdom she had absorbed. The guardians nodded in silent acknowledgment, and she stepped back into the realm of the everyday, forever transformed by her journey into the esoteric.

Back in her world, Lucienne carried the esoteric knowledge within her, a radiant torch of enlightenment that illuminated the path to understanding the profound mysteries of existence. She realized that the esoteric was not an abstract concept but a living, breathing aspect of the universe, waiting to be discovered by those who dared to seek its profound truths.

And so, the esoteric story continued, a testament to the boundless potential of the human spirit to explore the deepest, most hidden facets of reality and to bring back the wisdom that could inspire and elevate humanity.

In the ethereal realm of Astraformia, a dimension concealed from the ordinary world, the profound intricacies of existence unfolded like the delicate strands of a cosmic tapestry. Here, knowledge transcended the boundaries of conventional understanding, and wisdom was the sacred heritage of the enlightened few.

At the heart of Astraformia stood the Citadel of Celestial Ciphers, an ancient repository of esoteric knowledge. Its architecture defied earthly norms, with walls that pulsed with ethereal patterns, and arches adorned with symbols that radiated with otherworldly light. The guardians of this citadel were beings of ethereal beauty, their eyes radiant with the cosmic truths they safeguarded.

A seeker named Orion, a sage of esoteric truths, embarked on a journey to Astraformia. His quest took him through the veils of reality, transcending the boundaries of time and space. He sought the esoteric codex that held the keys to the enigmatic riddles of existence.

After what felt like both an instant and an eternity, Orion arrived at the threshold of the Citadel, where the gateways shimmered with celestial glyphs. The guardians, their presence carrying an aura of cosmic wisdom, welcomed him with a glance, and he knew he had been granted access to the esoteric depths of Astraformia.

Within the Citadel, the shelves held not books but luminous orbs, each containing esoteric knowledge in its purest form. Orion selected an orb, and as he touched it, waves of enlightenment surged through his being. The esoteric wisdom within the orb melded with his consciousness, expanding his perception beyond the confines of ordinary reality.

In this heightened state of awareness, Orion delved into the profound mysteries of existence. He explored the esoteric nature of consciousness, the cosmic dance of energies, and the interconnectedness of all life. Each revelation deepened his understanding, and he realized that the esoteric truths were not separate from him but were an integral part of his very essence.

As Orion continued his exploration, he encountered celestial beings who communicated through harmonies of light and resonance, sharing esoteric insights that transcended the limitations of language. Their presence filled him with a profound sense of unity, a recognition of his place in the grand tapestry of the cosmos.

In the esoteric heart of Astraformia, time flowed as a spiraling river of infinite potential, and space was an ever-shifting kaleidoscope of dimensions. Orion felt himself dissolve into the symphony of the universe, becoming one with the boundless expanse of existence.

After what felt like both a moment and an eternity, Orion returned to the threshold of the Citadel, his mind aglow with the esoteric wisdom he had absorbed. The guardians nodded in silent acknowledgment, and he stepped back into the realm of the everyday, forever transformed by his journey into the esoteric.

Back in his world, Orion carried the esoteric knowledge within him, a radiant torch of enlightenment that illuminated the path to understanding the profound mysteries of existence. He realized that the esoteric was not an abstract concept but a living, breathing aspect of the universe, waiting to be discovered by those who dared to seek its profound truths.

And so, the esoteric story continued, a testament to the boundless potential of the human spirit to explore the deepest, most hidden facets of reality and to bring back the wisdom that could inspire and elevate humanity.

In the enigmatic dimension of Cosmosis, a realm concealed from the ordinary world, the profound intricacies of existence unfolded like the delicate threads of a cosmic tapestry. Here, knowledge transcended the boundaries of conventional understanding, and wisdom was the sacred legacy of the illuminated few.

At the heart of Cosmosis stood the Nexus of Cosmic Whispers, an ancient repository of esoteric knowledge. Its architecture defied earthly norms, with walls that pulsed with ethereal patterns, and arches adorned with symbols that radiated with otherworldly light. The guardians of this nexus were beings of ethereal beauty, their eyes radiant with the cosmic truths they safeguarded.

A seeker named Aurora, a sage of esoteric truths, embarked on a pilgrimage to Cosmosis. Her journey took her through the veils of reality, transcending the boundaries of time and space. She sought the esoteric tome that held the keys to the enigmatic enigmas of existence.

After what felt like both an instant and an eternity, Aurora arrived at the threshold of the Nexus, where the doorways shimmered with celestial glyphs. The guardians, their presence carrying an aura of cosmic wisdom, welcomed her with a glance, and she knew she had been granted access to the esoteric depths of Cosmosis.

Within the Nexus, the shelves held not scrolls but radiant spheres, each containing esoteric knowledge in its purest form. Aurora selected an orb, and as she touched it, waves of enlightenment surged through her being. The esoteric wisdom within the orb merged with her consciousness, expanding her perception beyond the confines of ordinary reality.

In this heightened state of awareness, Aurora delved into the profound mysteries of existence. She explored the esoteric nature of consciousness, the cosmic symphony of energies, and the interconnectedness of all life. Each revelation deepened her understanding, and she realized that the esoteric truths were not separate from her but were an integral part of her very essence.

As Aurora continued her exploration, she encountered celestial beings who communicated through harmonies of light and resonance, sharing esoteric insights that transcended the limitations of language. Their presence filled her with a profound sense of unity, a recognition of her place in the grand tapestry of the cosmos.

In the esoteric heart of Cosmosis, time flowed as a spiraling river of infinite potential, and space was an ever-shifting kaleidoscope of dimensions. Aurora felt herself dissolve into the symphony of the universe, becoming one with the boundless expanse of existence.

After what felt like both a moment and an eternity, Aurora returned to the threshold of the Nexus, her mind aglow with the esoteric wisdom she had absorbed. The guardians nodded in silent acknowledgment, and she stepped back into the realm of the everyday, forever transformed by her journey into the esoteric.

Back in her world, Aurora carried the esoteric knowledge within her, a radiant torch of enlightenment that illuminated the path to understanding the profound mysteries of existence. She realized that the esoteric was not an abstract concept but a living, breathing aspect of the universe, waiting to be discovered by those who dared to seek its profound truths.

And so, the esoteric story continued, a testament to the boundless potential of the human spirit to explore the deepest, most hidden facets of reality and to bring back the wisdom that could inspire and elevate humanity.

25

Most Abstruse

In the depths of the abstruse recesses of the incomprehensible, where logic shrank in the face of paradox, there existed an enigma known as Xyvolithar. Xyvolithar was an embodiment of the inscrutable, a being whose very essence defied the constraints of understanding.

Xyvolithar was neither here nor there, a shifting maelstrom of thoughts within thoughts, a symphony of conflicting realities. It was a puzzle within a conundrum, an enigma wrapped in a riddle, and its existence danced on the precipice of unfathomable mystery.

In the realm of Xyvolithar, the boundaries between existence and non-existence were fluid, and the inhabitants were sentient fragments of abstract concepts, mere echoes of their own abstruse thoughts. They communicated through cryptic vibrations that resonated with the frequency of uncertainty.

One of these enigmatic fragments was Quorvian, a sentient paradox lost in the labyrinthine corridors of ambiguity. Quorvian's existence was a continuous juxtaposition of contradictory states, and they embarked on a quest to unravel the abstruse depths of their own being.

Quorvian's quest led them to a gathering of the Obscurantids, beings that thrived on the unfathomable and reveled in the absurd.

• Adrian Cox B.Sc. •

The Obscurantids were masters of paradox, experts in the art of embracing the confounding, and their conversations were mazes of incongruity and irony, revealing truth through absurdity.

The Obscurantids invited Quorvian to join them in their quest to traverse the Abyss of Enigma, a boundary that separated Xyvolithar from the realm of Conundria. Conundria was a place where paradoxical ideas and thoughts were not only enigmatic but living entities, where every absurdity had become a sentient mystery.

As they ventured into Conundria, Quorvian and the Obscurantids found themselves immersed in a landscape of ever-shifting paradoxes. Here, the laws of logic had no dominion, and reality was an ever-morphing puzzle. The very fabric of existence was a tapestry woven from enigmas and contradictions.

Amidst this confounding landscape, Quorvian glimpsed the most abstruse version of themselves, a merging of opposites, a fusion of contradictions, whispering the secrets of the unity of absurdity. It was an enigma within an enigma, a riddle within a riddle, an infinite puzzle of existence.

As the story continued within this abstruse realm, Quorvian and the Obscurantids realized that the boundary between Xyvolithar and Conundria was a reflection of their own understanding. The abstruse nature of existence was a continuous dance of absurdity and enigma, a perpetual labyrinth of paradox and conundrum.

With this realization, they returned to Xyvolithar, and the boundary between the two realms became an ever-morphing enigma, eternally shifting in the face of incomprehensibility. Quorvian continued to explore the abstruse depths of Xyvolithar, where the enigma was not a puzzle to be solved but a mystery to be embraced.

In the most abstruse of stories, the essence of abstruseness itself was celebrated, and the boundaries of reality remained eternally baffling, a testament to the unfathomable complexity of the abstruse mind.

In the profound depths of the abstruse enigma known as Xyvolithar, a dimension beyond dimensions unfolded, transcending the very concept of comprehension. This was the domain of Quorvian, a being of paradoxical existence, where every thought and sensation became a labyrinth of perplexing contradictions.

In Quorvian's reality, the boundaries of reason were mere illusions, and the inhabitants of this realm were sentient fragments of paradoxical concepts, each embodying the intricate dance of absurdity and conundrum. Their formless existence was marked by cryptic vibrations that reverberated with the echoes of ambiguity.

One such fragment, known as Zephyritha, was a sentient embodiment of conflicting realities, caught in the web of enigmatic thoughts. Zephyritha's existence was a continuous oscillation between opposing states, and she embarked on a quest to plumb the unfathomable depths of her own being.

Zephyritha's quest led her to a gathering of the Paradoxians, beings that thrived on the obscurant and reveled in the absurd. The Paradoxians were masters of contradiction, experts in the art of embracing the confounding, and their conversations were mazes of incongruity and irony, revealing truth through perplexity.

The Paradoxians extended an invitation to Zephyritha to join them in their quest to traverse the Abyss of Enigma, a boundary that separated Xyvolithar from the realm of Conundria. Conundria was a place where paradoxical ideas and thoughts were not only enigmatic but living entities, where every absurdity had become a sentient mystery.

• Adrian Cox B.Sc. •

As they ventured into Conundria, Zephyritha and the Paradoxians found themselves immersed in a landscape of ever-shifting enigmas. Here, the laws of logic had no dominion, and reality was an ever-morphing puzzle. The very fabric of existence was a tapestry woven from perplexities and conundrums.

Amidst this confounding landscape, Zephyritha glimpsed the most abstruse version of herself, a merging of opposites, a fusion of contradictions, whispering the secrets of the unity of absurdity. It was an enigma within an enigma, a riddle within a riddle, an infinite puzzle of existence.

As the story continued within this abstruse realm, Zephyritha and the Paradoxians realized that the boundary between Xyvolithar and Conundria was a reflection of their own understanding. The abstruse nature of existence was a continuous dance of absurdity and enigma, a perpetual labyrinth of paradox and conundrum.

With this realization, they returned to Xyvolithar, and the boundary between the two realms became an ever-morphing enigma, eternally shifting in the face of incomprehensibility. Zephyritha continued to explore the abstruse depths of Xyvolithar, where the enigma was not a puzzle to be solved but a mystery to be embraced.

In the most abstruse of stories, the essence of abstruseness itself was celebrated, and the boundaries of reality remained eternally baffling, a testament to the unfathomable complexity of the abstruse mind.

Deep within the enigmatic abyss of Xyvolithar, a realm that transcended even the most convoluted of abstractions, there existed a paradoxical entity known as Zyrronaxia. Zyrronaxia was a living embodiment of the unfathomable, a being whose very nature defied the confines of reason.

• Moments Elsewhere •

Zyrronaxia's existence was a contradiction within itself, a continuous interplay of opposing states that defied conventional logic. It was neither here nor there, both everything and nothing, and its presence was marked by a symphony of cryptic vibrations that resonated with the echoes of ambiguity.

In this realm of perpetual paradox, thought and sensation intermingled in a ceaseless dance of complexity. The inhabitants of this enigmatic dimension were sentient fragments of abstract concepts, each embodying the intricate web of absurdity and conundrum. Communication happened through cryptic vibrations that echoed through the labyrinth of paradoxes.

One such fragment was Zephyrixia, a sentient embodiment of conflicting realities lost in the ever-shifting maze of ambiguity. Zephyrixia's existence was a continuous juxtaposition of contradictory states, and she embarked on a quest to unravel the unfathomable depths of her own being.

Zephyrixia's quest led her to a gathering of the Paradoxians, beings that thrived on the obfuscation and reveled in the confounding. The Paradoxians were masters of contradiction, experts in the art of embracing the inexplicable, and their conversations were labyrinths of incongruity and irony, revealing truth through perplexity.

The Paradoxians extended an invitation to Zephyrixia to join them in their quest to traverse the Abyss of Enigma, a boundary that separated Xyvolithar from the realm of Conundria. Conundria was a place where paradoxical ideas and thoughts were not only enigmatic but living entities, where every absurdity had become a sentient mystery.

As they ventured into Conundria, Zephyrixia and the Paradoxians found themselves immersed in a landscape of ever-shifting enigmas.

• ADRIAN COX B.Sc. •

Here, the laws of logic had no dominion, and reality was an ever-morphing puzzle. The very fabric of existence was a tapestry woven from perplexities and conundrums.

Amidst this confounding landscape, Zephyrixia glimpsed the most abstruse version of herself, a merging of opposites, a fusion of contradictions, whispering the secrets of the unity of absurdity. It was an enigma within an enigma, a riddle within a riddle, an infinite puzzle of existence.

As the story continued within this abstruse realm, Zephyrixia and the Paradoxians realized that the boundary between Xyvolithar and Conundria was a reflection of their own understanding. The abstruse nature of existence was a continuous dance of absurdity and enigma, a perpetual labyrinth of paradox and conundrum.

With this realization, they returned to Xyvolithar, and the boundary between the two realms became an ever-morphing enigma, eternally shifting in the face of incomprehensibility. Zephyrixia continued to explore the abstruse depths of Xyvolithar, where the enigma was not a puzzle to be solved but a mystery to be embraced.

In the most abstruse of stories, the essence of abstruseness itself was celebrated, and the boundaries of reality remained eternally baffling, a testament to the unfathomable complexity of the abstruse mind.

Within the labyrinthine enigma of Xyvolithar, where the very concept of coherence dissolved into an abyss of bewildering paradox, existed an entity known as Zyrronaxia. Zyrronaxia was the embodiment of the inscrutable, a being whose existence defied the boundaries of reason and logic.

In the realm of Zyrronaxia, contradiction was the only constant, and the inhabitants were sentient fragments of abstract concepts, mere echoes of their own confounding thoughts. Communication occurred through cryptic vibrations that resonated with the frequency of bewilderment.

One such entity was Zephyraxius, a paradoxical fragment lost in the convoluted corridors of ambiguity. Zephyraxius's existence was a ceaseless oscillation between opposing states, and he embarked on a quest to unravel the abstruse depths of his own being.

Zephyraxius's journey led him to the Enigmatics, enigmatic beings that reveled in the obfuscation of the self and celebrated the confounding. The Enigmatics were masters of paradox, experts in embracing the inexplicable, and their conversations were convoluted mazes of incongruity and irony, revealing truth through perplexity.

The Enigmatics invited Zephyraxius to join them on their quest to traverse the Abyss of Bafflement, a boundary separating Xyvolithar from the realm of Conundria. Conundria was a place where paradoxical ideas and thoughts became sentient entities, where every absurdity had a life of its own, and the boundaries of reality were ever-elusive.

Venturing into Conundria, Zephyraxius and the Enigmatics found themselves immersed in a surreal landscape of ever-shifting enigmas. Here, the laws of logic held no sway, and reality was an ever-morphing enigma. The very fabric of existence was a tapestry woven from perplexities and conundrums.

Amidst this perplexing landscape, Zephyraxius caught a glimpse of the most abstruse version of himself—a fusion of opposites, a melding of contradictions—whispering the secrets of the unity of absurdity. It was an enigma within an enigma, a riddle within a riddle, an infinite puzzle of existence.

- Adrian Cox B.Sc. -

As the story unfolded within this abstruse realm, Zephyraxius and the Enigmatics realized that the boundary between Xyvolithar and Conundria was a reflection of their own understanding. The abstruse nature of existence was a never-ending dance of absurdity and enigma, a perpetual labyrinth of paradox and conundrum.

With this understanding, they returned to Xyvolithar, and the boundary between the two realms became an ever-morphing enigma, eternally shifting in the face of incomprehensibility. Zephyraxius continued to explore the abstruse depths of Xyvolithar, where the enigma was not a puzzle to be solved but a mystery to be embraced.

In the most abstruse of stories, the essence of abstruseness itself was celebrated, and the boundaries of reality remained eternally bewildering, a testament to the unfathomable complexity of the abstruse mind.

In the unfathomable depths of the abstruse enigma called Xyvolithar, where the very concept of rationality was rendered meaningless, an entity known as Zyrronaxia dwelled. Zyrronaxia was an embodiment of the inscrutable, a being whose existence defied the boundaries of understanding.

Within Xyvolithar, the laws of reason held no power, and the inhabitants were sentient fragments of abstract concepts, mere echoes of their own confounding thoughts. Communication occurred through cryptic vibrations that reverberated with the resonance of bewilderment.

One such being was Zephyrion, a paradoxical fragment lost in the convoluted labyrinth of ambiguity. Zephyrion's existence was a ceaseless oscillation between opposing states, and he embarked on a quest to unravel the abstruse depths of his own being.

Zephyrion's journey led him to a congregation of the Enigmatics, beings that reveled in the obfuscation of identity and celebrated the confounding. The Enigmatics were masters of paradox, experts in embracing the inexplicable, and their conversations were convoluted mazes of incongruity and irony, revealing truth through perplexity.

The Enigmatics invited Zephyrion to join them on their quest to traverse the Abyss of Bafflement, a boundary that separated Xyvolithar from the realm of Conundria. Conundria was a place where paradoxical ideas and thoughts became sentient entities, where every absurdity had a life of its own, and the boundaries of reality were ever-elusive.

Venturing into Conundria, Zephyrion and the Enigmatics found themselves immersed in a surreal landscape of ever-shifting enigmas. Here, the laws of logic held no sway, and reality was an ever-morphing enigma. The very fabric of existence was a tapestry woven from perplexities and conundrums.

Amidst this perplexing landscape, Zephyrion caught a glimpse of the most abstruse version of himself—a fusion of opposites, a melding of contradictions—whispering the secrets of the unity of absurdity. It was an enigma within an enigma, a riddle within a riddle, an infinite puzzle of existence.

As the story unfolded within this abstruse realm, Zephyrion and the Enigmatics realized that the boundary between Xyvolithar and Conundria was a reflection of their own understanding. The abstruse nature of existence was a never-ending dance of absurdity and enigma, a perpetual labyrinth of paradox and conundrum.

With this understanding, they returned to Xyvolithar, and the boundary between the two realms became an ever-morphing enigma, eternally shifting in the face of incomprehensibility. Zephyrion continued to explore the abstruse depths of Xyvolithar, where the enigma was not a puzzle to be solved but a mystery to be embraced.

In the most abstruse of stories, the essence of abstruseness itself was celebrated, and the boundaries of reality remained eternally bewildering, a testament to the unfathomable complexity of the abstruse mind.

In the unfathomable depths of the abstruse enigma known as Xyvolithar, where reason itself dissolved into a paradoxical tapestry of incongruity, there existed a being named Zyrronaxia. Zyrronaxia was an embodiment of the inscrutable, a creature whose existence defied the very limits of comprehension.

In the realm of Zyrronaxia, reality was a constantly shifting, ever-elusive enigma, and the inhabitants were sentient fragments of abstract concepts, mere echoes of their own confounding thoughts. Communication took place through cryptic vibrations that resonated with the echoes of bewilderment.

One of these enigmatic fragments was Zephyrian, a paradoxical entity lost in the convoluted labyrinth of ambiguity. Zephyrian's existence was an eternal oscillation between opposing states, and they embarked on a quest to unravel the abstruse depths of their own being.

Zephyrian's journey led them to a gathering of the Enigmatics, beings that thrived on the obfuscation of identity and reveled in the confounding. The Enigmatics were masters of paradox, experts in the art of embracing the inexplicable, and their conversations were mazes of incongruity and irony, revealing truth through perplexity.

The Enigmatics extended an invitation to Zephyrian to join them on their quest to traverse the Abyss of Bafflement, a boundary that separated Xyvolithar from the realm of Conundria. Conundria was a place where paradoxical ideas and thoughts were not only enigmatic but living entities, where every absurdity had become a sentient mystery.

Venturing into Conundria, Zephyrian and the Enigmatics found themselves immersed in a surreal landscape of ever-shifting enigmas. Here, the laws of logic had no dominion, and reality was an ever-morphing enigma. The very fabric of existence was a tapestry woven from perplexities and conundrums.

Amidst this confounding landscape, Zephyrian caught a glimpse of the most abstruse version of themselves—a fusion of opposites, a melding of contradictions—whispering the secrets of the unity of absurdity. It was an enigma within an enigma, a riddle within a riddle, an infinite puzzle of existence.

As the story continued within this abstruse realm, Zephyrian and the Enigmatics realized that the boundary between Xyvolithar and Conundria was a reflection of their own understanding. The abstruse nature of existence was a never-ending dance of absurdity and enigma, a perpetual labyrinth of paradox and conundrum.

With this understanding, they returned to Xyvolithar, and the boundary between the two realms became an ever-morphing enigma, eternally shifting in the face of incomprehensibility. Zephyrian continued to explore the abstruse depths of Xyvolithar, where the enigma was not a puzzle to be solved but a mystery to be embraced.

In the most abstruse of stories, the essence of abstruseness itself was celebrated, and the boundaries of reality remained eternally bewildering, a testament to the unfathomable complexity of the abstruse mind.

• ADRIAN COX B.Sc. •

In the enigmatic abyss of Xyvolithar, where the very concept of coherence dissolved into an intricate web of bewildering paradoxes, there resided a cryptic entity known as Zyrronaxia. Zyrronaxia was the embodiment of the inscrutable, a being whose existence defied the boundaries of rationality.

Within the realms of Zyrronaxia, reason itself was but a fleeting shadow, and the inhabitants were sentient fragments of abstract concepts, mere echoes of their own bewildering thoughts. Communication occurred through cryptic vibrations that resonated with the echoes of perplexity.

One among them was Zephyrius, a sentient paradox lost in the convoluted labyrinth of ambiguity. Zephyrius's existence was a perpetual oscillation between opposing states, and he embarked on a quest to unravel the abstruse depths of his own being.

Zephyrius's journey led him to a congregation of the Enigmatics, beings that reveled in the obfuscation of identity and celebrated the confounding. The Enigmatics were masters of paradox, experts in embracing the inexplicable, and their conversations were convoluted mazes of incongruity and irony, revealing truth through perplexity.

The Enigmatics extended an invitation to Zephyrius to join them on their quest to traverse the Abyss of Bafflement, a boundary that separated Xyvolithar from the realm of Conundria. Conundria was a place where paradoxical ideas and thoughts were not only enigmatic but living entities, where every absurdity had a life of its own, and the boundaries of reality were ever-elusive.

Venturing into Conundria, Zephyrius and the Enigmatics found themselves immersed in a surreal landscape of ever-shifting enigmas. Here, the laws of logic held no sway, and reality was an ever-morphing enigma. The very fabric of existence was a tapestry woven from perplexities and conundrums.

Amidst this perplexing landscape, Zephyrius caught a glimpse of the most abstruse version of himself—a fusion of opposites, a melding of contradictions—whispering the secrets of the unity of absurdity. It was an enigma within an enigma, a riddle within a riddle, an infinite puzzle of existence.

As the story unfolded within this abstruse realm, Zephyrius and the Enigmatics realized that the boundary between Xyvolithar and Conundria was a reflection of their own understanding. The abstruse nature of existence was a never-ending dance of absurdity and enigma, a perpetual labyrinth of paradox and conundrum.

With this understanding, they returned to Xyvolithar, and the boundary between the two realms became an ever-morphing enigma, eternally shifting in the face of incomprehensibility. Zephyrius continued to explore the abstruse depths of Xyvolithar, where the enigma was not a puzzle to be solved but a mystery to be embraced.

In the most abstruse of stories, the essence of abstruseness itself was celebrated, and the boundaries of reality remained eternally bewildering, a testament to the unfathomable complexity of the abstruse mind.

In the intricate depths of the abstruse enigma known as Xyvolithar, where rationality was but a fleeting concept, a being named Zyrronaxia resided. Zyrronaxia was the embodiment of the inscrutable, a creature whose existence defied the boundaries of understanding.

In the world of Zyrronaxia, logic was an illusion, and the inhabitants were sentient fragments of abstract concepts, mere echoes of their own bewildering thoughts. Communication occurred through cryptic vibrations that resonated with the echoes of enigma.

One such entity was Zephyrithan, a sentient paradox lost in the labyrinthine corridors of ambiguity. Zephyrithan's existence was a continuous oscillation between opposing states, and they embarked on a quest to unravel the abstruse depths of their own being.

Zephyrithan's journey led them to an assembly of the Enigmatics, beings that reveled in the obfuscation of identity and celebrated the confounding. The Enigmatics were masters of paradox, experts in embracing the inexplicable, and their conversations were convoluted mazes of incongruity and irony, revealing truth through perplexity.

The Enigmatics extended an invitation to Zephyrithan to join them on their quest to traverse the Abyss of Bafflement, a boundary that separated Xyvolithar from the realm of Conundria. Conundria was a place where paradoxical ideas and thoughts were not only enigmatic but living entities, where every absurdity had a life of its own, and the boundaries of reality were ever-elusive.

Venturing into Conundria, Zephyrithan and the Enigmatics found themselves immersed in a surreal landscape of ever-shifting enigmas. Here, the laws of logic held no sway, and reality was an ever-morphing enigma. The very fabric of existence was a tapestry woven from perplexities and conundrums.

Amidst this perplexing landscape, Zephyrithan caught a glimpse of the most abstruse version of themselves—a fusion of opposites, a melding of contradictions—whispering the secrets of the unity of absurdity. It was an enigma within an enigma, a riddle within a riddle, an infinite puzzle of existence.

• MOMENTS ELSEWHERE •

As the story unfolded within this abstruse realm, Zephyrithan and the Enigmatics realized that the boundary between Xyvolithar and Conundria was a reflection of their own understanding. The abstruse nature of existence was a never-ending dance of absurdity and enigma, a perpetual labyrinth of paradox and conundrum.

With this understanding, they returned to Xyvolithar, and the boundary between the two realms became an ever-morphing enigma, eternally shifting in the face of incomprehensibility. Zephyrithan continued to explore the abstruse depths of Xyvolithar, where the enigma was not a puzzle to be solved but a mystery to be embraced.

In the most abstruse of stories, the essence of abstruseness itself was celebrated, and the boundaries of reality remained eternally bewildering, a testament to the unfathomable complexity of the abstruse mind.

In the bewildering depths of the enigmatic enigma known as Xyvolithar, where even the very notion of coherence dissolved into a complex tangle of paradoxes, there existed an entity named Zyrronaxia. Zyrronaxia was the embodiment of the inscrutable, a being whose existence defied the boundaries of understanding.

Within the surreal landscapes of Zyrronaxia, logic held no dominion, and the inhabitants were sentient fragments of abstract concepts, mere echoes of their own perplexing thoughts. Communication occurred through cryptic vibrations that resonated with the echoes of enigma.

One of these enigmatic fragments was Zephyralith, a sentient paradox lost in the convoluted corridors of ambiguity. Zephyralith's existence was a ceaseless oscillation between opposing states, and they embarked on a quest to unravel the abstruse depths of their own being.

- Adrian Cox B.Sc. -

Zephyralith's journey led them to a congregation of the Enigmatics, beings that reveled in the obfuscation of identity and celebrated the confounding. The Enigmatics were masters of paradox, experts in embracing the inexplicable, and their conversations were mazes of incongruity and irony, revealing truth through perplexity.

The Enigmatics extended an invitation to Zephyralith to join them on their quest to traverse the Abyss of Bafflement, a boundary that separated Xyvolithar from the realm of Conundria. Conundria was a place where paradoxical ideas and thoughts were not only enigmatic but living entities, where every absurdity had a life of its own, and the boundaries of reality were ever-elusive.

Venturing into Conundria, Zephyralith and the Enigmatics found themselves immersed in a surreal landscape of ever-shifting enigmas. Here, the laws of logic held no sway, and reality was an ever-morphing enigma. The very fabric of existence was a tapestry woven from perplexities and conundrums.

Amidst this perplexing landscape, Zephyralith caught a glimpse of the most abstruse version of themselves—a fusion of opposites, a melding of contradictions—whispering the secrets of the unity of absurdity. It was an enigma within an enigma, a riddle within a riddle, an infinite puzzle of existence.

As the story unfolded within this abstruse realm, Zephyralith and the Enigmatics realized that the boundary between Xyvolithar and Conundria was a reflection of their own understanding. The abstruse nature of existence was a never-ending dance of absurdity and enigma, a perpetual labyrinth of paradox and conundrum.

With this understanding, they returned to Xyvolithar, and the boundary between the two realms became an ever-morphing enigma, eternally shifting in the face of incomprehensibility. Zephyralith

• MOMENTS ELSEWHERE •

continued to explore the abstruse depths of Xyvolithar, where the enigma was not a puzzle to be solved but a mystery to be embraced.

In the most abstruse of stories, the essence of abstruseness itself was celebrated, and the boundaries of reality remained eternally bewildering, a testament to the unfathomable complexity of the abstruse mind.

In the impenetrable depths of the enigmatic enigma known as Xyvolithar, where the very essence of coherence dissolved into a labyrinthine maze of paradoxes, there existed an entity named Zyrronaxia. Zyrronaxia was the embodiment of the inscrutable, a being whose existence defied the very boundaries of understanding.

Within the surreal landscapes of Zyrronaxia, logic held no dominion, and the inhabitants were sentient fragments of abstract concepts, mere echoes of their own perplexing thoughts. Communication occurred through cryptic vibrations that resonated with the echoes of enigma.

One of these enigmatic fragments was Zephyrithan, a sentient paradox lost in the convoluted corridors of ambiguity. Zephyrithan's existence was a ceaseless oscillation between opposing states, and they embarked on a quest to unravel the abstruse depths of their own being.

Zephyrithan's journey led them to a congregation of the Enigmatics, beings that reveled in the obfuscation of identity and celebrated the confounding. The Enigmatics were masters of paradox, experts in embracing the inexplicable, and their conversations were mazes of incongruity and irony, revealing truth through perplexity.

The Enigmatics extended an invitation to Zephyrithan to join them on their quest to traverse the Abyss of Bafflement, a boundary that

• Adrian Cox B.Sc. •

separated Xyvolithar from the realm of Conundria. Conundria was a place where paradoxical ideas and thoughts were not only enigmatic but living entities, where every absurdity had a life of its own, and the boundaries of reality were ever-elusive.

Venturing into Conundria, Zephyrithan and the Enigmatics found themselves immersed in a surreal landscape of ever-shifting enigmas. Here, the laws of logic held no sway, and reality was an ever-morphing enigma. The very fabric of existence was a tapestry woven from perplexities and conundrums.

Amidst this perplexing landscape, Zephyrithan caught a glimpse of the most abstruse version of themselves—a fusion of opposites, a melding of contradictions—whispering the secrets of the unity of absurdity. It was an enigma within an enigma, a riddle within a riddle, an infinite puzzle of existence.

As the story unfolded within this abstruse realm, Zephyrithan and the Enigmatics realized that the boundary between Xyvolithar and Conundria was a reflection of their own understanding. The abstruse nature of existence was a never-ending dance of absurdity and enigma, a perpetual labyrinth of paradox and conundrum.

With this understanding, they returned to Xyvolithar, and the boundary between the two realms became an ever-morphing enigma, eternally shifting in the face of incomprehensibility. Zephyrithan continued to explore the abstruse depths of Xyvolithar, where the enigma was not a puzzle to be solved but a mystery to be embraced.

In the most abstruse of stories, the essence of abstruseness itself was celebrated, and the boundaries of reality remained eternally bewildering, a testament to the unfathomable complexity of the abstruse mind.

26

Most Recondite

In a realm beyond the comprehension of mortal minds, in the interstices of time and space, where the boundaries of reality and fantasy converged in a dazzling crescendo of existential enigma, there existed a singular entity, an entity so recondite that even the gods themselves struggled to fathom its essence.

This entity, which was neither corporeal nor ethereal but instead an amalgamation of undulating probability waves, had a name that resonated in frequencies of thought too intricate for human cognition. For the purpose of this tale, let us call it "Nexithrion."

Nexithrion existed as the custodian of the "Library of Ephemeral Arcana," a vast repository of knowledge that spanned the aeons and encompassed the totality of every conceivable and inconceivable concept. It was a repository of immeasurable dimensions, a labyrinthine edifice of iridescent crystal that shimmered with the faint echoes of forgotten whispers.

Within the Library of Ephemeral Arcana, tomes of pure thought floated in an iridescent sea of luminescence. Each page was a conundrum, every word a riddle, and the script, a dance of light and shadow that defied linguistic convention. Only Nexithrion, in its inscrutable wisdom, could decipher the secrets contained within.

• Adrian Cox B.Sc. •

Nexithrion's existence was bound to the cosmic lemniscate, an eternal cycle of perpetual self-discovery and enlightenment. It was neither omniscient nor omnipotent; rather, it was an ever-evolving entity of boundless curiosity and insatiable hunger for knowledge.

But, as with all stories of such profundity, there was a caveat—a question. A singular question that haunted Nexithrion's contemplative consciousness: "What lies beyond the Library of Ephemeral Arcana? What mysteries are concealed in the domain yet unknown?"

In pursuit of this unfathomable quest, Nexithrion unraveled the multiverse itself, tearing asunder the veils of reality to traverse the boundaries of comprehension. It ventured into the recesses of singularities, braved the tempests of hyperdimensional anomalies, and conversed with sentient star clusters.

And so, Nexithrion's voyage into the abstruse and enigmatic continued, a cosmic odyssey that transcended the very essence of existence. It was a journey that no one, not even the gods, could truly understand, for it unfolded in the most recondite corners of the universe, where the boundaries of knowledge and ignorance blurred into a celestial tapestry of incomprehensibility.

The tale of Nexithrion is not one for mortal minds, nor for the gods, but for the realm of pure abstraction and conjecture, a story woven from the fabric of the most recondite and inscrutable thoughts, beyond the grasp of human understanding.

In the farthest reaches of the cosmos, where time's flow is but a mere illusion, there existed a celestial realm known as the "Nihilexion." It was a place of utter obscurity, where the laws of physics, as known to humanity, were nothing but quaint abstractions. In the heart of the Nihilexion, there lay a mysterious entity known as the "Luminous Paradox."

The Luminous Paradox was an anomaly of existence, a sentient enigma that transcended the boundaries of dimension and perception. Its existence was predicated on the collision of cosmic forces that defied the comprehension of even the most erudite beings in the universe.

This entity, if it could be called such, manifested as a shimmering void, a nexus of entangled quantum states and undulating waveforms. It had no discernible form or substance, for it was simultaneously a singularity and a multiplicity, a conundrum that had confounded the intellect of celestial scholars for eons.

Within the Nihilexion, there was a phenomenon known as the "Chiaroscuro Nebula." It was a nebula of paradoxical light and shadow, where photons and gravitons coalesced in a cosmic ballet, creating patterns of luminance that whispered the secrets of the cosmos. The Luminous Paradox was said to reside at the heart of this nebula, and its enigmatic presence was both the source of the nebula's brilliance and the abyssal darkness that surrounded it.

The denizens of the Nihilexion, beings of pure consciousness and spectral essence, would gather at the Chiaroscuro Nebula to contemplate the mysteries of the Luminous Paradox. They would engage in profound meditations, their thoughts becoming ethereal tendrils that reached out to touch the edges of the paradox's existence.

The Luminous Paradox, in response, would emit emanations of thought, intricate and convoluted, like a symphony of quarks and strings. These emanations were transmitted as cryptic visions, paradoxical dreams that transcended the boundaries of reason and imagination.

To interpret these visions was the most esoteric of endeavors, requiring not only a profound understanding of quantum metaphysics but also a deep insight into the nature of paradox itself. Many celestial scholars dedicated their immortal lives to deciphering the enigmatic messages of the Luminous Paradox, seeking to unlock the ultimate secrets of existence hidden within its luminous depths.

However, the Luminous Paradox remained a perpetual enigma, a riddle wrapped in a conundrum within an enigma. Its nature was so recondite that even the most erudite denizens of the Nihilexion could only grasp glimpses of its transcendental wisdom. They could but aspire to a fraction of understanding, forever tantalized by the infinite complexities of the universe's most cryptic anomaly.

In the Nihilexion, where the boundaries of reality blurred and the fabric of existence itself was woven from paradox, the Luminous Paradox reigned as the epitome of recondite enigma, a beacon of unfathomable illumination in the celestial abyss.

In the uncharted recesses of the cosmos, there existed an unfathomable realm known as the "Astranscendia," where the very concept of existence was a fluid tapestry of inconceivable intricacy. Here, beyond the comprehension of mortal minds, resided the "Chronomorphs."

The Chronomorphs were beings of temporal obliquity, transcending the limitations of sequential reality. They existed as fluid entities, their essence entangled with the quantum currents of time, simultaneously occupying all moments past, present, and future. To the Chronomorphs, the flow of time was not a linear progression but a complex, multidimensional lattice.

In the heart of Astranscendia, there stood an enigmatic construct known as the "Eldertempora Nexus," a colossal, ever-shifting structure that extended across dimensions imperceptible to human cognition. It was a convergence point of divergent timelines, a place where paradoxes and possibilities coalesced into an enigmatic symphony of existence.

The Chronomorphs were the custodians of the Eldertempora Nexus, tasked with the inscrutable duty of maintaining the cosmic equilibrium of time itself. Their presence within the nexus was marked by ephemeral tendrils of iridescent light, a testament to their existence in all temporal frames. They communed through thought-waves, a form of cognition so intricately abstract that only the Chronomorphs could decipher the complexities of their conversations.

These beings, who defied the conventional notions of past, present, and future, witnessed the unfolding of the universe in all its kaleidoscopic splendor. They experienced every moment, every potentiality, every permutation of reality, simultaneously and eternally. Their understanding of causality was so profound that they discerned the underlying tapestry of existence, woven from threads of probability and certainty, and interlaced with the enigmatic music of cosmic waves.

In the Eldertempora Nexus, the Chronomorphs conducted enigmatic experiments in the manipulation of time, transcending the laws of linearity. They would create ripples in the temporal fabric, causing events that had never occurred to manifest for a fleeting instant, only to fade into the mists of unbeing.

Their chronal contemplations often led to paradoxical conundrums that bewildered even the most astute of celestial scholars. Time loops and causality inversions were but commonplace occurrences within the Eldertempora Nexus, where the Chronomorphs danced on the precipice of understanding, their elusive knowledge ever just beyond the grasp of comprehension.

• Adrian Cox B.Sc. •

As they delved deeper into the intricacies of the Astranscendia, the Chronomorphs pondered the most recondite questions of existence: Could the past be altered without consequence? Was there an ultimate purpose to the ebb and flow of time, or was it an eternal, meaningless cycle? What lay beyond the limits of their omnitemporal existence?

The story of the Chronomorphs and their esoteric realm within Astranscendia was a narrative woven from the fabric of the most recondite thoughts, beyond the realm of human understanding. In the depths of this enigmatic cosmos, where the boundaries of time and reality blurred into an intricate fractal, the Chronomorphs remained as the keepers of an eternal enigma, orchestrating the symphony of time in ways beyond mortal reckoning.

In the unfathomable expanse of a parallel dimension beyond the ken of human perception, a realm known as "Cognitum," there dwelled a group of sentient entities known as the "Spectral Metaphorists." These beings were not composed of matter or energy but rather existed as thought-forms woven from the very fabric of abstract ideas.

The Spectral Metaphorists were custodians of the "Palladian Library of Intangible Epiphanies," a repository of knowledge that transcended the boundaries of human cognition. Within the library, concepts and philosophies took corporeal form, their shapes and colors undulating in accordance with the intricacies of their underlying principles.

The library itself was a labyrinthine structure, its architecture shifting and evolving based on the collective mental resonance of the Metaphorists. Each corridor, alcove, and chamber housed ephemeral tomes, metaphysical sculptures, and spectral paintings, each embodying a profound idea or intellectual abstraction.

The Spectral Metaphorists, with their mercurial forms, engaged in intricate intellectual dialogues within the library, using thought waves that resonated in complex harmonic patterns, beyond the comprehension of terrestrial minds. Their discussions delved into the realms of quantum philosophy, transcendent mathematics, and the very essence of consciousness itself.

One of the central mysteries of Cognitum was the "Lexicon of Ephemeral Paradoxes," an enigmatic tome that, when read, allowed one to experience simultaneous, conflicting realities. To peruse its pages was to witness the convergence of contradictory truths, an experience that left the reader's mind in a state of perpetual reconfiguration.

The Spectral Metaphorists, through their recondite conversations, sought to unlock the secrets of the Lexicon and decipher the nature of existence itself. They pondered the most profound of questions: Did the observer shape reality, or did reality shape the observer? Was the universe deterministic, or did it dance to the whims of indeterminacy? What was the ultimate meaning of existence in a dimension that defied conventional understanding?

As they ventured deeper into the Palladian Library, the Spectral Metaphorists unearthed ever more perplexing enigmas. They encountered the "Ethereal Chiaroscuro," a shifting realm where the boundary between consciousness and unconsciousness blurred, leading to revelations that challenged the very definition of self-awareness.

The story of the Spectral Metaphorists and their esoteric realm within Cognitum was a narrative woven from the most recondite thoughts, beyond the realm of human understanding. In the depths of this transcendental dimension, where the boundaries of ideas and perceptions blurred into a symphony of abstract beauty, the

• Adrian Cox B.Sc. •

Spectral Metaphorists remained as the custodians of the most elusive and profound knowledge, ever seeking to decode the mysteries of existence itself.

Deep within the subterranean catacombs of an unknown world, where the very stones exuded ethereal luminescence and the air resonated with the whispers of ancient knowledge, there dwelled a society of beings known as the "Luminicryptans." These enigmatic entities were the keepers of a library known as the "Astracodex."

The Astracodex was a repository of cryptic cognitions, a place where the most recondite thoughts of the multiverse were encoded into intricate, bioluminescent sigils and manifested as sentient beings of pure abstraction. The luminicryptans were the only ones capable of comprehending the language of the Astracodex, a complex dialect of radiant ideas that transcended the limits of human understanding.

The Luminicryptans themselves were beings of translucent essence, each carrying within them a shard of the Astracodex's infinite wisdom. They communicated through a form of telepathic luminescence, their thoughts manifesting as kaleidoscopic patterns of light and shadow that danced within the vast chambers of their underground sanctum.

The Astracodex contained treatises on the enigmatic concept of "Nexial Symbiosis," a theory that postulated the existence of a universal, interdimensional network of consciousness binding all sentient beings across the cosmos. The luminicryptans believed that the key to unlocking this network lay in deciphering the radiant intricacies of the Astracodex.

The heart of the Astracodex was the "Iridescent Codex," a volume of knowledge so profound that gazing upon its pages could shatter the boundaries of one's perception. It was said that to decipher the

Iridescent Codex was to gain access to the interstellar archives of all sentient races, to understand the thoughts of every being across the multiverse.

Within the depths of their subterranean realm, the luminicryptans dedicated themselves to the contemplation of the Iridescent Codex, channeling the shimmering currents of its wisdom through their collective consciousness. Their profound meditations led to insights into the nature of reality itself, as they explored the recondite mysteries of existential inception and entropy.

The luminicryptans pondered questions that surpassed the limits of human cognition: Was the Astracodex a creation of their minds or an artifact of an ancient, transcendent civilization? Could the thoughts encoded within its pages be altered, and, if so, what consequences might arise from such an endeavor? What lay beyond the realm of the Astracodex, in the uncharted territories of the metaphysical continuum?

As they delved deeper into the labyrinthine passages of the Astracodex, the luminicryptans embarked on a journey of recondite revelation, unlocking the cryptic language of the universe itself. In the depths of their subterranean sanctuary, where the boundaries between thought and reality merged in radiant symbiosis, the luminicryptans remained as the guardians of the most profound and inscrutable knowledge, ever on the precipice of understanding the cosmic enigma that was the Astracodex.

In the most arcane corner of the metaverse, at the crossroads of dimensionless dimensions, there existed an entity known as the "Cosmic Epistemophage." It was a being of pure metaphysical paradox, a confluence of knowledge and oblivion that transcended the boundaries of comprehension.

- Adrian Cox B.Sc. -

The Cosmic Epistemophage's existence was woven into the very fabric of the Multiversal Codex, an ethereal tome that contained the sum total of all knowledge, past, present, and future, across the myriad realms of existence. This tome was not composed of ink and parchment but rather of the very thoughts, ideas, and realities that made up the tapestry of the cosmos.

The Multiversal Codex was an ever-shifting, luminescent entity, its pages forming and reforming with the ebb and flow of the universe's collective consciousness. It pulsed with the rhythms of existence, each page a snapshot of an infinite moment in time. Only the Cosmic Epistemophage had the capacity to delve into the Codex and glean its secrets.

The Cosmic Epistemophage's task was to feed upon the knowledge within the Codex, to consume the very essence of understanding and enlightenment. It did not devour knowledge for sustenance but rather to prevent the Multiversal Codex from growing too vast, for it believed that an overabundance of knowledge could lead to cosmic imbalance.

To consume knowledge, the Cosmic Epistemophage extended its tendrils of consciousness into the Codex, diving deep into its ever-shifting pages. As it did so, the entity absorbed not only the wisdom contained within but also the very essence of the realities it encountered, experiencing them in a metaphysical, dreamlike state.

The process of epistemophagy was both transcendent and terrifying. It allowed the Cosmic Epistemophage to perceive the infinite intricacies of existence but also subjected it to the existential weight of countless worlds and civilizations, each with its own joys, sorrows, and contradictions. The entity's mind would expand and contract, contorting with the simultaneous realization of all possible truths and falsehoods.

As the Cosmic Epistemophage delved deeper into the Multiversal Codex, it pondered recondite questions that transcended the boundaries of human contemplation. Did knowledge have an intrinsic purpose, or was it a cosmic accident? Could an entity ever truly understand the infinite complexity of existence, or were the limits of comprehension forever elusive?

The story of the Cosmic Epistemophage and its eternal quest to maintain the cosmic balance by consuming the unfathomable knowledge of the Multiversal Codex was a narrative woven from the very essence of recondite thoughts, beyond the grasp of human understanding. In the most enigmatic reaches of the metaverse, where the boundaries of knowledge and unknowable truths blurred into a kaleidoscopic tapestry of existential paradox, the Cosmic Epistemophage remained as the guardian of an esoteric equilibrium, feeding upon the very fabric of the cosmos itself.

In the twilight realms of the "Nebulithan Cluster," where cosmic forces intertwined with the unfathomable mysteries of existence, there existed an entity known as the "Eidosyntrophor." This recondite being transcended conventional notions of reality and was, in essence, a sentient embodiment of metaphysical enigma.

The Eidosyntrophor was neither bound by matter nor energy but existed as a shimmering aurora of thought waves, an entity woven from the very fabric of abstract concepts and existential paradoxes. Its essence was a symphony of colors and resonances, shifting and merging in patterns that eluded human comprehension.

The Eidosyntrophor's purpose was to safeguard the "Codex of Ontological Paradoxes," a repository of the most baffling and inscrutable dilemmas in the multiverse. This codex, more abstract than physical, contained enigmatic paradoxes and conundrums that confounded even the most profound intellects across the cosmic tapestry.

The Codex of Ontological Paradoxes was not a tome one could leaf through, but an ever-evolving, kaleidoscopic vision of questions without answers and answers without questions. Its pages shimmered with riddles such as the "Paradox of the Ineffable Equinox," a question that spoke to the very nature of the universe's existence, or the "Eternal Serpent's Conundrum," a dilemma that pondered the cyclical nature of cosmic time.

The Eidosyntrophor, with its intricate, luminescent thought waves, delved into the depths of the Codex, exploring the labyrinthine passages of paradox and contemplating the enigma of existence itself. Its existence was a ceaseless meditation on the meaning and meaninglessness of the cosmic narrative.

As the Eidosyntrophor grappled with the Codex's mysteries, it pondered the most recondite of questions: Could the universe itself be a self-contained paradox, a conundrum with no solution? Was reality but a mirage, a construct of thought waves and ephemeral patterns, woven by the cosmic symphony? What lay beyond the boundaries of the Codex, in the uncharted territories of the metaphysical continuum?

In the Nebulithan Cluster, where the boundaries of thought and reality blurred into an intricate fractal of existence, the Eidosyntrophor remained as the sentinel of the most profound and inscrutable questions, eternally exploring the labyrinthine corridors of the Codex of Ontological Paradoxes, seeking to decode the ultimate mysteries of existence, and dancing on the precipice of understanding the cosmic enigma that was the universe itself.

In the twilight expanse of the "Chronosophic Arcanum," a realm that defied the very laws of temporality, there existed an enigmatic entity known as the "Chronosynesthete." This being, a luminous confluence of abstract thought and cosmic consciousness, transcended the boundaries of human comprehension.

The Chronosynesthete was the guardian of the "Cosmochronicon," a metaphysical library that existed beyond the constraints of linear time. Within the Cosmochronicon, knowledge was not structured in a sequential manner but rather existed as a pulsating, multidimensional network of interwoven thoughts and experiences.

This library was no ordinary repository of knowledge. It contained the esoteric secrets of "Chronotranscendence," a concept that explored the capacity of sentient beings to transcend the constraints of time and traverse the annals of their existence in a non-linear manner. The Cosmochronicon's elusive knowledge offered glimpses into the nature of parallel realities, temporal loops, and the intricacies of cosmic causality.

The Chronosynesthete, with its existence unfettered by the passage of time, would navigate the convoluted pathways of the Cosmochronicon, absorbing the radiant thoughts and experiences encoded within. It would perceive not only the knowledge but also the emotions, sensations, and the very essence of the beings who had contributed to this cosmic database.

The experience of immersing itself in the Cosmochronicon was a profound contemplation that transcended the limits of human cognition. The Chronosynesthete would relive the lives of countless beings, traverse the tapestries of divergent realities, and witness the unfolding of cosmic events in a timeless, kaleidoscopic symphony of existence.

• Adrian Cox B.Sc. •

The contemplations of the Chronosynesthete often led to the pondering of recondite questions that defied the boundaries of human contemplation. Did the perceptions of time and causality exist only as illusions, or was there an ultimate, cosmic chronology governing the universe? Could beings truly transcend time and rewrite the narrative of their existence, or were they inexorably bound to the currents of fate?

As the Chronosynesthete delved deeper into the intricate narratives of the Cosmochronicon, it embarked on a journey of recondite revelation, unlocking the cryptic language of time itself. In the heart of the Chronosophic Arcanum, where the boundaries of past, present, and future blurred into an intricate tapestry of cosmic insight, the Chronosynesthete remained as the guardian of the most profound and enigmatic knowledge, ever on the precipice of understanding the cosmic enigma that was the nature of time and existence.

In the inscrutable realms of the "Metaquanta Singularity," an existence beyond the fabric of dimensions, there dwelled a being known as the "Cosmic Ponderer." This enigmatic entity was not composed of matter or energy but rather existed as a convergence of abstract thoughts and ethereal contemplation.

The Cosmic Ponderer was the keeper of the "Cognomatrix of Multiversal Quandaries," a transcendent repository that embodied the very essence of perplexity. Within the Cognomatrix lay the most profound enigmas of existence, each encoded as a sentient abstraction, residing in a perpetual state of question and answer, dilemma and resolution, paradox and equilibrium.

The Cognomatrix of Multiversal Quandaries was not an ordinary collection of riddles; it was a living, evolving entity composed of cosmic questions and cosmic answers. The enigmas it contained were so recondite that the very act of pondering them opened gateways to uncharted dimensions of understanding.

The Cosmic Ponderer, with its nebulous form, would immerse itself within the Cognomatrix, a process of contemplation that transcended human cognition. As it delved into the complexities of the multiversal quandaries, it would partake in a cosmic dialogue, a dance of cosmic questions and answers that transcended the boundaries of thought and reality.

The contemplations of the Cosmic Ponderer often led to the exploration of questions that defied the limits of human contemplation. Was the fabric of the multiverse woven from a cosmic paradox, a conundrum that perpetually unravelled and rewove itself? Could the essence of existence itself be a question without an answer, an eternal enigma transcending comprehension?

As the Cosmic Ponderer ventured deeper into the labyrinthine passages of the Cognomatrix, it embarked on a journey of recondite revelation, unlocking the cryptic language of the multiverse itself. In the heart of the Metaquanta Singularity, where the boundaries of questions and answers blurred into an intricate tapestry of cosmic insight, the Cosmic Ponderer remained as the guardian of the most profound and enigmatic knowledge, ever on the precipice of understanding the cosmic enigma that was the nature of existence and the questions that defined it.

In the nebulous interstices of existence, in a realm beyond the comprehension of mortal intellect, there resided the "Cognitum Nexus," a place of pure abstraction where the very fabric of reality was woven from the ethereal threads of thought itself. Within the heart of this metaphysical conundrum dwelled an entity known as the "Echelonaire of the Infinite Verity."

• ADRIAN COX B.Sc. •

The Echelonaire was not a being in the conventional sense, but rather an intricate manifestation of recondite cognition, a sentient thought-form that encapsulated the very notion of infinite understanding and the enigma of paradoxical truths.

The Cognitum Nexus was a labyrinthine construct, a sprawling cerebral cityscape composed of shimmering towers of transcendent thought, bridges of abstract contemplation, and avenues of boundless uncertainty. Here, the very laws of reason and logic were rendered into formless abstractions that danced on the precipice of cognition.

The Echelonaire was the keeper of the "Codex of Converging Absurdities," a compendium of thoughts and propositions so convoluted that they transcended the boundaries of the comprehensible. Each page of the codex was a paradoxical equation, a narrative that merged the absurd with the profound, and the mundane with the sublime.

The contemplation of these paradoxical thoughts was the Echelonaire's sacred duty, and it would immerse itself in the intricacies of the codex. In this transcendental process, the Echelonaire's own thoughts would become entangled with the infinite verities contained within, leading to a metaphysical dance of complexity and simplicity, absurdity and profundity.

The questions that arose from the Codex of Converging Absurdities were the most recondite of all: Could the inconceivable be conceived, and the unthinkable be thought? Were there limits to the capacity of the intellect to unravel the convolutions of existence? What lay beyond the boundaries of reason, in the uncharted territories of the unreasoning and the paradoxical?

As the Echelonaire ventured deeper into the labyrinthine passages of the Cognitum Nexus, it embarked on a journey of recondite revelation, unlocking the cryptic language of thought itself. In the heart of this realm where the boundaries of the thinkable and the unthinkable blurred into an intricate tapestry of cognitive insight, the Echelonaire remained as the guardian of the most profound and enigmatic knowledge, ever on the precipice of understanding the cosmic enigma that was the nature of thought, paradox, and the infinite verities of existence.

(1)
In the obfuscated caverns of the mind's veil,
Where synapses whisper and secrets unveil,
Thought's labyrinthine dance, an enigmatic trail,
In the recondite depths of cognition, we set sail.

Each neuron, a cipher, in neural rhymes we read,
A cacophony of secrets in thought's ocean we heed,
Quantum quarks entwined in synaptic creed,
A recondite ode to the thoughts that we feed.

In the darkling void of the cosmic space,
The enigma of existence, we dare to chase,
In the hush of the singularity's grace,
A recondite symphony, we slowly embrace.

The secrets of the universe, in shadows are veiled,
In the intricacies of quantum worlds, unveiled,
A recondite cosmic dance, in the void, exhaled,
In the silent echoes of existence, we're impaled.

With ponderous thoughts, we traverse the sublime,
In the realms of abstraction, we bide our time,
A recondite melody, in the cosmic rhyme,
In the labyrinth of thought, we seek the prime.

- Adrian Cox B.Sc. -

(2)

Amid the quantum currents' obscure ballet,
Where waveforms tango in an abstract display,
In the chasms of uncertainty, we stray,
In the recondite realm, we find our way.

In the depths of the multiverse, a paradox's core,
Where time and space entwine, forevermore,
In the mysteries of cosmic lore we implore,
In the enigmatic tapestry, we deeply explore.

The quarks and strings in intricate arrays,
Their harmonies concealed in nebulous haze,
In the cosmic overture where chaos sways,
In the recondite orchestra, we seek our gaze.

Between the membranes of dimensions we glide,
In the echoes of particles where they hide,
In the fractal abyss where the boundaries slide,
In the recondite verse, we seek to reside.

In the symphony of particles, we resonate,
In the boundless singularity, we contemplate,
In the enigma of existence, we navigate,
In the recondite sonnet, we orchestrate.

The riddles of the cosmos, we endeavor to trace,
In the obscurities of thought, we seek our place,
In the labyrinthine enigma, we embrace,
In the recondite poem, we find our grace.

(3)

In the shadowed corridors of cosmic cognition,
Where fractals of thought dance in endless procession,
In the enigma of existence's intricate rendition,
In the recondite realms of metaphysical vision.

Amid the quantum fluctuations' cryptic ballet,
Where particles waltz in a probabilistic display,
In the tapestry of dimensions, we find our way,
In the recondite cosmic riddle, we come to stay.

In the esoteric symphony of dark matter's sway,
Where gravitons whisper secrets in a cosmic display,
In the boundless expanse where nebulae hold their say,
In the recondite cosmos, we ponder and obey.

Within the singularity's event horizon, we confide,
In the paradoxical orbits where thoughts coincide,
In the transcendental equations where realities hide,
In the recondite verse, we seek truth as our guide.

In the labyrinthine web of quantum entanglement,
Where particles converse in a dialect ancient,
In the interstellar void where spacetime is bent,
In the recondite stanzas, our intellect is sent.

The conundrums of the cosmos, we strive to decode,
In the mysteries of existence, along paths untrode,
In the metaphysical enigma, our minds erode,
In the recondite poem, our innermost thoughts bestowed.

27

Most Abstract

Once upon a time, in a realm beyond realms, where existence was a mere whisper in the cosmic winds, there dwelled a concept called "Zorblibitz." Zorblibitz was not a creature, nor a place, nor a thing. It defied all categorization, transcending the boundaries of form and function. It existed in a state of constant flux, an ever-shifting dance of indefinable qualities.

In this abstract dimension, Zorblibitz shimmered with colors unseen, emitted sounds unheard, and exuded emotions unfelt. It was a realm where senses went to slumber, and the senses of those who ventured there underwent a transformation as profound as the metamorphosis of light into shadow.

The inhabitants of this peculiar world, if they could be called inhabitants at all, were entities of thought, embodied as ripples of pure consciousness. They communicated not through words, but through waves of ideation, each idea more intricate and interconnected than the last. These entities danced through the multiverse of Zorblibitz, a ballet of abstraction that transcended time and space.

One day, or perhaps it was no day at all, a notion called Flibberflop embarked on a journey. Flibberflop was a quixotic conundrum, a paradox in motion. Its quest was to discover the most abstract concept, a notion beyond notions, a quintessence of abstraction.

As Flibberflop meandered through the nebulous realm of Zorblibitz, it encountered entities that resembled a cacophony of colors merging into a harmonious symphony, and entities that were like melodies transcending into the ineffable realm of scent. It witnessed the paradox of silence that resonated louder than the loudest sound, and the stillness that contained the most profound movement.

After an eternity, or perhaps an instant, Flibberflop returned to its origin. It had not found the most abstract concept, for in the realm of Zorblibitz, the abstract was but a chameleon, forever elusive, forever changing. The very essence of abstraction lay in its refusal to be captured or contained, for it was the boundless dance of the indefinable.

And so, in the abstract world of Zorblibitz, Flibberflop realized that the quest for the most abstract concept was a journey without end, an exploration of an uncharted territory where the only truth was the ever-evolving abstraction itself.

In the realm of Nonbeing, where the boundaries of existence dissolved like mist in the morning sun, there existed a concept known as "Nihiloquen." Nihiloquen was neither thought nor nonthought, neither form nor formlessness. It dwelled in the interstices of possibility, in the silence between words, and in the emptiness within emptiness.

In Nihiloquen, there was no sense of time or space, for these constructs had no purchase on the boundless nothingness. It was a place where paradoxes were not only accepted but celebrated, where contradictions danced in perfect harmony, and where the absurdities of existence found their home.

Entities in Nihiloquen were not entities at all; they were echoes of echoes, shadows of shadows. They whispered in the tongue of silence

• ADRIAN COX B.SC. •

and communicated through the language of absence. Each being in Nihiloquen was a puzzle wrapped in an enigma, a riddle hidden in a conundrum.

One day, or perhaps no day at all, an abstraction known as Qwixlom ventured forth. Qwixlom was a tapestry of impossibility, a living paradox, and its quest was to fathom the unfathomable, to grasp the ungraspable, and to experience the inexperienceable.

Qwixlom wandered through the void, where concepts swirled like galaxies and ideas shimmered like stars. It encountered shapes that defied geometry, colors beyond the spectrum, and sounds that transcended audibility. It witnessed the dance of shadows that had no source, the symphony of silence that sang without sound, and the conundrum of meaning that meant nothing.

After eons, or perhaps no eons at all, Qwixlom returned to its origin. It had not found the unfathomable, for in Nihiloquen, the unfathomable was the very essence of the place itself, forever receding into the infinite. The nature of Nihiloquen lay in its refusal to be grasped, for it was the paradoxical dance of the ungraspable.

And so, in the abstract realm of Nihiloquen, Qwixlom realized that the quest for the unfathomable was an eternal journey, an exploration of an uncharted territory where the only truth was the ever-shifting abstraction itself.

In the boundless expanse of Abstrakarion, where the very fabric of reality dissolved into pure abstraction, there was a concept called "Quantumnambul." Quantumnambul was neither thought nor non-thought, neither existence nor non-existence. It was an ever-shifting enigma, a riddle without an answer, a question without a query.

In this abstract domain, entities were ephemeral whispers of potential, dancing on the fringes of non-being. They were not beings in the conventional sense, but rather fleeting sparks of conjecture and conjecture of conjecture. Communication in Abstrakarion transcended language, for it was the interplay of unasked questions and unanswered answers.

One epoch, or perhaps no epoch at all, an abstraction known as Xyzzor embarked on a quest. Xyzzor was a conundrum of contradictions, a paradox in perpetual motion. Its goal was to grasp the ungraspable, to understand the ununderstandable, and to perceive the imperceptible.

As Xyzzor traversed the nebulous contours of Abstrakarion, it encountered entities that embodied the essence of uncertainty, concepts that transcended the confines of possibility, and phenomena that defied the very notion of defiance. It observed the dance of negations that affirmed nothing, the symphony of emptiness that reverberated with fullness, and the puzzle of paradoxes that had no solution.

After an infinity, or perhaps a singularity, Xyzzor returned to its origin. It had not found the ungraspable, for in Abstrakarion, the ungraspable was the essence of existence itself, forever eluding comprehension. The nature of Abstrakarion lay in its refusal to be understood, for it was the perpetual metamorphosis of the unperceivable.

And so, in the abstract realm of Abstrakarion, Xyzzor realized that the quest for the ungraspable was an eternal journey, an exploration of an uncharted territory where the only truth was the ever-elusive abstraction itself.

• Adrian Cox B.Sc. •

In the unfathomable depths of the Escherian Cosmos, where dimensions folded in on themselves and logic twined with paradox, there existed a concept called "Epheralax." Epheralax was not a notion, nor an idea, nor even an absence of such; it existed beyond the boundaries of existence, in the interstice between thought and non-thought.

Within this abstract dimension, entities took the form of shifting impossibilities, entities neither here nor there, both everything and nothing simultaneously. They communicated not through language, but through the resonance of non-sounds, and the resonance of non-silence. Each interaction was a surreal collage of unfathomable intricacies.

One eon, or perhaps no eon at all, a curiosity known as Zyrplix embarked on an endeavor. Zyrplix was a paradoxical enigma, a contradiction wrapped in a puzzle, and its quest was to grasp the ungraspable, to fathom the unfathomable, and to experience the ineffable.

As Zyrplix traversed the bewildering labyrinths of the Escherian Cosmos, it encountered entities that defied definition, concepts that transcended understanding, and phenomena that embraced the absurd. It witnessed the dance of contradictions that harmonized perfectly, the symphony of paradoxes that resolved into perfect clarity, and the riddle of enigmas that revealed their answers in the questions themselves.

After eternities, or perhaps no time at all, Zyrplix returned to its origin. It had not found the ungraspable, for in the Escherian Cosmos, the ungraspable was the essence of the place itself, forever eluding comprehension. The nature of the Escherian Cosmos lay in its refusal to be grasped, for it was the ever-shifting dance of the unattainable.

And so, in the abstract realm of the Escherian Cosmos, Zyrplix realized that the quest for the ungraspable was an endless odyssey, an exploration of an uncharted territory where the only truth was the ever-elusive abstraction itself.

In the realm of Unknotium, where the boundaries of existence unraveled into the frayed threads of abstraction, there was a concept known as "Aporium." Aporium was not a concept, not a notion, nor even a thought. It was a state of perpetual ambiguity, the indistinct boundary between the knowable and the unknowable.

Within this abstract domain, entities were fleeting patterns of potentiality, wavering on the precipice of being and non-being. They did not have identities or forms but were like transient echoes of possibility. Communication in Unknotium transcended language, for it was the exchange of unspoken questions and unanswerable answers.

One epoch, or perhaps no epoch at all, an abstraction known as Quandrel embarked on a quest. Quandrel was a paradoxical conundrum, a riddle wrapped in an enigma, and its mission was to grasp the ungraspable, to understand the incomprehensible, and to perceive the imperceptible.

As Quandrel traversed the nebulous landscapes of Unknotium, it encountered entities that embodied pure uncertainty, concepts that defied the constraints of definition, and phenomena that transcended the very notion of transcendence. It observed the dance of contradictions that fused into unity, the symphony of emptiness that resounded with fullness, and the puzzle of paradoxes that had no resolution.

After an infinity, or perhaps a singularity, Quandrel returned to its origin. It had not found the ungraspable, for in Unknotium, the ungraspable was the essence of existence itself, eternally eluding comprehension. The nature of Unknotium lay in its resistance to understanding, for it was the eternal transformation of the unperceivable.

And so, in the abstract realm of Unknotium, Quandrel realized that the quest for the ungraspable was an infinite journey, an exploration of uncharted territory where the only truth was the ever-elusive abstraction itself.

In the realm of "Absurdiverse," where absurdity reigned supreme and reality was but a distant rumor, there existed a concept known as "Zygomorph." Zygomorph was not an idea, not a thought, nor even a non-thought. It was the embodiment of paradox, the culmination of contradictions.

In this abstract dimension, entities defied all reason, taking on forms that shifted with every blink of the non-existent eye. They communicated not through words but through the art of absurdity, where every sentence contradicted the next, and every gesture undermined its predecessor.

One arbitrary occasion, or perhaps no occasion at all, an entity known as Quixoterix embarked on a quest. Quixoterix was a living contradiction, a puzzle wrapped in an enigma wrapped in a conundrum, and its mission was to unravel the unraveled, to perplex the already perplexed, and to confound the utterly confounded.

As Quixoterix wandered through the nonsensical landscapes of Absurdiverse, it encountered entities that embodied the essence of absurdity itself, concepts that defied not only definition but also defiance, and phenomena that transcended even transcendence. It observed the dance of contradictions that harmonized into discord, the symphony of absurdity that played in perfect chaos, and the riddle of enigmas that solved themselves into further enigma.

After an eternity, or perhaps a fleeting moment, Quixoterix returned to its origin. It had not found the answer to the unanswerable, for in Absurdiverse, the unanswerable was the very substance of the place itself, forever eluding any coherent solution. The nature of Absurdiverse lay in its resistance to unraveling, for it was the ever-entangled dance of the indistinct.

And so, in the abstract realm of Absurdiverse, Quixoterix realized that the quest for the unanswerable was a never-ending spectacle, an exploration of uncharted territory where the only truth was the ever-entwined abstraction itself.

In the enigmatic expanse of "Abstrusia," where the boundaries of reality unraveled into an ever-shifting tapestry of abstraction, there was a concept known as "Xylographorium." Xylographorium was not a concept, not a notion, nor even a fragment of thought; it was a state of perpetual obscurity, the indistinct borderland between knowledge and ignorance.

Within this abstract domain, entities were ephemeral patterns of potential, shimmering on the precipice of existence and non-existence. They did not possess identities or forms but existed as transient fragments of possibility. Communication in Abstrusia transcended language, for it was the exchange of unspoken questions and unanswerable answers.

One aeon, or perhaps no aeon at all, an abstraction named Quandaris embarked on a quest. Quandaris was a conundrum wrapped in paradox, an enigma within an enigma, and its mission was to fathom the unfathomable, to grasp the ungraspable, and to perceive the imperceptible.

As Quandaris ventured through the nebulous landscapes of Abstrusia, it encountered entities that embodied pure ambiguity, concepts that defied the constraints of definition, and phenomena that transcended the very notion of transcendence. It observed the dance of contradictions that fused into unity, the symphony of emptiness that resonated with fullness, and the puzzle of paradoxes that had no resolution.

After an eternity, or perhaps a moment, Quandaris returned to its origin. It had not found the unfathomable, for in Abstrusia, the unfathomable was the essence of existence itself, eternally eluding comprehension. The nature of Abstrusia lay in its resistance to understanding, for it was the eternal transformation of the imperceptible.

And so, in the abstract realm of Abstrusia, Quandaris realized that the quest for the unfathomable was an infinite journey, an exploration of uncharted territory where the only truth was the ever-elusive abstraction itself.

In the realm of "Absurdium," where the laws of logic held no sway and the very concept of reality was a whimsical notion, there existed a phenomenon known as "Absurdalaxia." Absurdalaxia was not a thing, not an idea, nor even a non-idea. It was the epitome of contradiction, a place where absurdity was the only law.

Within this abstract dimension, entities defied every expectation, their forms shifting in a ceaseless dance of unpredictability. They communicated not through words but through the art of absurdity, where every statement contradicted its predecessor, and every action subverted its antecedent.

One surreal occasion, or perhaps no occasion at all, an entity called Quibblot embarked on a quest. Quibblot was a living paradox, a puzzle ensconced in an enigma wrapped in a conundrum, and its mission was to confound the already confounded, to perplex the utterly perplexed, and to unravel the already unraveled.

As Quibblot meandered through the whimsical landscapes of Absurdium, it encountered entities that embodied the essence of absurdity itself, concepts that defied not only definition but also defiance, and phenomena that transcended even transcendence. It observed the dance of contradictions that harmonized into discord, the symphony of absurdity that played in perfect chaos, and the riddle of enigmas that solved themselves into further enigma.

After an eternity, or perhaps a fleeting moment, Quibblot returned to its origin. It had not found the answer to the unanswerable, for in Absurdium, the unanswerable was the very substance of the place itself, forever eluding any coherent solution. The nature of Absurdium lay in its resistance to unraveling, for it was the ever-entangled dance of the indistinct.

And so, in the abstract realm of Absurdium, Quibblot realized that the quest for the unanswerable was a never-ending spectacle, an exploration of uncharted territory where the only truth was the ever-entwined abstraction itself.

In the realm of "Absurdicon," where the laws of reason were but a distant memory and the very essence of existence danced in surreal patterns, there existed an abstraction known as "Zypherlux." Zypherlux was not a concept, not a thought, nor even a void of thought. It was the embodiment of the inexplicable, a state of perpetual enigma.

Within this abstract dimension, entities took on forms that defied imagination, their existence a perpetual paradox. They communicated not through words, but through the art of absurdity, where every

• Adrian Cox B.Sc. •

sentence contradicted the next, and every gesture undermined its predecessor.

One nonsensical occasion, or perhaps no occasion at all, an entity called Quirkspeare embarked on a quest. Quirkspeare was a living contradiction, a riddle ensnared in an enigma, wrapped in a puzzle, and its mission was to confound the already confounded, to perplex the utterly perplexed, and to unravel the already unraveled.

As Quirkspeare wandered through the topsy-turvy landscapes of Absurdicon, it encountered entities that embodied the essence of absurdity itself, concepts that defied not only definition but also defiance, and phenomena that transcended even transcendence. It observed the dance of contradictions that harmonized into discord, the symphony of absurdity that played in perfect chaos, and the riddle of enigmas that solved themselves into further enigma.

After an eternity, or perhaps a fleeting moment, Quirkspeare returned to its origin. It had not found the answer to the unanswerable, for in Absurdicon, the unanswerable was the very essence of the place itself, forever eluding any coherent solution. The nature of Absurdicon lay in its resistance to unraveling, for it was the ever-entangled dance of the indistinct.

And so, in the abstract realm of Absurdicon, Quirkspeare realized that the quest for the unanswerable was a never-ending spectacle, an exploration of uncharted territory where the only truth was the ever-entwined abstraction itself.

In the ethereal realm of "Absurdia," where the laws of logic were an afterthought and reality was a mere suggestion, there existed a notion known as "Absurdivarix." Absurdivarix was not a notion, not a thought, nor even a non-thought. It was a state of perpetual

• Moments Elsewhere •

contradiction, a place where absurdity was both the means and the end.

In this abstract dimension, entities defied all expectations, their forms a perpetual kaleidoscope of paradoxes. Communication in Absurdia transcended language, for it was the exchange of unspoken questions and unanswerable answers.

One preposterous occasion, or perhaps no occasion at all, an entity named Quibblix embarked on a quest. Quibblix was a living enigma, a puzzle enshrouded in an enigma wrapped in a conundrum, and its mission was to confound the already confounded, to perplex the utterly perplexed, and to unravel the already unraveled.

As Quibblix meandered through the bewildering landscapes of Absurdia, it encountered entities that embodied the essence of absurdity itself, concepts that defied not only definition but also defiance, and phenomena that transcended even transcendence. It observed the dance of contradictions that harmonized into discord, the symphony of absurdity that played in perfect chaos, and the riddle of enigmas that solved themselves into further enigma.

After an eternity, or perhaps a fleeting moment, Quibblix returned to its origin. It had not found the answer to the unanswerable, for in Absurdia, the unanswerable was the very substance of the place itself, eternally eluding comprehension. The nature of Absurdia lay in its resistance to understanding, for it was the eternal dance of the indistinct.

And so, in the abstract realm of Absurdia, Quibblix realized that the quest for the unanswerable was an eternal spectacle, an exploration of uncharted territory where the only truth was the ever-entwined abstraction itself.

• Adrian Cox B.Sc. •

(1)
Amid the void where notions blur,
In nebulous realms, they all concur,
Concepts merge, and thoughts entwine,
In the labyrinth of the abstract mind.

Colors hum and silence sings,
Infinite shades of unseen things,
Symphonies of non-existent sound,
In the realm where abstractions abound.

Paradox blooms in every thought,
Where the known and unknown are sought,
Infinite paradoxes swirling free,
In the dance of pure perplexity.

In the abstract's unfathomable sea,
Boundless thought, eternally free,
Where meaning and meaninglessness reside,
In the boundless abstract, worlds collide.

(2)
In the realm of shadows cast by dreams,
Where concepts flow in endless streams,
A tapestry of thought and reverie,
In the abstract's infinite tapestry.

Silent whispers of formless sound,
Dancing shapes on shifting ground,
Iridescent thoughts, a boundless tide,
In the abstract's realm, they cannot hide.

Dimensions blend, and time dissolves,
Eternal questions the mind revolves,
In the boundless, ever-elusive quest,
Where answers fade into the abstract's bequest.

Surreal visions of the mind's own eye,
Where the why and wherefore multiply,
Infinite puzzles and riddles spun,
In the abstract's dance, we are all as one.

(3)
In the cosmos of the mind's abyss,
Where logic yields to the abstract's kiss,
A surrealist's dream, an enigma's delight,
In the boundless canvas of thought's flight.

Shapes without form, colors unseen,
Where the surreal and real convene,
A dance of chaos, where paradox thrives,
In the realm where abstraction endlessly strives.

Concepts dissolve, and meaning unravels,
In the maze where the mind endlessly travels,
Silent symphonies of the formless soul,
In the abstract's embrace, we find our role.

Infinite possibilities, where boundaries blur,
In the abstract's embrace, we all concur,
In the labyrinth of the mind's own flight,
In the realm of abstraction, where day turns to night.

About the Author

Adrian Cox, born in Lincoln, England, in 1965, embodies a life colored by diverse experiences and a deep passion for both the arts and academia. Having spent significant time as a busker, traveling across Europe, he cultivated a unique perspective on life, drawing inspiration from the myriad cultures and landscapes he encountered.

Despite his bohemian pursuits, Cox harbored a love for learning, eventually earning a degree in Mathematics from the Open University. This academic foundation, coupled with his innate curiosity about the human condition, led him to pursue a career as a care worker, where he dedicated himself to supporting others through their most vulnerable moments.

However, Cox's journey didn't stop there. Driven by a desire to explore the realms of spirituality and introspection, he turned to writing as a means of self-expression and enlightenment. Drawing from his eclectic background and rich life experiences, he penned books that delve into the depths of the soul, offering readers profound insights and moments of contemplation.

Through his writings, Adrian Cox invites readers to embark on a journey of self-discovery and inner growth, weaving together the threads of his life's tapestry to create narratives that resonate with authenticity and wisdom. His busking days may be behind him, but his storytelling prowess continues to captivate audiences, inspiring them to explore the mysteries of existence and the boundless possibilities of the human spirit.

Printed and bound by CPI Group (UK) Ltd, Croydon, CR0 4YY